ANIMAL SCIENCE, ISSUES AND PROFESSIONS

ANIMAL PROTECTION: TREATMENT AND WELFARE ISSUES

ANIMAL SCIENCE, ISSUES AND PROFESSIONS

Additional books in this series can be found on Nova's website under the Series tab.

Additional E-books in this series can be found on Nova's website under the E-books tab.

ANIMAL SCIENCE, ISSUES AND PROFESSIONS

ANIMAL PROTECTION: TREATMENT AND WELFARE ISSUES

DENNIS G. CARLTON
EDITOR

Nova Science Publishers, Inc.
New York

For permission to use material from this book please contact us:
Telephone 631-231-7269; Fax 631-231-8175
Web Site: http://www.novapublishers.com

LIBRARY OF CONGRESS CATALOGING-IN-PUBLICATION DATA

Animal protection : treatment and welfare issues / editors, Dennis G. Carlton.
p. cm.
Includes index.
ISBN 978-1-61728-353-6 (hardcover)
1. Animal welfare--Law and legislation--United States. 2. United States. Humane Methods of Slaughter Act of 1978. I. Carlton, Dennis G.
KF3841. A96 2010
344.7304'9--dc22
2010022558

Published by Nova Science Publishers, Inc. ✦New York

CONTENTS

PREFACE

Animal protection activists in the United States have long sought legislation to modify or curtail some practices considered by U.S. agriculture to be acceptable or even necessary to animal health. USDA's Animal and Plant Health Inspection Service (APHIS) is responsible for enforcing the Animal Welfare Act, which requires minimum standards of care for certain warm-blooded animals bred for commercial sale, used in research, transported commercially, or exhibited to the public. The Human Methods of Slaughter Act governs the humane slaughter and handling of livestock at packing plants. This book examines the violations perpetrated under the Human Methods of Slaughter Act, and the Animal Welfare Act and advises where actions are needed to strengthen enforcement on the humane treatment of animal handling laws.

Chapter 1 - The Animal Welfare Act (AWA) was first passed in 1966 to prevent pets from being stolen for sale to research laboratories, and to improve the treatment and well-being of animals intended for research. Congress periodically has amended the act to strengthen enforcement, expand coverage to more animals and activities, or curtail practices viewed as cruel, among other things. Farm animals are not covered by the AWA, which is administered by the U.S. Department of Agriculture's Animal and Plant Health Inspection Service.

In the 110th Congress, 2007 legislation (H.R. 137; P.L. 110-22) was aimed at strengthening provisions against animal fighting, the sixth time that Congress has amended the act. It was amended again in 2008 when AWA provisions were included in the 2008 farm bill (P.L. 110-246). These provisions ban the importation of puppies under six months of age for resale, tighten prohibitions on dog and other animal fighting activities, and increase penalties for violation of the act.

Other AWA bills that were pending at the close of the 110th Congress included H.R. 1280/S. 714, to restrict where research facilities could obtain their dogs and cats; H.R. 1947, to make it unlawful for animal exhibitors and dealers (but not accredited zoos) to allow direct contact between the public and big cats such as lions and tigers; H.R. 2193, to prohibit the use of animals in marketing medical devices and products; and H.R. 6949/S. 3519, to require an AWA license from USDA of those who raise more than 50 dogs in a 12-month period and sell directly to the public.

Only one of these proposals—to restrict where research facilities could obtain their dogs and cats—was reintroduced in the first session of the 111th Congress. This proposal, the Pet

Safety and Protection Act of 2009, was introduced October 22, 2009, into the House as H.R. 3907 and into the Senate as S. 1834.

The Animal Welfare Act (AWA; 7 U.S.C. 2131 *et seq.*) is intended to ensure the humane treatment of animals that are intended for research, bred for commercial sale, exhibited to the public, or commercially transported. Under the AWA, businesses and others with animals covered by the law must be licensed or registered, and they must adhere to minimum standards of care. Farm animals are among those not covered by the act, which nonetheless provides a broad set of statutory protections for animals.[1]

The law was first passed in 1966 following several years of lobbying by animal welfare organizations and growing public outcry over allegations that large numbers of pets were being "dognapped" for sale to medical research laboratories. Congress amended the original law in 1970, 1976, 1985, 1990, and 2002. These amendments generally were intended to expand the scope of the AWA or to clarify various provisions. The U.S. Department of Agriculture's (USDA's) Animal and Plant Health Inspection Service (APHIS) administers the AWA. The House and Senate Agriculture Committees have exercised primary legislative jurisdiction over the act and its amendments.

Animal welfare advocacy organizations have continued to back proposals to further extend the reach of the AWA. Although a variety of such proposals were introduced in the 110th Congress, only one, the Pet Safety and Protection Act of 2009 (H.R. 3907/S. 1834), had re-emerged as of the end of the first session of the 111th Congress (see "Pet Safety and Protection Act of 2009," below).

Chapter 2 - Animal protection activists in the United States have long sought legislation to modify or curtail some practices considered by U.S. agriculture to be acceptable or even necessary to animal health. Members of Congress over the years have offered various bills that would affect animal care on the farm, during transport, or at slaughter; several proposals have been introduced in the 111th Congress. Members of the House and Senate Agriculture Committees generally have expressed a preference for voluntary rather than regulatory approaches to humane care. Meanwhile, animal activists have won initiatives in several states to impose some care requirements on animal producers.

Chapter 3 - Concerns about the humane handling and slaughter of livestock have grown; for example, a 2009 video showed employees at a Vermont slaughter plant skinning and decapitating conscious 1-week old veal calves. The Humane Methods of Slaughter Act of 1978, as amended (HMSA) prohibits the inhumane treatment of livestock in connection with slaughter and requires that animals be rendered insensible to pain before being slaughtered. The U.S. Department of Agriculture's (USDA) Food Safety and Inspection Service (FSIS) is responsible for HMSA.

GAO was asked to (1) evaluate FSIS's efforts to enforce HMSA, (2) identify the extent to which FSIS tracks recent trends in resources for HMSA enforcement, and (3) evaluate FSIS's efforts to develop a strategy to guide HMSA enforcement. Among other things, GAO received survey responses from inspectors at 235 plants and examined a sample of FSIS noncompliance reports and suspension data for fiscal years 2005 through 2009.

Chapters 4 through 8 feature testimony before the U. S. Senate.

Chapter 9 - This directive informs inspection program personnel of the requirements, verification activities, and enforcement actions for ensuring that the handling and slaughter of livestock, including the slaughter of livestock by religious ritual methods, is humane. This directive explains how inspection program personnel should approach these activities.

Chapters 10 and 11 feature testimony before the U. S. Senate.

Chapter 12 - This chapter contains brief summaries of federal animal protection statutes, listed alphabetically. It includes statutes enacted to implement certain treaties, but it does not include treaties. Additionally, this chapter includes statutes that concern animals but that are not necessarily animal protection statutes. For example, it discusses a statute authorizing the eradication of predators, because one of the statute's purposes is to protect domestic and "game" animals; and it includes statutes to conserve fish even though the ultimate purpose of such statutes may not be for the benefit of the fish. This chapter also includes statutes that allow the disabled to use service animals and statutes aimed at acts of animal rights advocates—i.e., the Animal Enterprise Protection Act of 1992, and the Recreational Hunting Safety and Preservation Act of 1994.

In: Animal Protection: Treatment and Welfare Issues
Editor: Dennis G. Carlton

ISBN: 978-1-61728-353-6

Chapter 1

THE ANIMAL WELFARE ACT: BACKGROUND AND SELECTED LEGISLATION*

Geoffrey S. Becker

SUMMARY

The Animal Welfare Act (AWA) was first passed in 1966 to prevent pets from being stolen for sale to research laboratories, and to improve the treatment and well-being of animals intended for research. Congress periodically has amended the act to strengthen enforcement, expand coverage to more animals and activities, or curtail practices viewed as cruel, among other things. Farm animals are not covered by the AWA, which is administered by the U.S. Department of Agriculture's Animal and Plant Health Inspection Service.

In the 110th Congress, 2007 legislation (H.R. 137; P.L. 110-22) was aimed at strengthening provisions against animal fighting, the sixth time that Congress has amended the act. It was amended again in 2008 when AWA provisions were included in the 2008 farm bill (P.L. 110-246). These provisions ban the importation of puppies under six months of age for resale, tighten prohibitions on dog and other animal fighting activities, and increase penalties for violation of the act.

Other AWA bills that were pending at the close of the 110th Congress included H.R. 1280/S. 714, to restrict where research facilities could obtain their dogs and cats; H.R. 1947, to make it unlawful for animal exhibitors and dealers (but not accredited zoos) to allow direct contact between the public and big cats such as lions and tigers; H.R. 2193, to prohibit the use of animals in marketing medical devices and products; and H.R. 6949/S. 3519, to require an AWA license from USDA of those who raise more than 50 dogs in a 12-month period and sell directly to the public.

Only one of these proposals—to restrict where research facilities could obtain their dogs and cats—was reintroduced in the first session of the 111th Congress. This proposal, the Pet

* This is an edited, reformatted and augmented version of a CRS Report for Congress publication, Report #RS22493, dated December 8, 2009.

Safety and Protection Act of 2009, was introduced October 22, 2009, into the House as H.R. 3907 and into the Senate as S. 1834.

The Animal Welfare Act (AWA; 7 U.S.C. 2131 *et seq.*) is intended to ensure the humane treatment of animals that are intended for research, bred for commercial sale, exhibited to the public, or commercially transported. Under the AWA, businesses and others with animals covered by the law must be licensed or registered, and they must adhere to minimum standards of care. Farm animals are among those not covered by the act, which nonetheless provides a broad set of statutory protections for animals.[1]

The law was first passed in 1966 following several years of lobbying by animal welfare organizations and growing public outcry over allegations that large numbers of pets were being "dognapped" for sale to medical research laboratories. Congress amended the original law in 1970, 1976, 1985, 1990, and 2002. These amendments generally were intended to expand the scope of the AWA or to clarify various provisions. The U.S. Department of Agriculture's (USDA's) Animal and Plant Health Inspection Service (APHIS) administers the AWA. The House and Senate Agriculture Committees have exercised primary legislative jurisdiction over the act and its amendments.

Animal welfare advocacy organizations have continued to back proposals to further extend the reach of the AWA. Although a variety of such proposals were introduced in the 110th Congress, only one, the Pet Safety and Protection Act of 2009 (H.R. 3907/S. 1834), had re-emerged as of the end of the first session of the 111th Congress (see "Pet Safety and Protection Act of 2009," below).

KEY PROVISIONS[2]

Animals Covered

The act applies to any live or dead dog, cat, nonhuman primate, guinea pig, hamster, rabbit, or other warm-blooded animal determined by the Secretary of Agriculture to be for research or exhibition, or used as a pet. The AWA explicitly excludes birds, rats, and mice bred for research; horses not used for research; and other farm animals used in the production of food and fiber.[3] Animals sold in retail facilities are not covered, unless they are wild or exotic animals. Cold- blooded animals like fish and reptiles also are excluded from coverage.

Businesses and Activities Covered

Generally, animal dealers and exhibitors must obtain a license, for which an annual fee is charged. APHIS does not issue a license until it inspects the facility and finds it to be in full compliance with its regulations. If a facility loses its license, it cannot continue its regulated activity. Those who conduct research, and general carriers that transport regulated animals, do not need a license but must still register with APHIS and undergo periodic inspections. Specific details follow.

Dealers, including pet and laboratory animal breeders and brokers, auction operators, and anyone who sells exotic or wild animals, or dead animals or their parts, must have an APHIS license for that activity. So-called Class A licensees are breeders who deal only in animals they breed and raise; all others are called Class B licensees. Exempt from the law and regulations are retail pet stores, those who sell pets directly to pet owners, hobby breeders, animal shelters, and boarding kennels.

Exhibitors must be licensed by APHIS as such. These so-called Class C licensees include zoos, marine mammal shows, circuses, carnivals, and promotional and educational exhibits. The law and regulations exempt agricultural shows and fairs, horse shows, rodeos, pet shows, game preserves, hunting events, and private collectors who do not exhibit, among others.

Animal transporters must be registered, including general carriers (e.g., airlines, railroads, and truckers). Businesses that contract to transport animals for compensation are considered dealers and must have licenses.

Research facilities must be registered. They include state and local government-run research institutions, drug firms, universities, diagnostic laboratories, and facilities that study marine mammals. Federal facilities, elementary and secondary schools, and agricultural research institutions are among those exempt from registration.

Animal fighting generally is prohibited by the AWA. The ban includes dogfights and bear and raccoon baiting; sponsors and exhibitors are subject to penalties. The AWA also has banned bird fights, except in the states where they are not prohibited by state law (namely Louisiana and New Mexico), and the sponsor or exhibitor was unaware that the transaction had occurred in interstate commerce.

Standards

All licensed and registered entities must comply with USDA-APHIS regulations, including recordkeeping and published standards of care. These standards deal with humane handling, shelter, space requirements, feeding, watering, sanitation, ventilation, veterinary care, and transport. (AWA regulations are at 9 C.F.R. § 1.1 *et seq.*)

Oversight and Enforcement

APHIS's Animal Care (AC) program oversees the AWA, under which approximately 10,300 facilities were licensed or registered in FY2008. That year, AC had total staff of approximately 200 and an annual budget of nearly $21 million.[4]

AC officials make unannounced inspections of registered and licensed facilities to ensure compliance with all rules. Under the AWA, research facilities are to be inspected at least annually. Inspection frequency for other AWA-regulated facilities is based on risk; for example, moderate- risk facilities are to be visited about once yearly. APHIS inspectors also conduct searches to identify unlicensed or unregistered facilities. Failure to correct deficiencies can result in confiscation of animals, fines, cease-and-desist orders, or license suspensions. AC inspectors conducted 18,343 inspections during FY2007, which included pre-licensing as well as compliance inspections, according to APHIS.

LEGISLATIVE HISTORY

Original Law

Although long known as the Animal Welfare Act, the original law was passed simply as P.L. 89- 544, the Act of August 24, 1966. The law requires dealers in dogs and cats for research purposes to obtain a USDA license and to abide by USDA-set humane treatment requirements. It also requires a research facility to register with USDA only if it uses dogs or cats and either (1) purchases them in interstate commerce or (2) receives federal research money. The law authorizes the Secretary of Agriculture to set humane handling standards for guinea pigs, nonhuman primates, rabbits, and hamsters as well as dogs and cats—but only dealers and research facilities with dogs and cats are subject to these standards. Farmers and pet owners are among those exempted from the law. Other provisions spell out recordkeeping requirements, enforcement authorities and penalties for noncompliance.

Animal Welfare Act of 1970

P.L. 91-579 expands animal coverage to include all warm-blooded animals determined by the Secretary to be used for experimentation or exhibition, except horses not used in research and farm animals used in food and fiber research. The 1970 law also incorporates exhibitors; defines research facilities; and exempts from coverage retail pet stores, agricultural fairs, rodeos, dog and cat shows.

Animal Welfare Act Amendments of 1976

P.L. 94-279 was passed mainly to clarify and expand previous regulations covering animal transport and commerce. This act for the first time addresses animal fighting, making it illegal to exhibit or transport interstate animals used in fighting ventures, such as dogs and roosters. Hunting animals are generally exempt, as are live fighting birds for states where such fighting is legal.

Improved Standards for Laboratory Animals Act

These amendments were passed as Title XVII, Subtitle F, of the Food Security Act of 1985 (P.L. 99-198, the omnibus 1985 farm bill). The law directs the Secretary to set new minimum standards of care for handling, housing, feeding, water, sanitation, ventilation, and so forth. One new provision that was highly contentious at the time singles out two species by requiring standards for the exercise of dogs and the psychological well-being of primates. The law provides that research facilities must have procedures that minimize pain and stress to the animals, and describes practices considered to be painful. Each research facility must establish an Institutional Animal Care and Use Committee to review research proposals that involve animal experimentation and to provide oversight of laboratories. The amendments also increase civil and criminal penalties for AWA violations, and establish an animal welfare information center at USDA's National Agricultural Library.

Protection of Pets

Section 2503 of the Food Agriculture, Conservation, and Trade Act of 1990 (P.L. 101-624, the 1990 farm bill) extends pet protections. It requires public and private animal shelters and research facilities that acquire dogs and cats to hold them for at least five days to allow time for either adoption or recovery by the original owner before they can be sold to a dealer. Dealers are prohibited from selling dogs and cats they did not breed unless they provide certified records on, among other things, the animals' origin. Other new recordkeeping requirements also are specified.

2002 Amendments

Title X, Subtitle D, of the Farm Security and Rural Investment Act of 2002 (P.L. 107-171, the omnibus 2002 farm bill) makes it a misdemeanor to ship a bird in interstate commerce for fighting purposes, or to sponsor or exhibit any bird in a fight with knowledge that any of the birds were so shipped (even fights within a state where the practice is permitted). The law also increases the maximum financial penalty for a violation (a misdemeanor) of the anti-fighting provisions of the AWA, to $15,000 from $5,000. The 2002 law also explicitly excludes from AWA coverage birds, rats, and mice bred for research purposes. The Secretary of Agriculture had previously published regulations excluding these animals from coverage, which the Animal Legal Defense Fund challenged in federal court. When USDA agreed to settle the case by essentially reversing its regulations, Congress (in P.L. 106-387, the FY2001 agriculture appropriation) blocked the action by prohibiting funds for such a rule change. The 2002 law made the exclusion a permanent part of the AWA.[5]

Animal Fighting Prohibition Enforcement Act of 2007

P.L. 110-22, signed into law May 3, 2007, makes a violation of the animal fighting provisions of the AWA a felony punishable by up to three years in prison, under Title 18 of the *U.S. Code* (Crimes and Criminal Procedure). The law, based on companion bills introduced by Representative Gallegly (H.R. 137) and Senator Cantwell (S. 261), also makes it a felony to trade, in interstate and foreign commerce, knives, gaffs, or other sharp objects designed for use in animal fighting, or to use the Postal Service or other "interstate instrumentality to trade in such devices, or to promote an animal fighting venture."

Proponents of various animal fighting bills had observed that in 2001, the House and Senate had approved strong animal fighting sanctions in their respective farm bills, but that conferees on the final 2002 farm bill (P.L. 107-171) removed the felony language. Stronger deterrents are needed because animal fighting is a brutal, inhumane practice that is closely associated with criminal activity, endangers children where aggressive dogs are being reared, and may contribute to the spread of avian influenza in the case of live birds, they argued. Opponents have countered that such measures would violate provisions in the U.S. Constitution that protect states' rights, including the Commerce Clause, and that recognize private citizens' right to travel for economic reasons. Completely banning and/or stiffening penalties for all animal fighting activities would drive them further underground, undermining efforts to protect animals and the public from any disease problems created by such activities, other opponents have argued.

2007-2008 Farm Bill

Animal Fighting

A new omnibus farm bill (P.L. 110-246, first passed as H.R. 2419) contains a number of amendments to the AWA. One section (§14207) strengthens further the definitions of, and penalties for, activities related to animal fighting. For example, maximum imprisonment rises to five years from the current three years. The animal fighting provision is based on language in S. 1880 and H.R. 3219—bills introduced shortly after the July 17, 2007, indictment of NFL quarterback Michael Vick on charges related to dog fighting—to more explicitly ban various dog fighting activities, and to define the term.[6]

Puppy Imports; Penalties for AWA Violations

The 2008 farm bill requires regulations to prohibit imports for resale of dogs unless they are at least six months of age, in good health, and have all necessary vaccinations, with exemptions for research, veterinary treatment, or imports into Hawaii from certain countries. Another section (Section 14214) increases the maximum penalty for a general violation of the act from the current $2,500 to $10,000 for each violation.

Dogs and Cats in Research

Both the House- and Senate-passed versions of the omnibus farm bill had contained the language of two other pending bills (the Pet Safety and Protection Act of 2007; H.R. 1280/S. 714) to restrict where research facilities could obtain their dogs and cats. This language was deleted by conferees; the final version instead directed USDA to review "any independent reviews by a nationally recognized panel of experts" on Class B use by researchers.

Conferees said in accompanying report language that they were aware of concerns regarding use of random source animals from Class B dealers. However, they observed that USDA's FY2008 appropriation (part of the Consolidated Appropriations Act, 2008, P.L. 110-161) had requested such an independent review, which was underway by the National Research Council (NRC) of the National Academies of Science (NAS). The results "will help provide Congress information regarding the value of Class B dogs and cats in medical research."

PET SAFETY AND PROTECTION ACT OF 2009

Critics have long asserted that the limited number of Class B dealers who still collect dogs and cats from random sources, including "free to a good home" classified ads, auctions, and flea markets, are more concerned about profit than animal welfare. Others have contended that passage would leave no viable sources of random source dogs and cats, which are needed by medical and veterinary researchers because of their genetic and age diversity; and that the majority of Class B dealers are in compliance with the AWA.

The NRC issued its report in May 2009. It concluded that random source dogs and cats may be desirable and necessary for certain types of biomedical research but that "it is not necessary to acquire them through Class B dealers, as there are adequate numbers of such animals from shelters and other sources." [7] The NRC noted that of the more than 1,000 Class B dealers in the United States, at last count only 11 of them acquired and sold live dogs and cats for research and teaching. The report's conclusions and recommendations apply only to these 11 dealers that may supply such animals for research funded by the National Institutes of Health, the authors stated.

The report discusses in more detail the advantages and disadvantages of random source dogs and cats, which constitute less than 1% of all laboratory animals; evaluates the Class B dealer system, under which (it found) animal standards of care appear to vary greatly; and offers alternative options for obtaining random source animals. These alternatives include partnering with pet owners, veterinarians, breeders, and others; obtaining animals from Class A dealers and through donations from small breeders and hobby clubs; and acquiring animals directly from pounds and shelters, among others.

On October 22, 2009, the Pet Safety and Protection Act was reintroduced as H.R. 3907/S. 1834. These bills would amend the AWA to limit the sources of random source dogs and cats to a licensed dealer (under Section 3 of the AWA) who has bred and raised the animal; a publicly owned or operated pound or shelter that meets certain qualifications; someone donating the dog or cat that bred and raised the animal or owned it for not less than one year; and research facilities licensed by the Secretary of Agriculture. The bill also would subject violators to a fine of $1,000 per violation, over and above any other applicable penalties.

OTHER SELECTED BILLS

The following bills were offered in the 110th Congress but did not re-emerge as proposals in the first session of the 111th Congress.

Animal Protection Accountability Improvement Act

H.R. 2193 would have amended the AWA to prohibit the use of animals in marketing medical devices and products, and increase the penalties for animal research facilities that violate this part of the act. This language was the House farm bill (H.R. 2419) but was deleted by conferees.

Interest in the proposal was stimulated at least in part by a sales demonstration in an Ohio medical facility, where a dog reportedly was given a brain aneurysm, repeatedly subjected to the medical device, and later put down. Proponents believe the incident highlighted an inhumane practice done for profit, not science or medicine. Opponents argue that the facility had not approved the demonstration and acted swiftly to address it, and that most research facilities even go beyond federal welfare requirements to ensure that research animals do not experience pain and suffering.

Haley's Act

This bill (H.R. 1947) would have amended the AWA to make it unlawful for animal exhibitors and dealers (but not accredited zoos) to allow direct contact between the public and big cats such as lions and tigers. The bill, which also would have increased penalties for AWA violations, was named for a teenager killed by a grown Siberian tiger in 2005 while having her picture taken with it at an APHIS-licensed facility. Opponents argue that the measure is unnecessary because federal regulations already ban such contacts with older cats (the facility presumably was out of compliance) and because zoos will gain a monopoly in exhibiting younger cats.

Puppy Mills

The proposed Puppy Uniform Protection and Safety (PUPS) Act (H.R. 6949/S. 3519) would have required those who breed dogs to obtain an AWA license from USDA if they raised more than 50 dogs in a 12-month period and sold directly to the public. The bills also would have set some minimum daily exercise requirements for dogs held by the dealers. Supporters of the bills contended that the Internet and other relatively recent marketing techniques have enabled importers and large commercial breeders, whom they call "puppy mills," to sell their animals directly to the public while evading the AWA licensing and humane handling requirements, even though they are selling large numbers of animals. (Wholesale breeders are already covered by the AWA.) Opponents countered that the measures would strain USDA resources and newly subject thousands of relatively small in-home and hobby breeders, as well as rescue organizations, to burdensome licensing and regulatory requirements that were designed for large commercial businesses.

The bills were similar in intent to measures offered in the 109th Congress, the Pet Animal Welfare Statute ("PAWS"; H.R. 2669; S. 1139). These bills would have required commercial dog and cat breeders to obtain AWA licenses if they sold more than six litters or more than 25 dogs or cats directly to the public each year, among other things.

End Notes

[1] Numerous other federal laws seek to protect other classes of animals, often those from the wild. Examples include the Marine Mammal Protection Act, the Lacey Act as amended, and the Wild Free-Roaming Horses and Burros Act. These and the others are described, with legal citations, in CRS Report 94-731, *Brief Summaries of Federal Animal Protection Statutes*, by Henry Cohen.

[2] Unless noted, sources on the AWA are various materials provided by APHIS.

[3] For example, rabbits raised for food are exempt from AWA coverage; those for pets are not.

[4] A portion of this amount, nearly $500,000, was used to administer the Horse Protection Act (15 U.S.C. §§1821-1831), which makes it a crime to exhibit or transport any "sore" horse, i.e., one whose feet have been injured to alter its gait.

[5] CRS Report 94-731, *Brief Summaries of Federal Animal Protection Statutes*, by Henry Cohen.

[6] Another bill, H.R. 3327, included the provisions of H.R. 3219 and S. 1880, as well as language to enable animal humane agencies to initiate civil actions where violations are alleged.

[7] NAS, *Scientific and Humane Issues in the Use of Random Source Dogs and Cats* (Report in Brief), May 2009. The entire report is at http://www.nap.edu/catalog.php?record_id=12641.

In: Animal Protection: Treatment and Welfare Issues
Editor: Dennis G. Carlton
ISBN: 978-1-61728-353-6

Chapter 2

HUMANE TREATMENT OF FARM ANIMALS: OVERVIEW AND ISSUES*

Geoffrey S. Becker

SUMMARY

Animal protection activists in the United States have long sought legislation to modify or curtail some practices considered by U.S. agriculture to be acceptable or even necessary to animal health. Members of Congress over the years have offered various bills that would affect animal care on the farm, during transport, or at slaughter; several proposals have been introduced in the 111th Congress. Members of the House and Senate Agriculture Committees generally have expressed a preference for voluntary rather than regulatory approaches to humane care. Meanwhile, animal activists have won initiatives in several states to impose some care requirements on animal producers.

BACKGROUND

USDA's Animal and Plant Health Inspection Service (APHIS) is responsible for enforcing the Animal Welfare Act (AWA; 7 U.S.C. 2131 et seq.), which requires minimum standards of care for certain warm-blooded animals bred for commercial sale, used in research, transported commercially, or exhibited to the public. However, the act excludes farm animals raised for food and fiber from coverage.[1]

The Humane Methods of Slaughter Act (7 U.S.C. 1901 et seq.), enforced by USDA's Food Safety and Inspection Service (F SIS), governs the humane slaughter and handling of livestock (but not poultry) at packing plants. Also, under the so-called Twenty-Eight Hour Law (49 U.S.C. 80502, last amended in 1994), many types of carriers "may not confine

* This is an edited, reformatted and augmented version of a CRS Report for Congress publication, Report #RS21978, dated January 15, 2010.

animals in a vehicle or vessel for more than 28 consecutive hours without unloading the animals for feeding, water, and rest."[2]

At the state level, laws to prevent deliberate animal cruelty sometimes apply to farm animals, but few states have prescribed on-farm treatment standards. That appears to be changing in states where animal activists have sponsored successful ballot measures to impose care standards on animal producers. In Florida, voters approved a 2002 ballot measure outlawing gestation crates for pigs; in Arizona, voters did the same, along with a veal stall ban, in 2006. In 2008, California voters approved so-called Proposition 2, which will require that veal calves, egg-laying hens, and pregnant pigs be allowed to lie down, stand up, fully extend their limbs and turn around freely. The California law, to take effect in 2015, subjects violators to misdemeanor penalties of up to $1,000 in fines and/or 180 days in jail.[3] Maine and Michigan also recently have passed laws regulating the housing of farm animals.

Criticisms of Animal Agriculture Practices

Many animal protection groups assert that today's intensive farming systems perpetuate standard practices that in their view are harmful to animals' well-being. Examples include:

- rearing large numbers of livestock or poultry in close confinement with little or no room for natural movement and activity (e.g., housing sows in small gestation crates, chickens in battery cages);
- isolating veal calves in small crates;
- performing surgery such as docking hog tails, dehorning cattle, and trimming poultry beaks (so that confined animals do not hurt each other or their handlers);
- permitting commercial movement of nonambulatory livestock ("downers") that are disabled due to sickness or injury; and
- not fully stunning poultry (which are not covered by the humane slaughter act) and, sometimes, livestock (most of which are covered) before slaughter.

Some of these groups link intensive animal agriculture with soil and water pollution, food safety problems (e.g., misuse of animal drugs, and foodborne bacterial illnesses), and the decline of smaller-scale, "family" farms.[4] They also believe that if regulators approve future applications of biotechnology—such as animal cloning, genetic alterations to improve productivity, and the use of livestock as "factories" for pharmaceuticals and human organs—animal well-being will be compromised. Some animal rights groups advance the more controversial argument that humans have no right to use animals for any purpose, including for food.

Defense of Animal Agriculture Practices

Farmers and ranchers maintain that they understand their animals' welfare needs and address them adequately. They express concern that efforts by poorly informed critics could lead to costly and counterproductive regulations harmful to their industry and the animals alike. Agricultural, food processing, and a number of animal science groups have argued that support for science, education, and voluntary guidelines are more effective ways of assuring animal welfare.

Recognizing that more customers are concerned about animal treatment, some major food retailers have developed humane animal care standards their suppliers must follow. Also, various industry groups have published voluntary standards for care that they encourage members to meet, including the American Meat Institute, American Sheep Industry Association, National Cattlemen's Beef Association, National Chicken Council, Pork Board, and United Egg Producers. Several of these, along with Certified Humane Raised and Handled, and Free Farmed of the American Humane Association, provide so-called third party certification programs intended to assure consumers that products were derived from producers who followed prescribed care standards. Some animal welfare groups contend that such voluntary industry standards are not strong or specific enough, are not enforceable, and/or are primarily marketing contrivances.

In Congress

Members of Congress have offered various proposals to require changes in the treatment of animals on the farm, during transport, or at slaughter. Members of the House and Senate Agriculture Committees, which generally have jurisdiction over such bills, have held hearings on various farm animal welfare issues, but they generally express a preference for voluntary rather than regulatory approaches to improving animal care.

On-Farm Care

In the 110th Congress, a key provision in the potentially sweeping Farm Animals Anti-Cruelty Act (H.R. 6202) stated, "[w]hoever, without justification, kills, mutilates, disfigures, tortures, or intentionally causes an animal held for commercial use pain or suffering, or has responsibility for an animal held for commercial use and fails to provide food, water, shelter, and health care as is necessary to assure the animal's health and well-being appropriate to the animal's age and species," is subject to penalties of up to one year in jail and/or $100,000 in fines. "Commercial use" would mean "use, or intended for use, as food or fiber or for food or fiber production." A separate bill, H.R. 1726, would have required the federal government to purchase products derived from animals only if they were raised according to humane standards (i.e., had adequate shelter with sufficient space to walk and move around with limbs fully extended, had adequate food and water with no starvation or force-feeding, and had adequate veterinary care). Similar legislation had not been introduced into the 111th Congress as of mid-January 2010.

Humane Slaughter

The treatment of farm animals reached center stage in February 2008, when USDA announced the largest-ever meat recall, by Hallmark/Westland Meat Packing Co. The recall came after USDA-FSIS found that the facility for at least two years did not always notify inspectors about cattle that had become nonambulatory after they had been inspected, but before they were slaughtered for food. FSIS regulations explicitly prohibit most nonambulatory ("downer") cattle in human food, because of their higher risk of bovine spongiform encephalopathy (BSE, or "mad cow disease"). Moreover, FSIS charged that the plant had violated the humane slaughter act, which first came to light after animal welfare advocates secretly videotaped what they described as employees inhumanely handling downer cattle before slaughter. The act stipulates, among other things, that "[n]o method of slaughtering or handling in connection with slaughtering shall be deemed to comply with the public policy of the United States unless it is humane."

In a number of subsequent 2008 hearings, FSIS came under strong criticism for failing to enforce the act. This was despite the fact that Congress had included, in the 2002 farm law (P.L. 107-171, Section 10305), a resolution urging USDA to fully enforce it and to report the number of violations to Congress annually. Since then, Congress—through annual USDA appropriations acts—has been directing millions of dollars to FSIS for full-time inspectors to oversee compliance, and for incorporation of a humane tracking system into the agency's field computer systems.

Downers

In 2005, the Senate-passed version of H.R. 2744, USDA's FY2006 appropriation, included a floor amendment, sponsored by Senator Akaka, to prohibit nonambulatory livestock (also called "downers") from being used for human food. The Akaka amendment would have applied not only to nonambulatory cattle (which by FSIS regulation are already generally banned from the food supply), but also to any sheep, swine, goats, horses, mules or other equines unable to stand or walk unassisted at inspection. The House version lacked such a ban, and conferees removed the Senate language prior to final passage (P.L. 109-97). The proposal re-emerged in the 110th Congress as S. 394 and H.R. 661—which also would have required that nonambulatory livestock be humanely euthanized rather than slaughtered. S. 2770 contained similar provisions and also would have set gradually increasing penalties for violations.

In the 111th Congress, the Senate-passed version of the American Recovery and Reinvestment Act of 2009 (H.R. 1) also included a provision to permanently prohibit the use of federal funds for inspecting any nonambulatory disabled cattle for use as human food, regardless of the reason or time the animal became nonambulatory. (Uninspected cattle cannot enter the food supply.) House-Senate conferees deleted the Senate provision from the final bill.

A freestanding bill (H.R. 4356) has since been introduced that would ban the slaughter of downed cattle and calves, require their euthanization, and extend coverage beyond slaughter facilities, to livestock markets. The measure, introduced on December 16, 2009, was referred to the House Agriculture Committee.

Horse Slaughter

For many years, horse protection groups have sought to end the slaughter of horses for human food. Policy issues focus on the acceptability of the practice and on how to dispose of or care for unwanted horses no longer being slaughtered. Until 2007, two foreign-owned plants in Texas and one in Illinois slaughtered horses for human food (105,000 in 2006), all for export. On January 19, 2007, however, a federal appeals court panel declared a Texas law banning commerce in horsemeat to be enforceable, effectively closing the two plants there. The remaining foreign plant in Illinois closed later in 2007 after a federal appeals court ruled that a new state law banning the practice was constitutional. The U.S. Supreme Court declined to hear the case in June 2008.

These developments had occurred as Congress considered a succession of measures to ban or otherwise limit equine slaughter. During respective floor debates on USDA's FY2006 appropriation (P.L. 109-97), the House and Senate approved amendments to ban use of appropriated funds to pay for the inspection of these horses. The presumption was that since inspection is required for any meat to enter the human food supply, a ban on inspection funding would halt the practice. However, the three plants petitioned USDA for voluntary ante-mortem inspection services, as authorized by the Agricultural Marketing Act of 1946, with the ante- mortem portion funded by user fees. USDA agreed to this plan, which took effect in early 2006. Subsequently, the FY2008 USDA appropriation (§ 741, Division A, of the Consolidated Appropriations Act, 2008, P.L. 110-161) both prohibited the use of appropriated funds to inspect horses prior to slaughter for human food, and also the USDA rule (see above) that provided for the collection of user fees.

Animal welfare groups have continued to seek new federal legislation, such as companion bills H.R. 503/S. 311, and H.R. 6598 in the 110th Congress, permanently ending horse slaughter for human food. The American Veterinary Medical Association (AVMA), which has opposed the bills, has asserted that horses that otherwise would have been transported and slaughtered in the United States—under more humane conditions—are now going to Mexico and Canada for processing. In 2007, more than 44,000 horses were shipped for slaughter to Mexico and 35,000 to Canada, respectively a 312% and 41% increase from 2006, according to AVMA. Bill supporters argued that one of the intents of H.R. 503/S. 311 and of H.R. 6598 was to prevent such exports; bill critics countered that once horses leave the country, enforcement and oversight would be problematic at best. A separately pending bill (H.R. 6278) would have prohibited the interstate transportation of horses in double-decked trailers. (See also CRS Report RS2 1842, *Horse Slaughter Prevention Bills and Issues*, by Geoffrey S. Becker.)

Both H.R. 503 and H.R. 6278 have been reintroduced into the 111th Congress, as H.R. 503 (Conyers)/S. 727 (Landrieu), respectively. The ban on transporting horses in double-decked trailers has been reintroduced as H.R. 305 (Kirk).

End Notes

[1] See CRS Report RS22493, *The Animal Welfare Act: Background and Selected Legislation*, by Geoffrey S. Becker.

[2] See also CRS Report 94-731, *Brief Summaries of Federal Animal Protection Statutes*, by Henry Cohen.

[3] California Secretary of State, Voter Information Guide on Proposition 2, accessed November 18, 2008 at http://www.voterguide.sos.ca.gov/title-sum/prop2-title-sum.htm.

[4] In the 111th Congress, companion bills (H.R. 1549, S. 619) have been introduced that would phase out the nontherapeutic use in food animals of seven specific classes of antibiotic drugs that can also be used to treat or prevent diseases and infections in humans. The legislation is aimed at addressing concerns that the widespread use of these drugs in animal agriculture has contributed to an increase in antibiotic resistance among sick patients; opponents assert that a link between animal usage and human health is not well established. See CRS Report R40739, *Antibiotic Use in Agriculture: Background and Legislation*, by Geoffrey S. Becker.

In: Animal Protection: Treatment and Welfare Issues ISBN: 978-1-61728-353-6
Editor: Dennis G. Carlton

Chapter 3

HUMANE METHODS OF SLAUGHTER ACT: ACTIONS ARE NEEDED TO STRENGTHEN ENFORCEMENT*

United States Government Accountability Office

WHY GAO DID THIS STUDY

Concerns about the humane handling and slaughter of livestock have grown; for example, a 2009 video showed employees at a Vermont slaughter plant skinning and decapitating conscious 1-week old veal calves. The Humane Methods of Slaughter Act of 1978, as amended (HMSA) prohibits the inhumane treatment of livestock in connection with slaughter and requires that animals be rendered insensible to pain before being slaughtered. The U.S. Department of Agriculture's (USDA) Food Safety and Inspection Service (FSIS) is responsible for HMSA.

GAO was asked to (1) evaluate FSIS's efforts to enforce HMSA, (2) identify the extent to which FSIS tracks recent trends in resources for HMSA enforcement, and (3) evaluate FSIS's efforts to develop a strategy to guide HMSA enforcement. Among other things, GAO received survey responses from inspectors at 235 plants and examined a sample of FSIS noncompliance reports and suspension data for fiscal years 2005 through 2009.

WHAT GAO RECOMMENDS

GAO is making recommendations to strengthen HMSA enforcement by, for example, establishing specific guidance on actions to take for HMSA violations. In commenting on a draft of this chapter, USDA did not state whether it agreed or disagreed with GAO's findings or recommendations. However, it stated that it plans to use them in improving efforts to enforce HMSA.

* This is an edited, reformatted and augmented version of a U. S. Government Accountability Office publication, Report #GAO-10-203, dated February 2010.

What GAO Found

GAO's survey results and analysis of FSIS data suggest that inspectors have not taken consistent actions to enforce HMSA. Survey results indicate differences in the enforcement actions that inspectors would take when faced with a humane handling violation, such as when an animal was not rendered insensible through an acceptable stunning procedure by forcefully striking the animal on the forehead with a bolt gun or properly placing electrical shocks. Specifically, as shown below, 23 percent of inspectors reported they would suspend operations for multiple unsuccessful stuns with a captive bolt gun whereas 27 percent reported that they would submit a noncompliance report. GAO's review of noncompliance reports also identified incidents in which inspectors did not suspend plant operations or take regulatory actions when they appeared warranted. The lack of consistency in enforcement may be due in part to the lack of clarity in current FSIS guidance and inadequate training. The guidance does not clearly indicate when certain enforcement actions should be taken for an egregious act—one that is cruel to animals or a condition that is ignored and leads to the harming of animals. A noted humane handling expert has stated that FSIS inspectors need clear directives to improve consistency of HMSA enforcement. According to GAO's survey, FSIS's training may be insufficient. For example, inspectors at half of the plants did not correctly answer basic facts about signs of sensibility. Some private sector companies use additional tools to assess humane handling and improve performance.

FSIS cannot fully identify trends in its inspection funding and staffing for HMSA, in part because it cannot track HMSA inspection funds separately from the inspection funds spent on food safety activities. FSIS also does not have a current workforce planning strategy for allocating limited staff to inspection activities, including HMSA enforcement. FSIS has strategic, operational, and performance plans for its inspection activities but does not clearly outline goals, needed resources, time frames, or performance metrics and does not have a comprehensive strategy to guide HMSA enforcement.

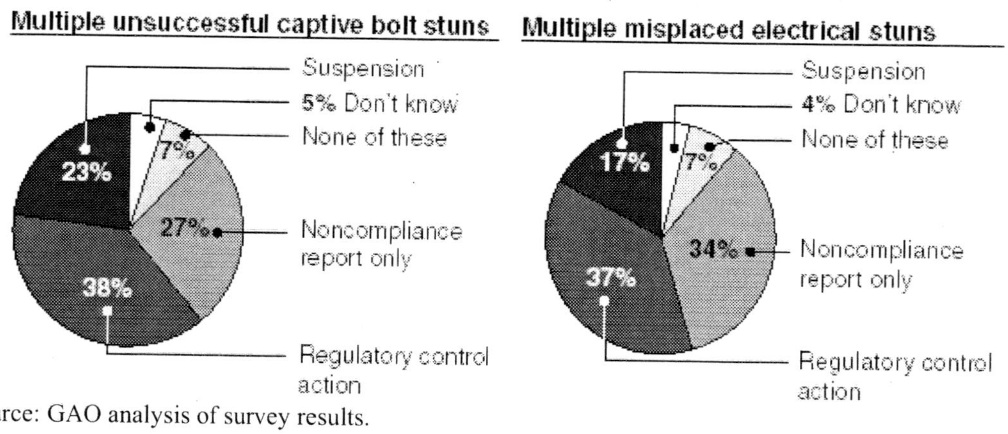

Source: GAO analysis of survey results.

Percentage of Inspectors Identifying Enforcement Actions for Stunning

ABBREVIATIONS

DVMS	district veterinary medical specialist
FSIS	Food Safety and Inspection Service
FTE	full-time equivalent
HMSA	Humane Methods of Slaughter Act of 1978
USDA	U.S. Department of Agriculture

February 19, 2010

The Honorable Darrell E. Issa
Ranking Member
Committee on Oversight and Government Reform
House of Representatives

The Honorable Dennis J. Kucinich
Chairman
Subcommittee on Domestic Policy
Committee on Oversight and Government Reform
House of Representatives

Concerns about the humane handling and slaughter of livestock have increased in recent years, particularly after a widely publicized video in 2008 of actions at a slaughter plant in California. The 2008 video showed employees at the plant delivering electric shocks to nonambulatory cows, spraying them with high-pressure water hoses, and ramming them with a forklift to force them to rise for slaughter. The U.S. Department of Agriculture (USDA) suspended operations at the California plant, citing the egregious nature of its actions and its failure to maintain and implement controls to prevent the inhumane handling and slaughter of nonambulatory cows at the facility. More recently, in October 2009, USDA received a video recording of employees at a Vermont slaughter plant that shows employees skinning and decapitating conscious veal calves, which are about 1-week old. USDA and the state of Vermont suspended the operating licenses for this plant, effectively shutting down operations, pending the results of an ongoing investigation. Such actions may violate the Humane Methods of Slaughter Act of 1978, as amended (HMSA). HMSA prohibits the inhumane treatment of livestock in slaughter plants and generally requires that animals be rendered insensible—typically referred to as stunning—before proceeding with slaughter.

USDA's Food Safety and Inspection Service (FSIS) is responsible for ensuring the safety of meat and other products in the United States, as well as for enforcing HMSA. Since 2002, Congress has urged USDA to fully enforce HMSA, directed it to enhance staffing for HMSA-related inspections and enforcement, and designated funding to develop and maintain a system for tracking the amount of time that inspectors spend on HMSA enforcement.

We have previously reported on weaknesses in FSIS's management of HMSA, particularly its reporting of violations and use of inconsistent criteria for enforcement.[1] In 2004, we recommended that FSIS take several actions to improve HMSA oversight, including providing informative data on HMSA violations and assessing whether FSIS resources are sufficient to effectively enforce the act. In 2008, USDA's Office of Inspector General reported that FSIS management controls over preslaughter activities could be strengthened to minimize the possibility of egregious humane handling events.[2]

In this context, you asked us to (1) evaluate FSIS's efforts to enforce HMSA, (2) identify the extent to which FSIS tracks recent trends in FSIS inspection resources for enforcing HMSA, and (3) evaluate FSIS's efforts to develop a strategy to guide HMSA enforcement.

To evaluate FSIS's efforts to enforce HMSA, we examined a sample of FSIS noncompliance reports, suspension data, and district veterinary medical specialist reports in all 15 of FSIS's district offices for fiscal years 2005 through 2009. To assess the reliability of these data, we examined the data for obvious errors in completeness and accuracy, reviewed existing documentation about the systems that produced the data, and questioned knowledgeable officials about the data and systems. We determined that the data were sufficiently reliable for the purposes of this chapter, with any limitations noted in the text. From May 2009 through July 2009, we also surveyed inspectors-in-charge—those responsible for reporting on humane handling enforcement in the plants—from a random sample of inspectors-in-charge at 257 livestock slaughter plants. We selected the sample of 257 plants, stratified by size, from a universe of 782 plants, and then surveyed inspectors-in-charge at the sample plants. Our sample allows us to make estimates about the observations and opinions of all inspectors-in-charge at U.S. slaughter plants. We obtained an overall survey response rate of 93 percent.[3] This chapter does not contain all of the results from our survey. The survey can be viewed at GAO-10-244SP. We also met with key officials from FSIS's Office of Field Operations who are responsible for implementing HMSA at the headquarters level. To understand district officials' perspectives on HMSA enforcement, we conducted semistructured interviews with each of FSIS's 15 district veterinary medical specialists (DVMS) and 15 district managers. We also obtained the views of experts in humane handling to understand key principles of humane handling techniques and enforcement. In particular, we consulted with Dr. Temple Grandin, a world-renowned expert on animal welfare, who provided her expert opinion on particular humane handling incidents we identified as possible HMSA violations.[4] To identify the extent to which FSIS tracks recent trends in inspection resources for enforcing HMSA, we reviewed FSIS funding and staffing data for each district. We also conducted semi-structured interviews with resource management analysts in each of FSIS's 15 district offices and interviewed key officials in the Resource Management and Planning Office within the Office of Field Operations. To assess FSIS's efforts to develop a strategy to enforce HMSA, we reviewed relevant FSIS strategies, including the most recent *FSIS Strategic Plan FY 2008 through FY 2013*, the *Office of Field Operations' Workforce Plan*, and other relevant planning documents. A more detailed description of our objectives, scope, and methodology is presented in appendix I.

We conducted this performance audit from October 2008 to February 2010, in accordance with generally accepted government auditing standards. Those standards require that we plan and perform the audit to obtain sufficient, appropriate evidence to provide a reasonable basis for our findings and conclusions based on our audit objectives. We believe that the evidence obtained provides a reasonable basis for our findings and conclusions based on our audit objectives.

BACKGROUND

In 2008, the most recently available data, more than 153 million cattle, sheep, hogs, and other animals ultimately destined to provide meat for human consumption were slaughtered at about 800 slaughter plants throughout the United States that engage in interstate commerce. Under federal law, meat-processing facilities that engage in interstate commerce must have federal inspectors on site. FSIS classifies plants according to size and the number of employees. Specifically, large plants have 500 or more employees; small plants have from 10 to 499 employees; and very small plants have fewer than 10 employees, or annual sales of less than $2.5 million. Under HMSA, FSIS inspectors are to ensure that animals are humanely treated from the moment they arrive at a plant until they are slaughtered. FSIS deploys these inspectors from 15 district offices nationwide. Figure 1 shows the states and territories in each FSIS district.

After livestock arrive at a slaughter plant, plant employees monitor their movements as they are unloaded from trucks to holding pens and eventually led into the stunning chute. Plant employees typically restrain an animal in the chute and stun it by using one of several devices—carbon dioxide gas, an electrical current, a captive bolt gun,[5] or a gunshot—that, as required by HMSA regulations, is rapid and effective in rendering the animal insensible. (See figure 2.) Under HMSA, animals must be rendered insensible—that is, unable to feel pain—on the first stun before being shackled, hoisted on the bleed rail, thrown, cast, or cut. According to the expert we consulted, animals on the bleed rail that exhibit any of the following signs are considered sensible and would therefore be need to be restunned:

- natural blinking,
- lifting head straight up and keeping it up (righting reflex),
- rhythmic breathing, and
- vocalizing.

Once the animals are considered stunned, they are shackled and hoisted onto a processing line, where their throats are cut, and they are fully bled before processing continues. HMSA exempts only ritual slaughter, such as kosher and halal slaughter, from the HMSA requirement that animals be rendered insensible on the first blow. See appendix II for a more detailed description of the movement of livestock through the plant.

FSIS has issued a variety of regulations and directives instructing FSIS inspectors on how to enforce HMSA. Overall, the regulations emphasize the minimization of "excitement and discomfort" to the animals and require that they are effectively stunned before being slaughtered. In 2003, FSIS guidance on humane handling enforcement stated that inspectors were to determine whether a humane handling incident does, or will immediately lead to, an injured animal or inhumane treatment. The guidance also specified the types of actions inspectors should take when these situations occur. Also in 2003, FSIS began providing "humane interactive knowledge exchange" scenarios as an educational tool to enhance inspectors' understanding of appropriate enforcement actions. These eight written scenarios, available on FSIS's Web site, provide examples of inhumane incidents and suggest enforcement actions.

In 2005, the agency issued additional guidance specifying egregious humane handling situations.[6] This guidance defines egregious as any act that is cruel to animals or a condition that is ignored and leads to the harming of animals. The guidance provided the following examples of egregious acts:

- making cuts on or skinning conscious animals,
- excessively beating or prodding ambulatory or nonambulatory disabled animals,
- dragging conscious animals,

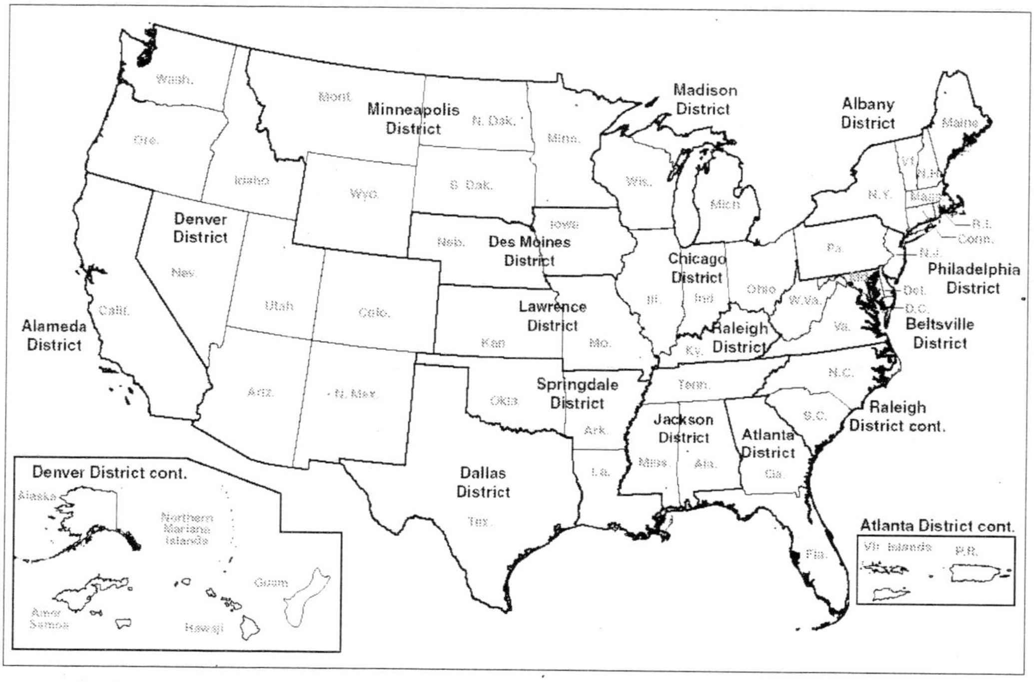

Sources: GAO analysis of FSIS data; Map Resources (map).

Figure 1. States and Territories Covered by FSIS District Offices

Source: FSIS *"Humane Handling Basics."*

Figure 2. Stunning Methods Consistent with HMSA

- driving animals off semitrailers over a drop-off without providing adequate unloading facilities so that animals fall to the ground,
- running equipment over animals,

- stunning animals and then allowing them to regain consciousness,
- leaving disabled livestock exposed to adverse climate conditions while awaiting disposition, or
- otherwise intentionally causing unnecessary pain and suffering to animals.

If inspectors determine that an egregious humane handling incident has occurred, they may suspend inspection at the plant immediately, effectively shutting down the plant's entire operation, and determine corrective actions with plant management and the district office.

In 2008, after the reported inhumane handling incident in California, which was at the Westland/Hallmark plant, FSIS expanded its guidance to include two more examples of egregious actions for which inspectors may suspend a plant: (1) multiple failed stuns, especially in the absence of corrective actions, and (2) dismemberment of live animals.

According to FSIS guidance, when FSIS inspectors observe a violation of HMSA or its implementing regulations and determine that animals are being injured or treated inhumanely, they are to take both of the following enforcement actions, which may restrict a facility's ability to operate:

- *Issue a noncompliance report.* This chapter documents the humane handling violation and the actions needed to correct the deficiency in cases where the animal may be injured or harmed. Inspectors are also directed to notify plant management when issuing a noncompliance report.

- *Issue a regulatory control action.* Inspectors place a regulatory control action or a reject tag on a piece of equipment or an area of the plant that was involved in harming or inhumanely treating an animal. This tag is used to alert plant management to the need to quickly respond to violations that they can readily address. The tag prohibits the use of a particular piece of equipment or area of the facility until the equipment is made acceptable to the inspector.
  When inspectors determine that an egregious humane handling incident has occurred, in addition to issuing a noncompliance report and regulatory control action, FSIS may also take the following actions:
- *Suspend plant operations.* An on-site FSIS supervisor—known as an inspector-in-charge—can initiate an action to suspend plant operations when an inspector observes egregious abuse to the animals. The inspector must document the facts that serve as the basis of the suspension action in a written memorandum of interview and promptly provide that information electronically to district officials. Ultimately, district officials assess the facts supporting the suspension, take any final action, and notify officials in headquarters.

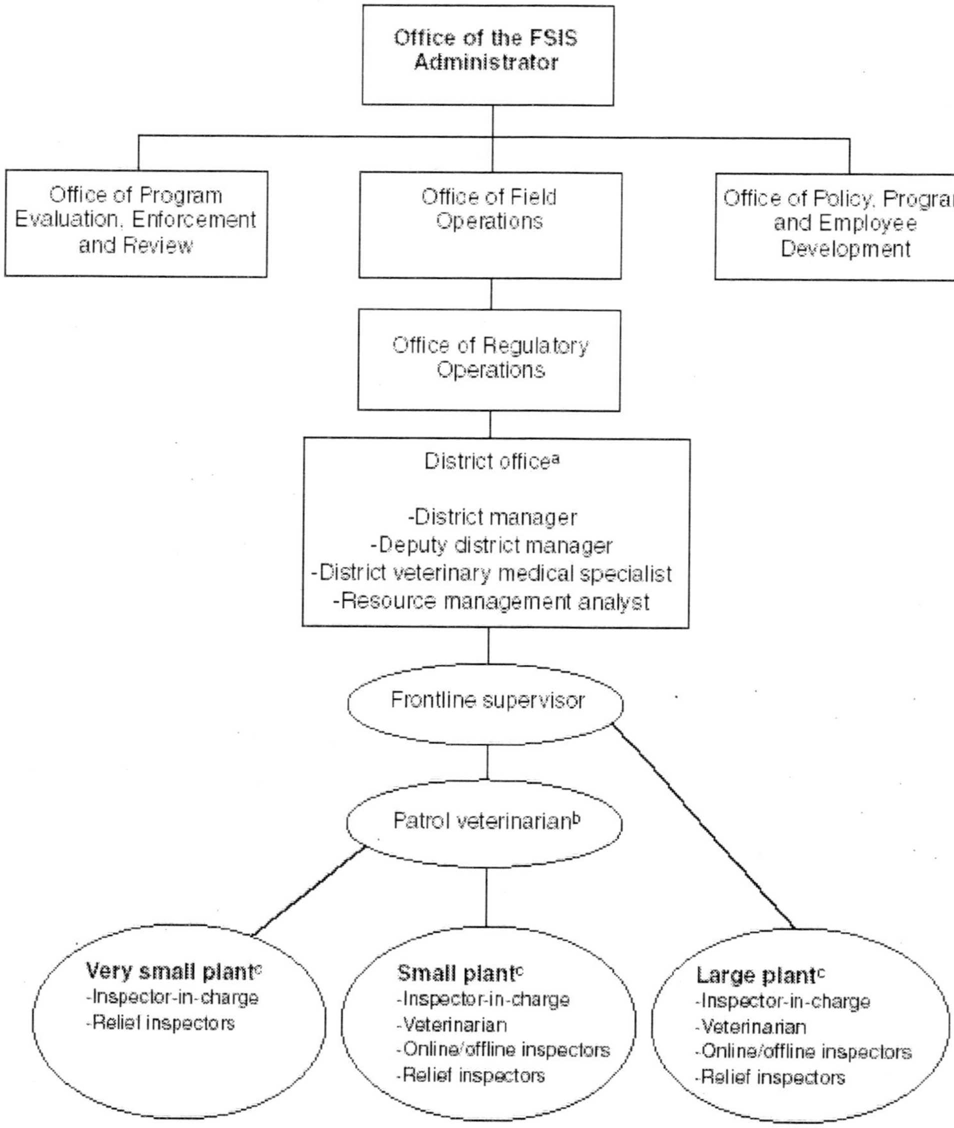

Source: GAO analysis of FSIS data.

[a] FSIS has a total of 15 district offices.

[b] Patrol veterinarians typically perform veterinarian duties at small and very small plants that do not have veterinarians.

[c] Three plants are shown for illustrative purposes only. A frontline supervisor may supervise more than one plant. According to FSIS documents, a very small plant has fewer than 10 employees; a small plant has 10 to 499 employees; and a large plant has 500 or more employees.

Figure 3. Key FSIS Inspection Personnel Involved in HMSA Enforcement

- *Withdraw the plant's grant of inspection.* If the plant fails to respond to FSIS's concerns about repeated and/or serious violations, the district offices may decide to withdraw all inspectors. Without FSIS inspectors on site, the plant's products cannot enter interstate or foreign commerce. The FSIS Administrator may file a complaint to withdraw the plant's grant of inspection and if the grant of inspection is withdrawn, the plant must then reapply for and be awarded a grant of inspection before it may resume operations.

FSIS employs inspectors at plants and in FSIS districts to help enforce HMSA and its food safety inspections. In the plant, FSIS employs inspectors-in-charge, online and offline inspectors, and relief inspectors. Inspectors-in-charge are the chief inspectors in the plant and may or may not be veterinarians. These inspectors are responsible for reporting humane handling activities for each shift, as well as carrying out food safety responsibilities, and making enforcement decisions in consultation with district officials when necessary. Online inspectors are typically assigned specific duties on the slaughter line, such as inspecting carcasses and animal heads; however, they may also perform some humane handling inspection duties as well. Offline inspectors conduct a variety of inspection activities throughout the plant and may also perform some humane handling inspection activities. FSIS also employs permanent relief inspectors, who step in for plant inspectors who are absent for a period of time, and may also observe humane handling. The plant inspectors and the inspectors-in-charge are supervised by frontline supervisors, who oversee multiple plants. Each plant has at least one FSIS veterinarian who is responsible for examining livestock prior to slaughter and performing humane handling activities. Some plants may require two veterinarians, depending on the volume of animals slaughtered at the plant and the number of operating shifts. Figure 3 provides an overview of FSIS personnel involved in the enforcement of HMSA.

Although FSIS does not require inspectors to observe the entire handling and slaughter process during a shift, it requires inspectors-in-charge to record the amount of time that the FSIS inspectors collectively devoted to observing humane handling during one shift. The inspectors-in-charge enter this information into a data tracking system known as the Humane Activities Tracking System.

At the district level, the DVMS in each of FSIS's 15 districts serves as the liaison between the district office and headquarters on all humane handling matters. These employees are directed to visit each plant within their district over a 12- to 18-month period and review the humane handling practices at each plant. DVMSs may also coordinate the verification of humane handling activities and educate plant inspectors on relevant humane handling information in directives, notices, and other information from headquarters through the district office to inspectors in the field.

Industry groups and animal welfare organizations have recently recommended actions to improve HMSA enforcement. As an expert witness, in 2008 testimony, Dr. Grandin proposed that FSIS guidance on humane handling be clearer—especially in determining when humane handling incidents at slaughter plants should be considered egregious violations of the HMSA.[7] She has also suggested that FSIS adopt a numerical scoring system—which has been adopted by the American Meat Institute—to determine how well animals were being stunned and handled at the plants. The system has different standards for different species of animal and can be adjusted to fit plants that slaughter fewer animals. Overall, the system seeks to reduce the subjective nature of inspections by using objective measures to help slaughter plants improve their humane handling performance. In addition, the Humane Society of the United States has proposed a variety of reforms to strengthen HMSA enforcement, including requiring FSIS inspectors to observe the entire humane handling and slaughter process during a shift.

WEAKNESSES PERSIST IN FSIS'S ENFORCEMENT, TRAINING AND GUIDANCE, AND DATA MANAGEMENT

According to our survey results and analysis of FSIS data, inspectors have not taken consistent actions to enforce HMSA once they have identified a violation. These inconsistencies may be due, in part, to weaknesses in FSIS's guidance and training for key inspection staff. While FSIS expects its inspectors to use their professional judgment based on the guidance in deciding enforcement actions, industry and others are using other tools to assist their efforts to improve humane handling performance. Furthermore, although FSIS has taken steps to correct data weaknesses in HMSA reporting that we noted in 2004, it has not used these data to analyze HMSA enforcement across districts and plants to identify inconsistent enforcement. For these reasons, FSIS cannot ensure that it is preventing the abuse of livestock at slaughter plants or that it is meeting its responsibility to fully enforce HMSA.

GAO Survey Results and FSIS Data Indicate Inconsistent Enforcement

According to FSIS officials, inspectors are to use their judgment in deciding whether to suspend a plant's operations or take the less stringent enforcement action (that is, issue a noncompliance report and a regulatory control action) when a humane handling violation occurs. For example, FSIS guidance is unclear on what constitutes excessive electrical prodding, such as the number of times an animal can be prodded before the inspector should consider the prodding to be excessive and therefore egregious. According to FSIS's guidance, if the inspector determines that the action was egregious, the inspector may also choose to suspend plant operations but is not required to do so.

U.S. meat industry representatives have expressed concerns in interviews about the inconsistency of HMSA enforcement across districts. For example, according to American Meat Institute officials, the inconsistency in HMSA enforcement is the single most critical issue for the industry; furthermore, one official noted that a number of the differences in interpretation of HMSA compliance are related to determining whether or not an animal is sensible after stunning. In addition, the expert we consulted testified in April 2008 that FSIS inspectors need better training and clear directives to improve consistency of HMSA enforcement.[8]

Our survey results indicate differences in the enforcement actions that inspectors reported they would take when faced with a humane handling violation. In our survey, we asked inspectors their views on electrically prodding over 50 out of 100 animals. Figure 4 shows the inspectors' responses to questions concerning electrical prodding. Under FSIS's guidance, inspectors are directed to issue a noncompliance report and take a regulatory control action in cases of excessive electrical prodding, but suspension is not required. However, the expert we consulted told us that she considers these cases to be egregious humane handling violations that should result in suspensions. In addition, according to an FSIS training scenario, electrical prods are never to be used on the anus, eyes, or other sensitive parts of the animal.

As figure 4 shows, 49 percent of the inspectors surveyed reported that they would either take a regulatory control action, such as placing a reject tag on a piece of equipment or suspending a plant's operations for electrical prodding of most animals, and 29 percent reported that they would take none of these actions or did not know what action to take for electrical prodding most animals. Furthermore, 67 percent of the inspectors surveyed reported that they would either take a regulatory control action or suspend operations for electrical prodding in the rectal area, and 10 percent reported that they would take none of these actions or did not know what action to take for electrical prodding in the rectal area. FSIS regulations prohibit electrical prodding that the inspector considers to be excessive.[9] FSIS guidance also states that excessive beating or prodding of ambulatory or nonambulatory disabled animals is egregious abuse—and may therefore warrant suspension of plant operations. From inspectors' compliance reports, we identified several specific incidents in which inspectors did not either take a regulatory control action or suspend plant operations. For example:

- In 2008, in the Denver district, the FSIS inspector reported observing a plant employee excessively using an electrical prod as his primary method to move the cattle—using the prod approximately 55 times to move about 46 head of cattle into the stun box. Cattle vocalized at least 15 times, which the inspector believed indicated a high level of stress. The FSIS inspector stated that this incident constituted excessive use of the electrical prod. As stated in FSIS guidance, excessive use of an electrical prod is an egregious violation that calls for the issuance of both a noncompliance report and a regulatory control action and for which an inspector may suspend plant operations. In this instance, the inspector stated that he had issued a noncompliance report. The inspector did not state that he took a regulatory control action and did not suspend operations at the plant, as the guidance allows. In the opinion of the expert we consulted, this was an egregious instance that should have resulted in a suspension.
- In 2007, in the Minneapolis district, an FSIS inspector reported observing plant employees using the electrical prods excessively to move hogs into the stunning chute. The animals became excited, jumping on top of one another, and vocalizing excessively. From the noncompliance report, it is unclear what, if any, regulatory actions were taken. According to FSIS regulations, electrical prods are to be used as little as possible in order to minimize excitement and injury; any use of such implements that an inspector considers excessive is prohibited.
- In 2008, in the Dallas district, the FSIS inspector reported that a plant employee used an electrical prod to repeatedly shock cows in the face and neck in an effort to turn them around in an overcrowded area. The inspector deemed the use of the electrical prod excessive, but the report does not indicate whether any regulatory control action was taken.

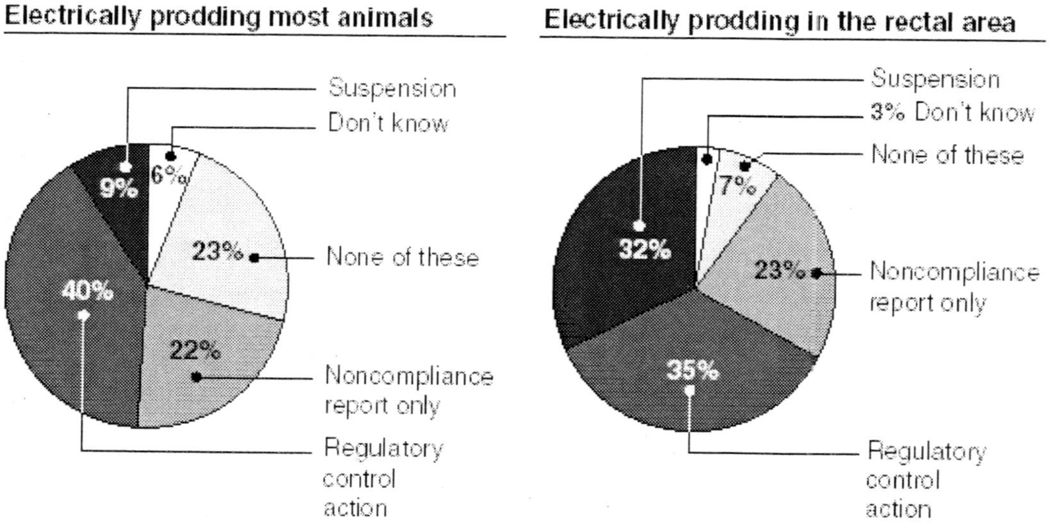

Source: GAO analysis of survey results.

Notes: This figure is based on the following survey question: "Do you believe that each of the following factors alone generally indicates that an establishment's action should result in a (1) suspension, (2) regulatory control action, (3) noncompliance report, or (4) none of these?" These factors included electrically prodding over 50 of 100 animals within acceptable voltage and electrically prodding one animal deliberately in the rectal area.

Percentages may not total 100 percent due to rounding.

Figure 4. Percentage of Inspectors Identifying Which Enforcement Action They Would Take for Electrical Prodding

With regard to stunning, our survey results and review of noncompliance records also show inconsistent enforcement actions when humane handling violations occurred. As figure 5 shows, 23 percent of inspectors reported they would suspend operations, while 38 percent would issue a regulatory control action for multiple unsuccessful captive bolt gun stuns. Similarly, 17 percent reported they would suspend operations for multiple misplaced electrical stuns, and 37 percent would issue a regulatory control action. According to FSIS guidance, egregious abuses that could result in a plant suspension include stunning animals and allowing them to regain consciousness and multiple attempts to stun an animal, especially in the absence of immediate corrective measures. However, it is unclear when a suspension is warranted, even if the acts are deemed to be egregious. FSIS's guidance simply states that an inspector-in-charge may immediately suspend the plant if there is an egregious humane handling violation— however, there is no clear directive to do so in guidance. In the opinion of the expert we consulted, if over 10 percent of the animals require a second shot or if over 5 percent of pigs had experienced an improperly placed electrical stun,[10] plant operations should be suspended. FSIS agreed that these incidents are troubling, and possibly egregious, but did not comment further. Figure 5 shows our survey results on stunning.

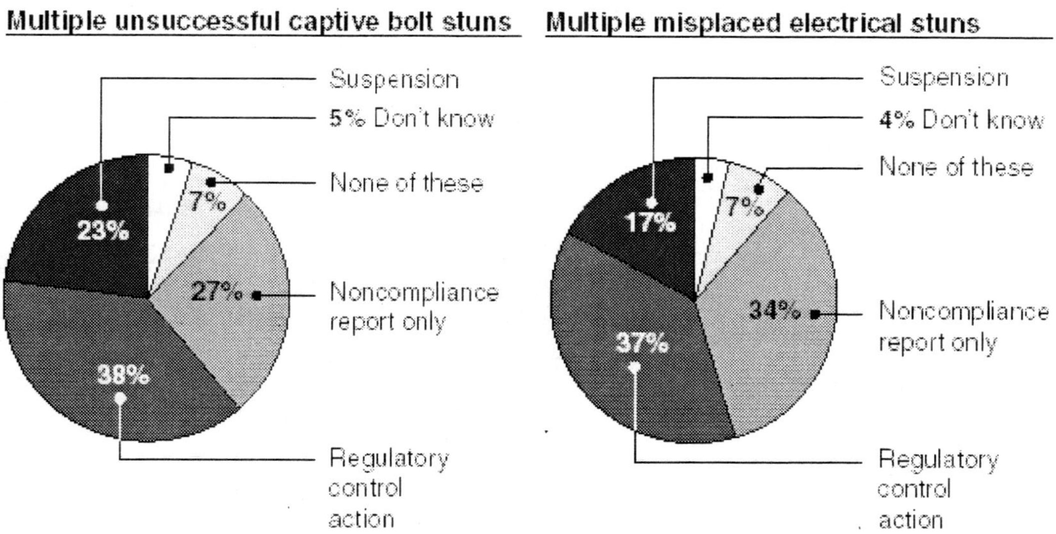

Source: GAO analysis of survey results.

Notes: This figure is based on survey question 11: "Do you believe that each of the following factors alone generally indicates that an establishment's action should result in a (1) suspension, (2) regulatory control action, (3) noncompliance report, or (4) none of these?"

Percentages may not total 100 percent due to rounding.

Figure 5. Percentage of Inspectors Identifying Which Enforcement Action They Would Take for Stunning

We also identified several incidents in FSIS's noncompliance reports in which inspectors did not suspend plant operations or take a regulatory control action. For example,

- In 2009, in the Raleigh district, a plant employee stunned a bull twice in the head with a captive bolt, but the bull remained sensible. Instead of restunning the animal with the captive bolt gun, the employee then drove a steel instrument used to sharpen knives into the open hole in the bull's head in an attempt to make the animal insensible. The bull rose to its feet and vocalized in apparent pain until it was eventually rendered insensible with a bullet to the head. FSIS regulations do not recognize this steel instrument as an acceptable stunning method.[11] However the inspector placed a reject tag on the stun box and cited the incident as egregious in the noncompliance report but did not suspend operations. In the opinion of the expert we consulted, this incident was an example of an egregious HMSA violation that should have resulted in a suspension.
- In 2008, in the Denver district, the inspector reported that the first attempt to stun a bull with a captive bolt stunner appeared to misfire, resulting in smoke and the smell of powder and no response by the bull.[12] A second stunning attempt appeared to render the bull unconscious in the stun box. However, it was followed by a third stunning attempt while the bull was still in the stun box. The employee then allowed the bull to roll out into the pit for shackling. The bull appeared unconscious but still was breathing rhythmically, indicating that the animal was still sensible. The employee then entered the pit and stunned the bull again and started conversing with another employee. The bull once again started breathing rhythmically while being

shackled, a sign that the bull still had not been rendered insensible to pain as the law requires. In response, the DVMS asked the employee to stun the bull again, and this stun rendered the bull unconscious and no longer breathing rhythmically. According to the report, the plant received a noncompliance report, but no regulatory control action was taken, as called for by guidance. In the opinion of our expert consultant, a regulatory control action should have been taken in this case because of multiple stuns that left the animal breathing rhythmically.

We also identified several other types of humane handling violations for which inspectors took inconsistent enforcement actions. For example, according to FSIS's regulations, animals are not to be moved from one area to another faster than a normal walking speed, with minimum excitement and discomfort. A faster speed could result in animals being driven over each other. Furthermore, animals in a holding pen are to have access to water and, if held longer than 24 hours, access to food. According to the expert we consulted, deliberately driving animals over the top of other others and failing to provide water for animals held over a weekend are egregious humane handling violations and, in her opinion, these actions should result in plant suspensions. However, as figure 6 shows, although most inspectors would take an enforcement action, including a regulatory control action, for these violations, 40 percent of inspectors surveyed would suspend plant operations for driving animals over each other, and 55 percent would suspend plant operations for failing to provide water over a weekend.

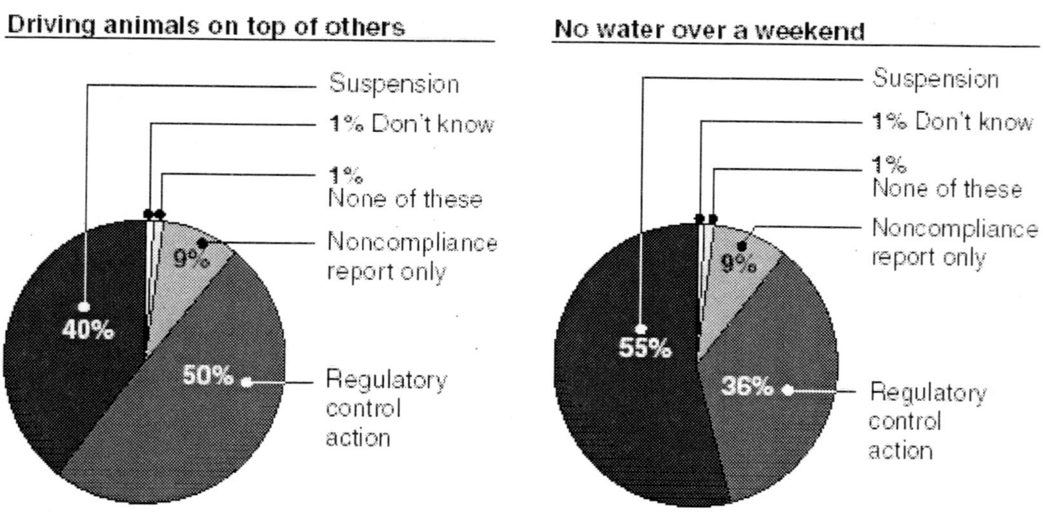

Source: GAO analysis of survey results.

Notes: This figure is based on survey question 11: "Do you believe that each of the following factors alone generally indicates that an establishment's action should result in a (1) suspension, (2) regulatory control action, (3) noncompliance report, or (4) none of these?"

Percentages may not total 100 due to rounding.

Figure 6. Percentage of Inspectors Identifying Which Enforcement Action They Would Take for Other Violations

The lack of consistency in enforcement actions is highlighted by inspectors' responses to our question about when they would suspend plant operations. According to our survey results, less than one-third of the inspectors-in-charge in the very small and small plants reported that they would be likely to suspend plant operations for multiple incorrect placements of electrical stunners and electrical prodding of most animals. Inspectors-in-charge at large plants with more frequently reported plant suspensions had more stringent views on enforcement actions than those at very small plants. For example, inspectors-in-charge at large plants more frequently reported suspensions as the enforcement actions that should be taken compared with inspectors-in-charge at very small plants. Figure 7 illustrates three humane handling scenarios in which significant differences were observed between large and very small plants. For example, large plants were more likely than very small plants to suspend plant operations for multiple incorrect electrical stuns, driving animals over the top of others, and electrically prodding most animals.

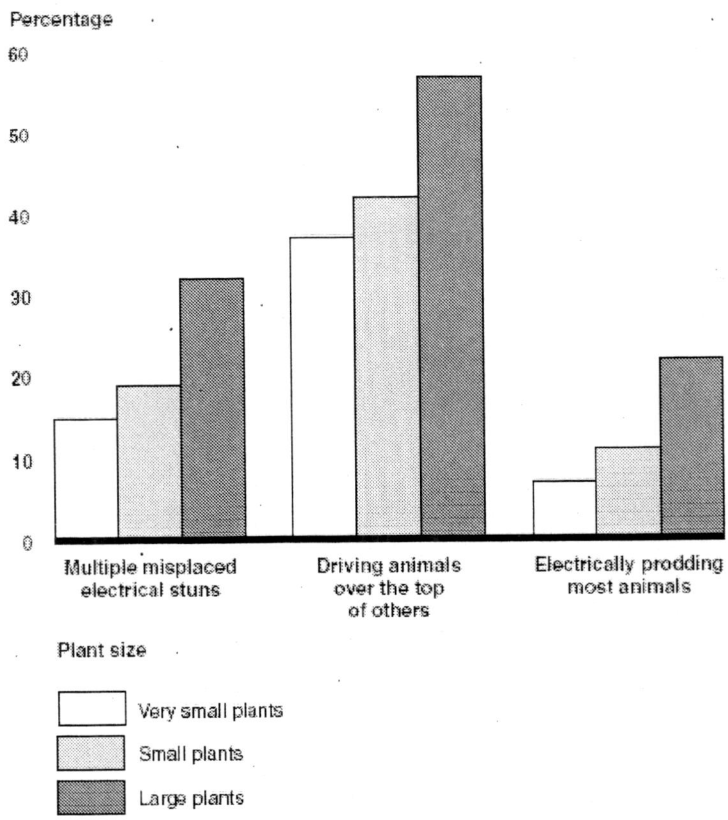

Source: GAO analysis of survey results.

Notes: Inspectors-in-charge at large plants more frequently reported suspensions than inspectors-in-charge at very small plants for 6 out of the 14 humane handling scenarios presented in our survey. Estimates by plant size have a margin of error of less than 15 percentage points.

This figure is based on survey question 11: "Do you believe that each of the following factors alone generally indicates that an establishment's action should result in a (1) suspension, (2) regulatory control action, (3) noncompliance report, or (4) none of these?"

Figure 7. Percentage of Inspectors-in-Charge Identifying Suspension as the Appropriate Enforcement Action, by Plant Size

We found similar indications of inconsistent enforcement across districts. According to our analysis of FSIS data, from calendar years 2005 through 2007, 10 districts of 15 FSIS districts—responsible for overseeing 44 percent of all animals slaughtered nationwide—suspended 35 plants for HMSA violations. The remaining 5 districts—responsible for overseeing 56 percent of all livestock slaughtered nationwide—did not suspend any plants.[13] For example, the Des Moines and the Chicago districts, which oversee the first and second highest volume of livestock slaughtered nationwide, respectively, were among the 5 districts that had never issued a suspension until February 2008, according to our analysis.

Before 2008, these five districts issued noncompliance reports, sometimes with regulatory control actions, such as a reject tag on a piece of equipment, rather than suspending an entire plant's operations. For example, in 2007, in the Lawrence district, a hog was observed walking around the stunning chute grunting and bleeding from the mouth and forehead. The animal had been stunned improperly, and plant personnel stated that both stun guns were not working and were being repaired. Because the plant did not have an operable stun device, the animal suffered for at least 10 minutes while the plant repaired the gun. The FSIS inspector applied a reject tag to the stunning box; stunning operations in the area were halted until the plant had taken corrective actions, but the record did not state the amount of time that stunning was stopped. According to FSIS's guidance, however, stunning animals and then allowing them to regain consciousness is considered egregious.

Suspensions increased overall following the February 2008 Westland/Hallmark incident in California. For calendar years 2007 and 2008, more than three-quarters of all suspensions were for stun-related violations for all districts. In the 10 districts that suspended operations for calendar years 2005 and 2006, over 40 percent of those suspensions were for stunning violations. (See app. III for detailed information on the number of HMSA enforcement actions over the period we reviewed.) Furthermore, following that incident, FSIS directed the inspectors to increase the amount of time they devoted to humane handling by 50 to 100 percent for March through May 2008. FSIS found that, when the amount of time spent on humane handling was increased, the number of noncompliance reports increased as well.

The Westland/Hallmark incident highlighted the problems that could occur when inspection staff inconsistently apply their discretion in determining which enforcement actions to take for humane handling violations. According to the USDA Inspector General's 2008 report that followed the Westland/Hallmark incident, between December 2004 and February 2008, FSIS inspectors did not write any noncompliance reports or suspend operations for humane handling violations at the Westland/Hallmark plant. Nevertheless, FSIS personnel acknowledged that at least two incidents of humane handling violations had occurred at the Westland/Hallmark plant during this period, both of which involved active abuse of animals. Instead of taking an enforcement action, the inspectors verbally instructed plant personnel to discontinue the action or practice in question. The report also stated that Westland/Hallmark had an unusual lack of noncompliance reports and that inspectors did not believe they should write a noncompliance report if an observed violation was immediately resolved.

Finally, our analysis of FSIS enforcement data for calendar years 2005 through August 2009 shows that suspensions were not consistently used to enforce HMSA. Figure 8 shows the total number of suspensions over the period and reveals that suspensions spiked from a low of 9 in calendar year 2005 to a high of 98 in 2008—a nearly 11-fold increase overall—and, as of August 2009, FSIS had suspended operations at 50 plants. Based on our review of the suspension records, it appears that this spike followed the February 2008 Westland/Hallmark incident. Also, more than three- quarters of these suspensions resulted from failure to render at least one animal insensible on the first stun. From calendar year 2005 through 2008, the number of noncompliance reports issued for humane handling decreased overall, while the number of animals slaughtered increased from about 128 million in 2004 to about 153 million in 2008.

While we cannot determine the extent to which HMSA violations were overlooked from FSIS data and inspection reports, we attempted to determine whether a much higher rate of enforcement actions were taken on the days that DVMSs conducted their audits for humane handling. However, according to FSIS officials, the records of DVMS audit visits are incomplete, and we were therefore unable to conduct a complete analysis. As a result, we could not fully determine how often DVMSs conducted humane handling audit visits nor whether there is a higher rate of enforcement actions on the days that DVMSs conducted their audits for humane handling. Furthermore, our survey found that 85 to 95 percent of inspectors-in-charge who had taken some type of enforcement action reported that their immediate supervisor, the DVMS, and other district management personnel were moderately or very supportive of their actions.

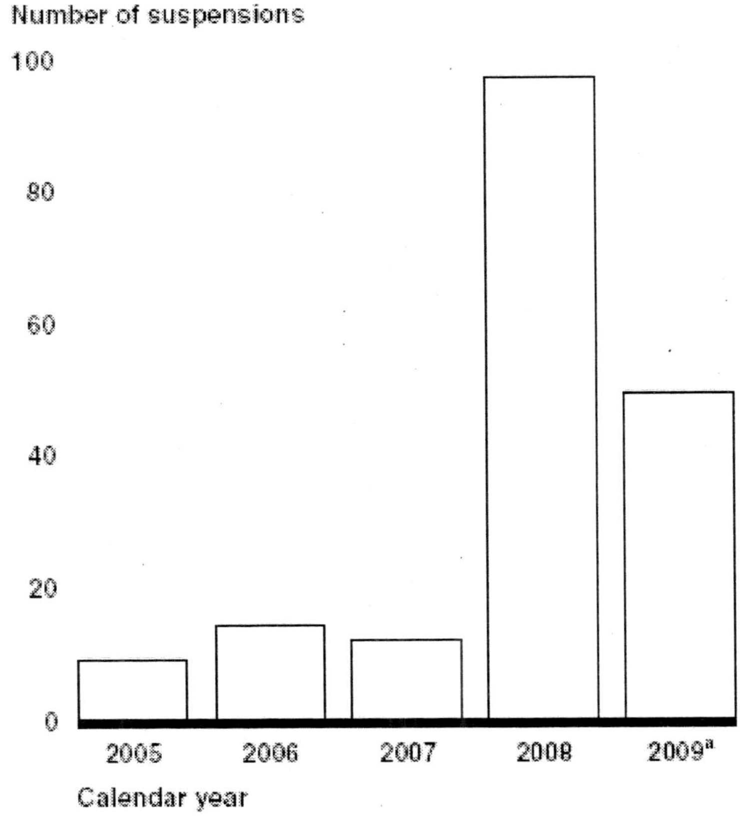

Source: GAO analysis of FSIS data.

[a] Calendar year 2009 data are as of August 2009.

Figure 8. Number of Plant Suspensions Nationwide, Calendar Years 2005 through August 2009

Weaknesses in Guidance and Training May Contribute to Inconsistent Enforcement

We found that incomplete guidance and inadequate training may contribute to the inconsistent enforcement of HMSA. Specifically, according to our survey results, inspectors at the plants we surveyed would like more guidance and training in seven key areas, as figure 9 shows.

Furthermore, an estimated 457 inspectors-in-charge, or those at more than half the plants surveyed, reported that additional FSIS guidance or training is needed on whether a specific incident of electrical prodding requires an enforcement action. In addition, of the 80 inspectors who provided detailed responses to our survey, 15 noted the need for additional guidance, including clarification on what actions constitute egregious actions. Similarly, 25 of the 80 inspectors who provided written comments identified a need for additional training in several key areas.

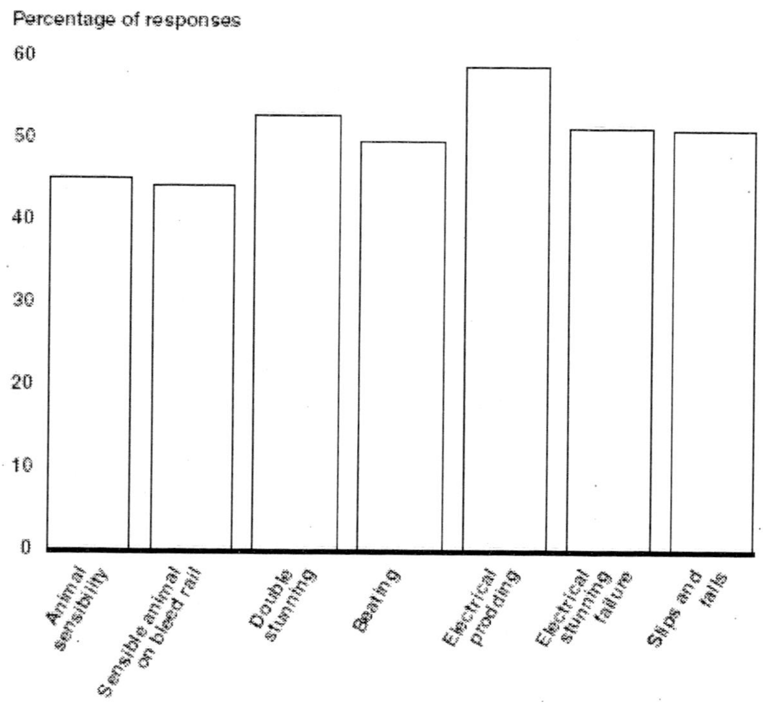

Source: GAO analysis of survey results.

Note: This figure is based on survey question 12: "Would additional guidance and/or training be helpful in the following areas? (1) determining when an animal is sensible or returning to sensibility; (2) determining what, if any, action to take for a sensible animal on the rail; (3) determining what, if any, action to take for double stunning; (4) determining when the use of a driving instrument or tool becomes beating; (5) determining whether a specific incidence of electric prodding requires a suspension, regulatory control action, or noncompliance report; (6) determining whether electrical stunning of an animal fails to render and maintain insensibility; and (7) assessing situations involving slipping and falling."

Figure 9. Inspectors Identified the Need for Additional Guidance and/or Training in Seven Key Areas of Humane Handling Enforcement

With respect to guidance, in 2004, we had recommended that FSIS establish additional clear, specific, and consistent criteria for district offices to use when considering whether to take enforcement actions because of repeat violations.[14] FSIS agreed with this recommendation and delegated to the districts the responsibility for determining how many repeat violations should result in a suspension. However, incidents such as those at the Bushway Packing plant in Vermont suggest that this delegation was not successful. To date, FSIS has not issued additional guidance.

Operations at this Vermont plant were suspended three times in May, June, and July 2009 for egregious humane handling violations. Two of the suspensions were for dragging nonambulatory conscious veal calves that were about 1-week old. According to a document describing the third incident, an employee threw a calf from the second tier of a truck to the first so that the calf landed on its head and side. FSIS has not issued any guidance to the district offices on how many suspensions should result in a request for a withdrawal of a grant of inspection. If specific guidance had been available on when to request a withdrawal of grant of inspection, the district office might have decided to request such a withdrawal before the October 2009 incident. If FSIS ultimately withdrew the grant, it would have required the plant to reapply for, and be awarded, a grant of inspection license before it could resume operations.

Regarding training, FSIS relies primarily on "on-the-job" training by DVMSs—who are directed to visit each plant within their district over a 12- to 18-month period. In addition, supervisory veterinarians and inspectorsin-charge provide on-the-job training. FSIS officials we spoke with said that the on-the-job training needs to be integrated into a formal training program and that efforts are under way to do so. FSIS also provides some humane handling training electronically. For example, in February 2009, all inspectors assigned to slaughter plants were required to complete a mandatory 1-hour basic humane handling course online, which the agency can track centrally. FSIS officials also stated that, since 2005, incoming inspectors have been required to complete some humane handling training during orientation. According to FSIS officials we spoke with, the agency has asked the districts to begin entering data on the completion of other humane handling courses so that this information can also be tracked centrally.

Our survey results suggest, however, that even inspectors-in-charge who had to complete mandatory humane handling training in February 2009 may not have been sufficiently trained. For example, an estimated 449, or 57 percent, of the inspectors-in-charge at the plants we surveyed from May through July 2009, reported incorrect answers on at least one of six possible signs of sensibility.[15] Specifically, an estimated 133, or 18 percent, of the inspectors–in-charge, failed to identify rhythmic breathing as a sign of sensibility. In addition, in 2004, we had reported that inspectors did not have the knowledge they needed to take enforcement actions when appropriate.[16] At that time, most of the deputy district managers, and about one-half of the DVMSs, noted that an overall lack of knowledge among inspectors about how they should respond to an observed noncompliance had been a problem in enforcing the HMSA.

Several outside observers have also commented on the need for better FSIS training.[17] Specifically:

- In November 2008, USDA's Office of Inspector General found that FSIS does not have a formal, structured developmental program and system in place to ensure that all of its inspection and supervisory staff receive both formal and on-the-job trainingto demonstrate that they possess the competencies essential for FSIS's mission-critical functions. The Inspector General recommended a structured training and development program that includes continuing education to provide the organizational control needed to demonstrate the competency of the inspection workforce. The Inspector General also stated that the workforce needs to be certified annually.

- In 2009, the National Academies' Institute of Medicine recommended testing and improved training, with special emphasis on the quality and consistency of noncompliance reports for food safety issues.[18] The institute noted that the decision to issue a noncompliance report is subjective and inspectors' experience levels and training differ. Supervisory review by inspectors-in-charge may likewise be variable or subject to bias and, therefore, unreliable.
- In 2009, representatives of the three major industry associations—the American Meat Institute, the American Association of Meat Processors, and the National Meat Association—told us that more training on humane handling is needed for FSIS inspectors. Specifically, the American Meat Institute identified insensibility as a critical issue in enforcement and noted that additional training on the signs of insensibility, such as blinking and the righting reflex, would be helpful.
- In 2009, the Humane Society of the United States recommended that FSIS inspectors receive adequate in-person, on-the-ground training so they can properly assess the conditions and treatment of animals.

FSIS officials stated that it launched a voluntary HMSA training program for plant employees at small slaughter plants in 2009. These plants represent the highest humane handling risk, according to FSIS officials, because plant management may not have sufficient resources to fully train plant employees on HMSA practices.

FSIS Has Only Recently Begun to Consider Using Additional Tools to Evaluate HMSA Performance

In recent years, the meat industry has adopted numerical scoring and video surveillance to improve plants' humane handling performance overall. According to FSIS officials, the agency does not require the use of such objective measures or scoring to aid judgment for enforcement purposes because situations are highly variable, and inspectors and higher-level officials are to use their judgment in conjunction with FSIS guidance. However, in December 2009, FSIS provided DVMSs with guidance on what it characterized as, an objective system to facilitate determinations of the problems that plants in their districts need to address.[19] Several of the DVMSs we interviewed acknowledged that they have been using a form of numerical scoring on their own to assist their efforts in evaluating HSMA enforcement at the plants.

The numerical scoring system was developed in 1996 by Dr. Grandin to determine how well animals were being stunned and handled at the plants. The system has different standards for different species of animal and can be adjusted to fit plants that slaughter fewer animals. This system seeks to reduce the subjective nature of inspections and uses the scoring system to help identify areas in need of improvement. For example, in a large plant, if more than 5 out of 100 animals were not rendered insensible on the first stun, the plant would fail the evaluation. Other standards include the percentage rates for slips and falls and the number of animals moved by an electrical prod. Once the plant is aware of the weaknesses, it can consider its options to improve its humane handling performance, such as repairing equipment and floors to provide better footing for the animals and targeting employee training in those specific areas.

The numerical scoring system has been adopted by industry and animal welfare organizations, as well as one federal agency. At the federal level, according to agency officials, USDA's Agricultural Marketing Service uses this system to rate slaughter plants to determine whether to approve or deny them to provide meat to the National School Lunch Program. In addition, the American Meat Institute and independent audit firms employed by restaurant chains, such as Burger King and McDonald's, have adopted this numerical scoring system to evaluate humane handling at their associated slaughter plants. According to industry experts, a publicized humane handling incident at their plants would potentially damage their business interests. Recently, the Canadian Food Inspection Agency proposed adoption of numerical scoring for federally inspected plants in Canada.

FSIS officials have stated that while the numerical scoring system may be useful in helping plants determine their humane handling performance; it should not be used to assess compliance with HMSA. Because the numerical scoring system allows for a certain percentage of stunning failures, using it would be inconsistent with the HMSA requirement that all animals must be rendered insensible on the first blow. However, as we noted earlier, this requirement has not been met consistently by slaughter plants because of human error, equipment failures, and animal movement, leaving FSIS to exercise its discretion in determining which violations require enforcement action.

Video surveillance is another tool being increasingly used by slaughter plants. Specifically, slaughter plants can hire specialized video technology companies to record plant operations and audit plant performance through remote video surveillance and the use of the American Meat Institute numerical scoring system to assess humane handling performance at the plant. These video technology companies can also provide slaughter plant management with continuous feedback and customized progress reports documenting humane handling performance at their plants. According to the testimony of one video surveillance company, this technology helps plant management provide positive reinforcement to the workers who are performing well and helps identify workers who may need further training.

In November 2008, the Office of the Inspector General recommended that FSIS determine whether FSIS-controlled, in-plant video monitoring would be beneficial in preventing and detecting animal abuses. However, FSIS officials responded that FSIS-controlled video cameras would not provide the definitive data needed to support enforcement of humane handling requirements, as compared with the direct, ongoing and random verification of humane handling practices at the plants.[20] According to the Humane Society of the United States, while video surveillance might serve as a supplemental tool, it does not negate the need for real-time inspectors' observations. According to our survey results, between 52 to 66 percent of inspectors-in-charge at large plants reported that video surveillance would be moderately or very useful in each of the five plant areas. Figure 10 illustrates our survey results on the usefulness of video surveillance for all plants. FSIS officials recently told us that they are exploring potential uses of video surveillance, but the agency had not released any official policy change, as of November 2009.

In addition, of 96 inspectors who provided written comments on the usefulness of video surveillance in our survey, most frequently reported that video surveillance would facilitate more inspections in different plant locations and provide a true picture of animal handling while plant staff do not know that the inspector is watching. Since video surveillance can provide continuous footage of ongoing activities in the plant, it may provide evidence regarding alleged violations when inspectors do not directly observe humane handling. For example, according to 39 percent of inspectors-in-charge at large plants, plant staff improved their handling behavior upon the inspectors' arrival. Furthermore, 25 percent of inspectors-in-charge at the large plants in our survey reported that plant staff often, or always, alert each other about inspectors' movements between areas by radio or whistle, for example.

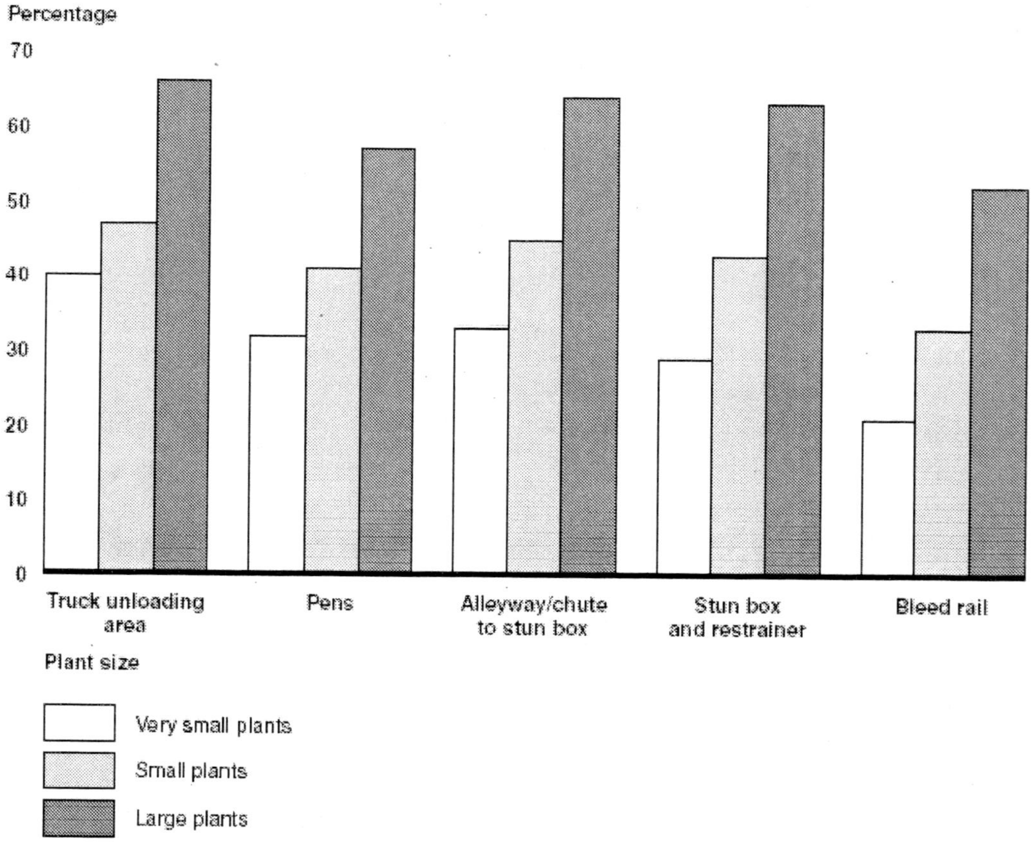

Source: GAO analysis of survey results.

Notes: This figure is based on survey question 31: "If FSIS were to issue regulations addressing the use of video surveillance, how useful would it be for you to have access to video of each of the following areas at this establishment (1) stun box and restrainer; (2) the bleed rail; (4) pens; (5) alleyway/chute to the stun box; and (6) area where the trucks are unloaded?"

Estimates by plant size have a margin of error of less than 9 percentage points.

Figure 10. Percentage of Inspectors-in-Charge Reporting Video Surveillance as Very or Moderately Useful in Five Plant Areas

FSIS Has Not Fully Analyzed Humane Handling Data to Consistently Enforce HMSA

Although FSIS collects humane handling data, we found that it is not fully analyzing and using these data to help ensure more consistent HMSA enforcement. For example, we found substantial differences in the range of time devoted to humane handling for large plants that slaughter market swine when we compared the amount of time devoted to humane handling activities for plants of similar size and species in an effort to determine if there were any inconsistencies among districts. Specifically, out of the six slaughter plants that kill between 700,000 to 900,000 market swine, the average time that a plant would devote to humane handling ranged from 1.8 to 9.7 hours per shift in 2008. For the nine plants that slaughter between 2 and 3 million market swine, we found that the average amount of time per shift ranged from 2.7 to 5.2 hours per shift in 2008.

In January 2004, we also reported that FSIS was not adequately analyzing the narrative found in noncompliance reports. As of November 2009, FSIS headquarters officials told us that they had not begun an effort to analyze the narratives in noncompliance reports. Instead, they told us, they rely on district officials to monitor whether plant inspectors have taken consistent enforcement action for each incident. Headquarters officials also stated that they only review the percentage of humane handling activities that are recorded as noncompliant in an FSIS database, known as the Performance-Based Inspection System. However, without analyzing the narrative, FSIS cannot readily provide the reasons for the noncompliance reports—for example, whether these reports were issued for one or two failed stuns, which is not uncommon, rather than three or four failed stuns, which might be considered an egregious violation. Thus, FSIS cannot easily analyze noncompliance reports across the districts to identify trends or patterns in plant violations or potential enforcement inconsistencies across districts.

Also in 2004, we reported that FSIS was not tracking humane handling activities. In response to the tracking issue, FSIS created the Humane Activities Tracking System, a database that inspectors use to record the amount of time they devote to humane handling activities in each plant. Inspectors are directed to record the total amount of time devoted to humane handling activities for each plant shift in 15-minute increments. According to our survey results, inspectors have differing views on the accuracy of the amount of time recorded in the tracking system. Specifically, 19 percent reported that the time recorded in this system was slightly or not at all accurate. However, 45 percent of the inspectors reported that the time was very accurate, and 36 percent reported that the time was moderately accurate.

Furthermore, of the 93 inspectors who provided written responses detailing inspectors' views of the reasons for the tracking database's inaccuracies, 56 pointed out that breaking out activities into 15-minute increments limited their ability to record their actual time spent, and 29 stated that humane handling activities are concurrent with other inspection activities. In addition, 14 responses noted that supervisors or district offices had placed either a minimum or maximum on the amount of time that could be charged to humane handling. Also, several of the DVMSs we interviewed reported that the Humane Activities Tracking System does not readily produce the types of reports that are needed to oversee and manage humane handling activities in their districts. For example, they reported that the system lacked the capability to readily produce comparative analyses of similar plants to help identify trends or anomalies across districts.

FSIS began analyzing data across districts from the Humane Activities Tracking System in 2008—4 years after it developed the system. Also in 2008, FSIS established the Data Analysis Integration Group in headquarters, with staff in the regional field offices to support district offices' data needs. The group began reporting quarterly on HMSA enforcement, including the amount of time inspectors have devoted to HMSA, the number of plants suspended, and the number of noncompliance reports issued in 2009, although FSIS has not analyzed the narrative in the noncompliance reports.

FSIS Cannot Fully Identify and Plan Resource Needs for HMSA Enforcement

FSIS cannot fully identify trends in its inspection resources—specifically, funding and staffing—for HMSA enforcement, in part because it cannot track humane handling inspection funds separately from the inspection funds spent on other food safety activities. Furthermore, FSIS does not have a current workforce planning strategy to guide its efforts to allocate staff to inspection activities, including humane handling.

FSIS Does Not Track HMSA Enforcement and Other Inspection Funds Separately

According to FSIS officials, funds for humane handling come primarily from two sources: (1) FSIS's general inspection account and (2) the account used to support the Humane Activities Tracking System. The general inspection account supports all FSIS inspection activities, both food safety and other activities, including humane handling enforcement.

Because the same inspectors may carry out these tasks concurrently, FSIS cannot track humane handling funds separately, according to FSIS officials.

According to FSIS officials, for the most part, inspectors are to devote 80 percent of their time to food safety inspection activities and 20 percent of their time to humane handling inspection and other activities. However, our analysis of resources shows that this is not the case. As table 1 shows, we estimated that the percentage of funds dedicated to HMSA enforcement has been above 1 percent of FSIS's total annual inspection appropriation, although it rose slightly in 2008, the year in which suspensions spiked following the 2008 Westland/Hallmark incident in California. While FSIS does not track humane handling inspection activities separately, FSIS's budget office estimates the funds needed to carry out these activities. Using FSIS's budget estimate for HMSA enforcement for fiscal years 2005 through 2008, we estimated the percentage of FSIS's total annual appropriation for its federal food safety inspection account that would have gone to HMSA enforcement. [21]

Table 1. Total Specified in Annual Appropriations for FSIS Inspections, Estimated Amount FSIS Dedicated for Humane Handling Enforcement, and Estimated Percentage of FSIS Annual Inspection Appropriation for Humane Handling, Fiscal Years 2005 through 2008

Dollars in millions			
Fiscal year	Total amount specified for FSIS inspection in the agency annual appropriation[a]	Estimated amount of FSIS funds dedicated to humane handling enforcement	Percentage of FSIS annual appropriation for inspection devoted to humane handling
2005	$742.3	$9.1	1.23%
2006	753.3	10.9	1.45%
2007	a	10.0	b
2008	829.8	$12.1	1.46%

Sources: GAO's analysis of the Budget of the United States and FSIS data.

[a]The FSIS inspection fund includes other activities, such as livestock slaughter, poultry slaughter, processing inspection, egg inspection, import inspection, in-commerce compliance, district office activities, and food safety enforcement activities. Congress did not designate an amount from FSIS's general appropriation for federal food safety inspection in fiscal year 2007.

[b]Because Congress did not specify an amount for federal food safety inspection in fiscal year 2007, no percentage of total inspection activities devoted to humane handling was calculated. Appropriation amounts come from federal food safety inspection activities specified in FSIS annual appropriations and do not consider rescissions or supplemental appropriations.

In contrast to FSIS's inability to track humane handling in its general inspection fund, FSIS officials noted; the DVMSs—whose primary responsibility is humane handling activities—have a special activity code that enables FSIS to track their portion of expenses, including salaries and travel; however, these expenses represent only a small portion of the total amount FSIS spends on humane handling inspection activities.

Although FSIS does not track funds spent on humane handling inspection activities separately from other inspection activities, it does track the funds specifically dedicated to supporting the Humane Activities Tracking System. For fiscal years 2005 through 2009, Congress designated a total of nearly $13 million specifically for the Humane Activities Tracking System, and FSIS has spent roughly that amount on the system, according to our review of FSIS budget data. For fiscal year 2005 and for fiscal year 2006, FSIS was required to spend the funding designated for the Humane Activities Tracking System within 2 years of the appropriation. However, beginning with fiscal year 2008, Congress folded the funding for the Humane Activities Tracking System into a larger FSIS information technology initiative, and the funding is available to FSIS until it is expended. As of November 2009, FSIS had not completed integrating the Humane Activities Tracking System into the information technology initiative, and FSIS officials could not provide an estimate of when the agency expected to do so.

FSIS Does Not Have a Long-term Plan for Addressing HMSA Staffing

Although FSIS cannot directly account for the funding designated for humane handling activities, Congress in recent years has required FSIS to devote a minimum amount of full-time equivalent (FTE) staff to humane handling.[22] Accordingly, FSIS estimates the total number of FTEs devoted to humane handling and reports this information to Congress every year. FSIS develops this estimate using Humane Activities Tracking System data on time spent on humane handling inspection activities and average inspector and veterinarian salaries. Table 2 shows that FSIS has reported exceeding Congress's minimum FTE requirements for humane handling enforcement, according to FSIS's calculation.

For fiscal year 2010, FSIS officials told us, they planned to use $2 million of their inspection funds to enhance oversight of humane handling enforcement by hiring 24 inspectors, including both public health veterinarians and inspectors. FSIS officials planned to strategically place these additional inspectors at locations where they are most needed to support humane handling enforcement in addition to their other food safety responsibilities. FSIS officials stated that the agency determined staffing needs on the basis of such factors as the highest number of animals condemned on postmortem, the number of animals inspected and passed for human consumption, and the amount of time spent conducting humane handling inspection activities. In addition, FSIS officials stated that the agency intends to establish a headquarters-based humane handling coordinator position. This coordinator will be primarily responsible for consistently overseeing humane handling activities.

While FSIS has increased its hiring, it has not done so in the context of an updated strategic workforce plan. Such a plan would help FSIS align its workforce with its mission and ensure that the agency has the right people in the right place performing the right work to achieve the agency's goals. In February 2009, we reported that the FSIS veterinarian workforce had decreased by nearly 10 percent since fiscal year 2003 and that the agency had not been fully staffed over the past decade.[23] We reported that, as of fiscal year 2008, FSIS had a 15 percent shortage of veterinarians and the majority of these veterinarians work for slaughter plants. The FSIS 2007 strategic workforce plan—the most recently available—identifies specific actions to help the agency address some of the gaps in recruiting and retaining these mission-critical occupations over time. However, it does not address specific workforce needs for HMSA enforcement activities.

Table 2. Minimum Number of FTEs Required by Congress for Humane Handling Compared with the FTEs Reported by FSIS, Fiscal Years 2005 through 2009

Fiscal year	Minimum congressionally required FTEs for humane handling	FTEs reported by FSIS
2005	63	110
2006	63	124
2007	[a]	121
2008	83	157
2009	120	157

Sources: GAO's analysis of appropriation acts and FSIS data.

[a] Congress did not specify any FTEs for humane handling enforcement in fiscal year 2007.

FSIS officials stated that workforce planning occurs at the district level and is determined using regulations that govern the number of inspectors required at each slaughter plant. According to district officials, they have discretion in deciding where to deploy relief inspectors. Therefore, they can deploy these inspectors at plants that they believe may require more HMSA oversight. However, more than one-third of the inspectors, who provided written comments in our survey, noted the need for additional staff or the lack of time to perform humane handling activities. Furthermore, inspectors at 80 percent of large plants stated that covering for others' responsibilities because of leave or vacancies has reduced the time spent on humane handling activities in those plants. While FSIS officials may need flexibility at the district level to allocate inspection resources, without an updated strategic workforce plan, the agency cannot effectively determine inspection needs across districts and adjust the inspection workforce to reflect changes in the industry and in FSIS resources.

Although the strategic workforce plan indicates that the agency performs this assessment annually, FSIS officials acknowledged that the agency has not updated its strategic workforce plan since 2007. We recommended in January 2004 that FSIS periodically reassess whether the level of inspection resources is sufficient to effectively enforce HMSA. As of November 2009, FSIS officials had told us that they were in the process of developing a workforce strategy but could not provide an estimated completion date.

FSIS Does Not Have a Comprehensive Strategy for Enforcing HMSA

Our body of work on results-oriented management calls for organizations to identify clearly defined goals that are aligned to available resources, develop time frames for achieving these goals, and develop performance metrics for measuring progress in meeting their goals.

We have recommended that all agencies adopt strategies that include these key elements. By implementing results-oriented management principles, agencies demonstrate their efforts to resolve long-standing management problems that undermine program efficiency and congressional decision making by providing more objective information on program performance.[24]

Although FSIS has strategic, operational, and performance plans for its inspection activities, these plans do not specifically address HMSA enforcement. That is, they do not clearly outline the agency's goals for enforcing HMSA, identify expected resource needs, specify time frames, or lay out performance metrics. Specifically, *FSIS Strategic Plan FY 2008 through FY 2013* provides an overview of the agency's major strategic goals and the means to achieve those goals. However, this plan does not clearly articulate or list goals related to HMSA enforcement. Instead, the plan generally addresses agency goals, such as improving data collection and analysis, maintaining information technology infrastructure to support agency programs, and enhancing inspection and enforcement systems overall to protect public health.

FSIS Office of Field Operations officials agreed that the plan does not specifically address humane handling, but they explained, the operational plans and policy performance plans contain the details concerning humane handling performance. However, as we indicate below, we did not find that these two plans provide a comprehensive strategy for HMSA enforcement:

- *Office of Field Operations' Operational Plan* identifies specific FSIS projects or initiatives and aligns them with the appropriate strategic goal identified in the *FSIS Strategic Plan for FY 2008 through FY 2013*. It also specifies the estimated dates for completion and recent information on the status of the project or initiative. According to our analysis of the July 2009 version of the operational plan, the most recent version available, humane handling activities fall under FSIS's first strategic goal—enhance inspection and enforcement systems and operations to protect public health. While the plan identifies tasks related to humane handling inspection activities, it does not identify any humane handling program goals linked to these tasks or explain how these tasks can be completed. For example, one of the plan's listed tasks is conducting humane handling information outreach, but the plan neither indicates how this task aligns with HMSA enforcement-related goals, nor does it specify resources needed. The plan also does not set priorities for proposed activities or identify milestones that could be used to measure progress or make improvements. Additionally, the document does not match the activities with resources needed to accomplish those tasks. According to FSIS officials, the Office of Field Operations' operational plan is an evolving document that is continually updated throughout the course of the year.
- *Office of Policy and Program Development Strategic Plan Fiscal Years 2008-2013* identifies policy goals that support the overall FSIS Strategic Plan. However, this plan does not clearly articulate or list goals related to HMSA enforcement.

Furthermore, FSIS does not have a set of performance measures for assessing the overall performance of humane handling enforcement across the districts. For example, FSIS is unable to determine whether the districts have improved their ability to enforce humane handling or may be weak in their enforcement. Although FSIS officials stated that the agency collects information such as the number of noncompliance reports, the number of egregious humane handling violations, and the number of humane handling activities performed on a routine basis by the DVMS, there is no indication of how these activities demonstrate improved enforcement of HMSA. Collecting and analyzing this type of information could be useful in identifying gaps or anomalies in performance and then developing a strategy to address them.

CONCLUSIONS

It is difficult to know whether the reported incidents of egregious animal handling at the slaughter plants in California and Vermont are isolated cases or indicative of a more widespread problem. Either way, it is evident from our survey results and our analysis of HMSA enforcement data that inspectors did not consistently identify and take enforcement action for humane handling violations for the period we reviewed. Furthermore, our survey results suggest that inspectors are not consistently applying their discretion as to which actions to take when egregious humane handling incidents occur, or when they are repeated, in part because the guidance is unclear. That is, the guidance states that inspectors-in-charge "may" suspend plant operations. Consequently, plants cited for the same type of humane handling incident may be subject to different enforcement actions. In January 2004, we recommended that FSIS establish additional clear, specific, and consistent criteria for enforcement actions to take when faced with repeat violations. FSIS responded by delegating this responsibility to the districts. However, incidents such as those at the Vermont plant suggest that this delegation has not been effective. While FSIS has stated that inspectors require discretion in enforcement, that discretion needs to be informed by an agency policy that ensures a consistent level of enforcement within plants and across districts. Without consistent enforcement actions, FSIS does not clearly signal its commitment to fully enforce HMSA. In addition, to improve plants' humane handling performance, the Agricultural Marketing Service, DVMSs, and others have adopted objective industry tools, such as numerical scoring, to help identify weaknesses. However, inspectors-incharge, who are responsible for assessing daily HMSA performance at the plants, are not directed to use such scoring tools.

Effective oversight of HMSA enforcement also requires FSIS to use available data to effectively manage the program, including allocating resources. FSIS has only recently begun to do so. Until 2009, FSIS did not routinely track and evaluate HMSA enforcement data—by geographic location, species, plant size, and history of compliance across districts. Although these analyses will be useful, FSIS has yet to analyze the narratives of humane handling incidents found in noncompliance reports, which would also help the agency identify weaknesses and trends in enforcement and develop appropriate strategies. Furthermore, we reiterate our January 2004 recommendation, which FSIS has not yet acted on, to periodically reassess whether its estimates still accurately reflect the resources necessary to effectively enforce the act. Finally, because FSIS does not have a comprehensive strategy for enforcing HMSA that aligns the agency's available resources with its mission and goals, and that identifies time frames for achieving these goals and performance metrics for meeting its goals, it is not well positioned to improve its ability to enforce HMSA.

RECOMMENDATIONS FOR EXECUTIVE ACTION

We are making the following four recommendations to the Secretary of Agriculture to strengthen the agency's oversight of humane handling and slaughter methods at federally inspected facilities.

To ensure that FSIS strengthens its enforcement of the Humane Methods of Slaughter Act of 1978, as amended, we recommend that the Secretary of Agriculture direct the Administrator of FSIS to take the following three actions:

- establish clear and specific criteria for when inspectors-in-charge should suspend plant operations for an egregious HMSA violation and when they should take enforcement actions because of repeat violations;

- identify some type of objective tool, such as a numerical scoring mechanism, and instruct all inspectors-in-charge at plants to use this measure to assist them in evaluating the plants' HMSA performance and determining what, if any, enforcement actions are warranted; and
- strengthen the analysis of humane handling data by analyzing the narrative in noncompliance reports to identify areas that need improvement.

To ensure that FSIS can demonstrate how efficiently and effectively it is enforcing HMSA, we recommend that the Secretary of Agriculture direct the Administrator of FSIS to develop an integrated strategy that clearly defines goals, identifies resources needed, and establishes time frames and performance metrics specifically for enforcing HMSA.

AGENCY COMMENTS AND OUR EVALUATION

We provided USDA with a draft of this chapter for review and comment. USDA did not state whether it agreed or disagreed with our findings and recommendations. However, it stated that it plans to use both our findings and recommendations to help improve efforts to ensure that establishments comply with HMSA and humane handling regulations. USDA also recognized the need to improve the inspectors' ability to identify trends in humane handling violations and work with academia, industry, and others to identify practices that will achieve more consistent HMSA enforcement.

USDA commented that the report contained some misstatements of fact that present a false picture of FSIS's humane handling verification and enforcement program and policies. We believe that we have fairly described FSIS policy and guidance on HMSA enforcement. In response to updated information that FSIS provided, we made appropriate revisions to clarify certain points. For example, we revised our report by deleting the portion of our analysis related to suspension data that occurred on the days that DVMSs conducted humane handling audits because on the basis of new information provided we believe that FSIS records of DVMS audit visits are incomplete.

USDA also questioned whether the results of our survey of FSIS inspectors provide evidence of systemic inconsistencies in enforcement. We believe they do, and would encourage USDA to consider the views of inspectors at the plants who are responsible for daily HMSA enforcement. Our survey results are based on strict adherence to GAO standards and methodology to ensure the most accurate results possible. Furthermore, our efforts were fully coordinated with FSIS before we distributed the survey.

Specifically, we vetted all of the questions with FSIS management in advance to ensure that these questions elicit responses that would reveal whether or not inspectors-in-charge understand how to fully enforce HMSA. In addition, we conducted numerous pre-tests of the survey with inspectors to ensure that we would receive the most accurate responses possible. We also coordinated with several humane handling experts who serve as FSIS consultants on training and enforcement issues to ensure that our questions would elicit the most accurate responses.

USDA also provided technical comments, which we have incorporated into this chapter as appropriate. USDA's written comments and our responses are presented in appendix IV.

As agreed with your offices, unless you publicly announce the contents of this chapter earlier, we plan no further distribution until 30 days from the report date. At that time, we will send copies of this chapter to appropriate congressional committees; the Secretary of Agriculture; the Director, Office of Management and Budget; and other interested parties. The report also will be available at no charge on the GAO Web site at http://www.gao.gov.

APPENDIX I. OBJECTIVES, SCOPE, AND METHODOLOGY

This chapter examines (1) U.S. Department of Agriculture Food Safety and Inspection Service's (FSIS) efforts to enforce the Humane Methods of Slaughter Act of 1978, as amended (HMSA); (2) the extent to which FSIS tracks recent trends in FSIS inspection resources for enforcing HMSA; and (3) FSIS's efforts to develop a strategy to guide HMSA enforcement.

To evaluate FSIS's efforts to enforce HMSA, we interviewed officials and collected documents from FSIS's Office of Field Operations; Office of Policy and Program Development; Office of Program Evaluation, Enforcement and Review; and the 15 district offices. We examined a nonprobability sample of FSIS noncompliance reports to provide illustrative examples of humane handling violations. In doing so, we searched for the words "prod" and "stun" in 533 noncompliance reports for 2007 and 589 noncompliance reports for 2008. Of these 1,122 reports, 272 reports included either the word "stun" or "prod" in reference to a violation. We then selected several of the reports that described violations appearing to be egregious and provided these reports to the expert we consulted for her assessment. This expert determined that the violations described in some of these reports were not sufficiently clear or detailed to determine whether they represented egregious violations, while others were clearly egregious in her judgment.

We also reviewed FSIS suspension data, data from the humane handling tracking system and district veterinary medical specialist reports in all 15 of FSIS's district offices for fiscal years 2005 through 2009. To assess the reliability of these data, we examined them for obvious errors in completeness and accuracy, reviewed existing documentation about the systems that produced the data, and questioned knowledgeable officials about the data and systems. We determined that the data were sufficiently reliable for the purposes of our review, with any limitations noted in the text. We also reviewed the HMSA enforcement reports produced by FSIS's Office of Data Analysis and Integration Group, as well as meeting minutes from the monthly district veterinary medical conferences. To understand FSIS policy and guidance on humane slaughter enforcement, we reviewed relevant regulations and FSIS instructions. From May 2009 through July 2009, we also surveyed inspectors-in-charge—those responsible for reporting on humane handling enforcement in the plants—from a random sample of inspectors at 257 livestock slaughter plants that were stratified by size—very small, small, and large. We adopted FSIS definition for small, very small, and large plants. We obtained an overall survey response rate of 93 percent.[25]

Table 3 shows the population and sample size distribution of slaughter plants by large, small and very small plant size. Each of the inspectors-incharge had a nonzero probability of being included, and that probability could be computed for any inspector-in-charge. Each inspector-in-charge was subsequently weighted in the analysis to account statistically for all the members of the population, including those who were not selected.

We analyzed all responses, including the written responses that we received from the survey by conducting a content analysis and categorizing the responses accordingly. The results of our survey are presented in a special publication titled *Humane Methods of Slaughter Act: USDA Inspectors' Views on Enforcement* that can be viewed at GAO-10-244SP.

Table 3. Universe of Plants and Sample Description

Plant size	Number of plants in universe	Number of plants in sample	Number of plants with inspectors-in-charge responding	Percentage response rate
Large	63	63	56	89%
Small	188	85	75	89%
Very small	531	109	104	95%
Total	**782**	**257**	**235**	**93%**

Source: GAO analysis of survey data.

We met with key officials from FSIS's Office of Field Operations who are responsible for implementing HMSA at the headquarters level. To understand district officials' perspectives on HMSA enforcement, we conducted semistructured interviews with each of FSIS's 15 district veterinary medical specialists (DVMS), 15 district managers, and 15 resource management analysts. We also performed a content analysis on all semistructured interviews to determine the districts' perspective on training, guidance, and resources available for humane handling enforcement. To understand the perspective of animal welfare groups and the meat industry, we met with representatives from the Humane Society of the United States, the Animal Welfare Institute, the American Meat Institute, the National Meat Association, and the American Association of Meat Processors. We reviewed these organizations' proposed reforms for HMSA enforcement. We also attended the 2009 American Meat Institute Humane Handling Conference in Kansas City, Missouri. To gain a better understanding of how the industry evaluates HMSA performance, we attended the Professional Animal Auditor Certification Organization training for meat plants in Denison, Iowa, in November 2008 and visited pork and beef slaughter plants that use a numerical scoring system. We also consulted animal handling expert Dr. Temple Grandin, who is a world-renowned expert on animal welfare who has served as a consultant to industry and FSIS, written extensively on modern methods of livestock handling, and designed slaughter facilities that have helped improve animal welfare in the United States and in other countries. Dr. Grandin provided her expert opinion on select humane handling incidents that we identified as possible HMSA violations. In addition to Dr. Grandin, we also spoke with animal welfare and food safety consultants to understand key principles of humane handling techniques and enforcement. We also met with representatives of the U.S. Department of Agriculture's Agricultural Marketing Service to understand how the agency uses numerical scoring to evaluate humane handling at the plants that provide meat to the National School Lunch Program. In order to understand FSIS training efforts, we attended an FSIS training seminar for small and very small plants held in Dallas, Texas, in February 2009, and met with

FSIS officials at the agency's Center for Learning in Washington, D.C., as well as with FSIS consultants who provide training in HMSA enforcement.

To identify the extent to which FSIS tracks recent trends in inspection resources for enforcing HMSA, we reviewed FSIS funding and staffing data for each district. We also conducted semistructured interviews with resource management analysts in each of FSIS's 15 district offices and interviewed key officials in the Resource Management and Planning Office within the Office of Field Operations. We performed a content analysis on all semistructured interviews to determine each districts' perspective on inspection resources available for humane handling enforcement. In order to understand how FSIS reports its annual full-time equivalent staff for humane handling to Congress, we collected funding and other relevant data and met with key officials in FSIS's Office of Field Operations and Office of Management and Office of the General Counsel, as well as the U.S. Department of Agriculture's Office of Budget and Program Analysis.

To assess FSIS's efforts to develop a strategy to enforce HMSA, we reviewed relevant FSIS strategies, including the *FSIS Strategic Plan FY 2008 through FY 2013, and the FSIS 2007 Strategic Workforce Plan*. We also reviewed the July 2009 version of the *Office of Field Operations' Operational Plan and the Office of Policy and Program Development Strategic Plan Fiscal Years 2008-2013*. Furthermore, we reviewed humane handling performance data from the Office of Policy and Program Development. We met with representatives of the FSIS Office of Management on human capital issues and officials from the Office of Personnel Management in Washington, D.C. To identify the key elements of a strategic plan, we reviewed the Government Performance and Results Act of 1993, as well as past GAO reports.

We conducted this performance audit for our work from October 2008 to February 2010, in accordance with generally accepted government auditing standards. Those standards require that we plan and perform the audit to obtain sufficient, appropriate evidence to provide a reasonable basis for our findings and conclusions based on our audit objectives. We believe that the evidence obtained provides a reasonable basis for our findings and conclusions based on our audit objectives.

APPENDIX II. LOCATION OF INSPECTORS OBSERVING HMSA COMPLIANCE AT TYPICAL MID-SIZED PLANT

Figure 11 illustrates the areas in a typical, mid-sized plant from which inspectors can observe HMSA compliance, although inspectors are not always present in all areas.

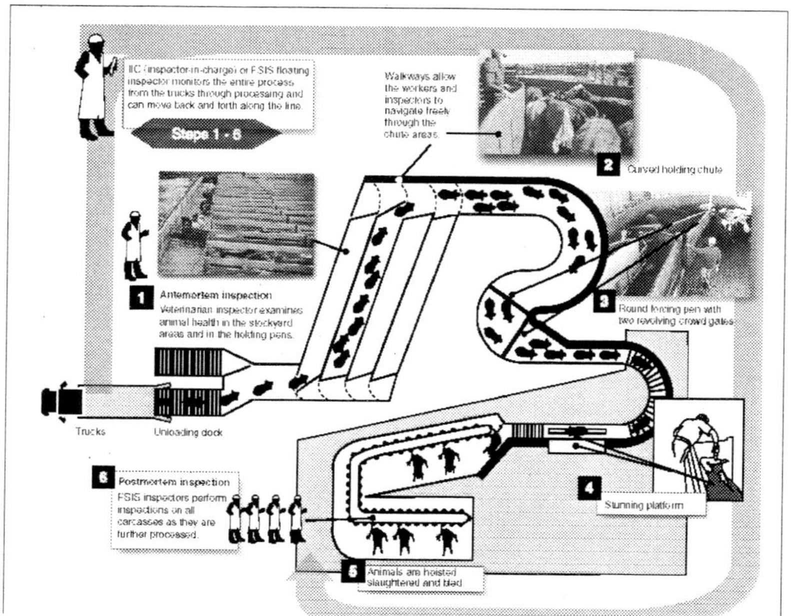

Sources: GAO graphic based on GAO analysis of information provided by FSIS and Dr. Temple Grandin, a humane handling expert.

Figure 11. Location of Inspectors Observing Compliance with the HMSA at a Typical Mid-Sized Plant

APPENDIX III. HMSA SUSPENSIONS FOR FSIS DISTRICTS

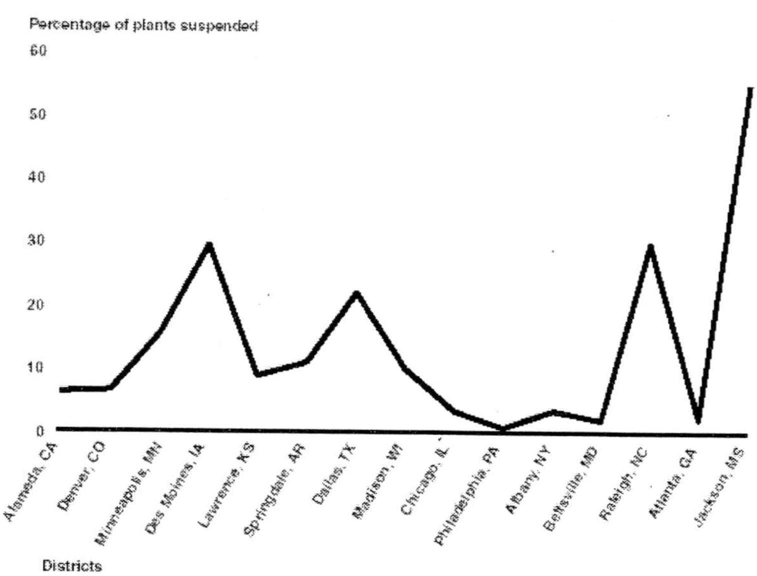

Source: GAO analysis of FSIS data.

Figure 12. Percentage of Suspensions by District, Calendar Year 2008

Figure 12 provides an overview of the percentage of plant suspensions for HMSA enforcement that occurred in each district for calendar year 2008. The percentages were determined based on the total number of plants in each districts and the number of reported suspensions. As the figure illustrates, the Jackson district had the highest percentage of suspensions.

APPENDIX IV. COMMENTS FROM THE U.S. DEPARTMENT OF AGRICULTURE

Note: GAO comments supplementing those in the report text appear at the end of this appendix.

USDA

United States Department of Agriculture

Office of the Secretary
Washington, D.C. 20250

Lisa Shames
Director, Natural Resources and Environment
United States Government Accountability Office
441 G Street, NW
Washington, DC 20548

JUL 22 2010

Dear Ms. Shames:

USDA appreciates the opportunity to comment on the GAO draft report. "Humane Methods of Slaughter Act: Actions are Needed to Strengthen Enforcement." We will be providing responses to the audit recommendations within 60 days of the publication of the report, as is required by 31 U.S.C. 720.

USDA's Food Safety and Inspection Service (FSIS) enforces the Humane Methods of Livestock Slaughter Act (HMSA), authorizing the agency to regulate the handling of livestock prior to slaughter, as well as the method of slaughter, at establishments. I want to be clear that this mandate is a high priority for FSIS. Ensuring that livestock are handled and slaughtered humanely is a responsibility FSIS is committed to, along with our mission to protect public health. When Congress passed the HMSA, it found that humane slaughter prevented needless suffering, resulted in safer and better working conditions for employees at slaughter establishments, and provided benefits to producer and consumers through better products and improved flow of livestock and livestock products. FSIS inspectors are in plants every day, working to ensure that Congressional intent to require humane slaughter at every slaughter plant is a priority and is carried out effectively.

FSIS has worked with the Government Accountability Office (GAO) during this audit to provide an accurate picture of how the agency enforces the HMSA. We appreciate this collaboration, and we plan to use both GAO's findings and recommendations as we improve our efforts to ensure that establishments comply with this law and our humane handling regulations. For example, FSIS recognizes the need to improve our inspectors' ability to identify trends in humane handling violations. The agency also needs to work with academia, industry, the non-profit sector, and animal health experts to identify practices that will achieve more consistent enforcement of the HMSA.

Actions that FSIS will take in response to this report will build on the considerable work already being done by FSIS to improve our performance in verifying humane handling at slaughter establishments. For example, as highlighted in the GAO report, FSIS will soon fill a humane handling coordinator position. This senior employee will provide oversight of inspectors' enforcement and strengthen our comprehensive strategy for enforcing HMSA, areas that GAO highlights in this report as needing improvement. In February 2009, FSIS inspection program personnel assigned to livestock slaughter establishments were required to complete refresher training on the Agency's humane handling policies. This training included information on how

See comment 1.

See comment 2.

See comment 3.

See comment 4.

to determine insensibility, documenting noncompliance, and suspending inspection for egregious situations. This training is in addition to the classroom instruction provided to entry level employees. FSIS is planning further workforce training activities related to humane handling for fiscal year 2010.

Recent enforcement also demonstrates the Agency's strong commitment to enforcing the HMSA. In 2008, FSIS issued a total of 178 suspensions to federally inspected establishments, 54 percent (97 suspensions) of which were for humane handling violations witnessed by inspection personnel. Of these 97 inhumane handling suspensions, 75 were initial suspensions and 22 were repeat suspensions. In 2009, FSIS issued a total of 164 suspensions to federally inspected establishments, 53 percent (87 suspensions) of which were for humane handling violations witnessed by inspection personnel. Of these 87 inhumane handling suspensions, 71 were initial suspensions and 16 were repeat suspensions. As noted by GAO in this report, both of these figures show a significant increase in humane handling enforcement (pages 21 and 22) since the events at Hallmark/Westland.

While GAO has provided the agency with useful information on how we might improve our oversight of humane handling and slaughter, this report also contains numerous substantive misstatements of fact that we believe warrant your further attention. We believe that these inaccuracies present a false picture of FSIS humane handling verification and enforcement programs and policies. In order to appropriately and accurately identify areas where improvements are needed in FSIS's oversight of humane handling, we ask that our general and specific comments below be published in the report.

General Comments on Themes in the Report Findings

These are FSIS's comments on themes in findings from the report, presented roughly in the order the findings first appear. In some cases, misstatements corrected in FSIS' specific comments are referenced.

Suspension of Inspection and District Veterinary Medical Specialist (DVMS) visits
In the initial summary of findings, on page 22 of the report and elsewhere, GAO states that 61% of suspensions of inspection related to humane handling "occurred during DVMSs humane handling audit visits," implying that FSIS verification of humane handling is deficient since DVMSs are directing the majority of suspensions, while spending so little time in individual establishments themselves. This is incorrect. Of the 97 suspensions related to humane handling violations in CY 2008, 84.5% (82 suspensions) were initiated by in-plant veterinarians or inspection personnel. Only 15.5% (15 suspensions) occurred during DVMS visits.

Withdrawal and Suspension of Inspection and the Incident at Bushway Packing
The description on page 9 of the process to "withdraw the plant's grant of inspection" is incorrect. A District office may not simply decide to withdraw a grant of inspection by withdrawing inspection program personnel. Although the district manager recommends the filing of a complaint for withdrawal, per the regulations in 9 CFR 500.6, if an establishment handles or slaughters livestock inhumanely, only the FSIS Administrator may file a complaint to

See comment 5.

See comment 6.

withdraw a grant of Federal inspection in accordance with the Uniform Rules of Practice, 7 CFR Subtitle A, part 1, subpart H. This correction is included in our specific comments, but it also informs our following comment on GAO's discussion of events at Bushway Packing on page 24 of the audit report.

On page 24, GAO criticizes FSIS for not issuing "any guidance to the district offices on how many suspensions should result in a withdrawal of inspectors" and claims that had the Agency done so, the November 2009 incident of inhumane handling at Bushway might have been prevented. FSIS does not agree that a fixed number of suspensions should necessitate a request for withdrawal of the grant of inspection. The decision to suspend inspection, as well as to request a withdrawal of the grant of inspection, is based on numerous qualitative factors and can be made only by weighing all of the evidence for a specific case. But even if there were such a threshold for requesting withdrawal, given the legal requirements cited above, it is not certain that a withdrawal of Bushway's grant of inspection would have occurred prior to November 2009.

Also on page 24, on page 40, and elsewhere in the report, GAO references the Bushway situation in concluding that FSIS's delegation of humane handling enforcement procedures to district offices "has not been effective." However, as stated above, suspensions for humane handling effected by Districts significantly increased during 2008 and 2009; they were in fact approximately twice the number of suspensions effected for other food safety related reasons.

Adoption of a Scoring System

On page 11, pages 27-29, and elsewhere in the document, GAO criticizes FSIS for not adopting a numerical scoring system for verification of compliance with humane handling requirements. FSIS has, in fact, provided a scoring tool to its DVMSs, the "Humane Handling and Slaughter Verification Tool," which was included in FSIS Directive 6910.1, Revision 1, published on December 7, 2009. FSIS has already conducted DVMS training on the scoring tool in August 2009. FSIS provided a draft of the tool to GAO during the audit.

The scores in the tool concern various indicators of humane handling, including stunning efficacy, and are based on industry standards. It is correct, as GAO points out on page 28 of the report, that the scoring is not regulatory in nature. Rather, the scores are used as guidance by the DVMS for discussions with the establishment. FSIS does not use the scoring alone for enforcement because the scoring, which allows for stunning failures, is inconsistent with the HMSA requirements for rendering livestock insensible to pain prior to slaughter "with a single blow or gunshot" (7 USC 1902(a)). Although it is true that establishments sometimes fail to stun livestock effectively with a single blow, FSIS does not enforce requirements less stringent than those mandated by the HMSA. Instead, FSIS uses its discretion to enforce in different ways, depending on the severity of and factors surrounding the stunning violation. In the case of an observed stunning failure, FSIS inspection program personnel are, at a minimum, to issue a noncompliance record (FSIS Directive 6900.2, Revision 2, Parts IV (C) and VI (A) and (B)).

See comment 7.
See comment 8.
See comment 8.
See comment 9.
See comment 9.

Strengthen the analysis of humane handling data

FSIS will be significantly strengthening its analysis of humane handling data later this year. In an effort to dramatically improve its data collection and analysis, FSIS will launch the Public Health Information System (PHIS) later this year. PHIS will enhance FSIS's data infrastructure through integration of all data streams, including data collected in the Humane Activities Tracking System (HATS), a system that FSIS currently uses to document humane handling verification activities. PHIS will allow us to provide ongoing, real-time assessment, analysis and surveillance of public health, food defense, and humane handling data. Once PHIS is implemented, FSIS will have a critical tool to carry out more effective oversight of humane handling at livestock slaughter establishments.

GAO Survey of FSIS Inspection Program Personnel

GAO draws many of its audit findings from the results of its survey of FSIS inspection program personnel. FSIS has acknowledged inconsistencies in enforcement of the humane handling requirements and plans to examine the GAO survey results as it continues to improve its humane handling verification and enforcement training and policies. But, for a number of reasons, FSIS questions whether the survey results provide evidence of systemic inconsistencies in enforcement, as suggested by the report.

Owing to the language of the HMSA and the nature of livestock slaughter operations, verification and enforcement of humane handling requirements are activities that require qualitative judgments. The HMSA does not establish quantitative standards for humane handling and every livestock slaughter operation is different - in size, construction, layout, and staffing. Some of the survey questions however, as well as some of GAO's conclusions based on the survey results, seem to presuppose and depend on a necessary correlation between frequencies of events and specific regulatory responses.

For example, questions 11 and 12 ask inspection program personnel to state what specific regulatory action they would take (suspension, regulatory control action, noncompliance record only) in response to specific frequencies of events, e.g. "Electrically prodding between 26 to 50 of 100 animals within acceptable voltage." Because inspection program personnel answered these types of questions differently, GAO concludes that HMSA enforcement is inconsistent. FSIS counters, though, that because there are no quantitative statutory requirements for humane handling and because each livestock slaughter establishment is unique, the responses show only that inspection program personnel were answering in the context of their experiences with specific establishments and livestock slaughter scenarios. Depending on the situation, any of the three regulatory responses often could be correct. Additionally, FSIS had not previously provided the potential frequencies of noncompliance found in the survey to in-plant personnel. This fact also likely contributed to the highly variable results.

Finally, in regard to the GAO survey, it is important to note that the results show that there is overwhelming consistency among inspection program personnel responses concerning certain humane handling situations that require action. The questionnaire shows that significant percentages of employees consider action necessary in response to these problem situations. We

See comment 10.
See comment 11.
See comment 4.
See comment 4.
See comment 12.
See comment 13.

see this as a starting point for using the GAO survey results in our efforts to improve HMSA verification and enforcement.

Specific Comments

Although some of our specific comments correct simple misstatements of fact, many address what FSIS sees as substantive misstatements of FSIS programs and policies. We believe that these misstatements, when taken together, create an inaccurate picture of FSIS humane handling verification and enforcement.

- Page 6 – The report states that "HMSA exempts only ritual slaughter, such as kosher and halal slaughter, from the HMSA requirements." This is incorrect. Under 7 U.S.C. 1902(b), kosher and halal slaughter are defined as "humane," not exempted from the requirements of the Act.
- Page 8 The report states that when inspection program personnel observe a violation of the HMSA they are *both* to issue a noncompliance record (NR) and a regulatory control action. This is incorrect. FSIS Directive 6900.2, Rev 1, section VI (A) (3) directs inspection program personnel to take a regulatory control action only if "an establishment fails to adequately respond to an NR or fails to take its immediate and further preventive actions ..."
- Page 8, bottom -- The sentence above the last bullet incorrectly describes the regulatory response to an egregious incident of humane handling. When the inspectors-in-charge (IIC) determines that an egregious incident has occurred, he or she applies the regulations at 9 CFR 500.3(b) in accordance with the instructions in FSIS Notice 21-09: "the IIC is to take an appropriate regulatory control action to prevent continued egregious inhumane handling and orally notify plant management of an immediate suspension action.".
- Page 9, bullet – The description of the process for withdrawing a grant of inspection is incorrect and misleading. A District office may not simply "decide" to withdraw a grant of inspection by withdrawing inspection program personnel. Although the district manager recommends the filing of a complaint for withdrawal, per the regulations in 9 CFR 500.6, if an establishment handles or slaughters livestock inhumanely, only "The FSIS Administrator may file a complaint to withdraw a grant of Federal inspection in accordance with the Uniform Rules of Practice, 7 CFR Subtitle A, part 1, subpart H."
- Page 9 – In the second sentence, GAO states that IICs "may or may not be vets." IICs typically are veterinarians, i.e. in all but the smallest slaughter facilities. Additionally, FSIS does not "certify" livestock prior to slaughter, as stated in the third to last sentence.
- Page 10 -- The chart references a "patrol veterinarian", which is only applicable to multi-IPPS (in-plant performance system) assignments. The term is not applicable, as shown, to large plants or most small plants.

See comment 14.
See comment 15.
See comment 3.
See comment 16.
See comment 17.

- Page 12 – In the incomplete paragraph at the top of the page, GAO states that FSIS has not used "data to analyze HMSA enforcement across districts and plants to identify inconsistent enforcement." FSIS disagrees. In FY09, FSIS issued four quarterly reports on HMSA enforcement, analyzing FY09 data across Districts. These have been made available to and discussed with the District Offices during the monthly DVMS calls.

- Page 15 -- In the second to last sentence, GAO states that in regard to suspension of inspection in response to egregious inhumane handling, "there is no directive to do so in guidance." This is misleading. FSIS Notice 21-09, which has the same force as an FSIS Directive and provides specific examples of egregious inhumane handling, states:

> However, if the observed inhumane treatment is of an egregious nature, the regulations at 9 CFR 500.3(b) apply. The regulations state, 'FSIS also may impose a suspension without providing the establishment prior notification because the establishment is handling or slaughtering animals inhumanely.' Therefore, the IIC is to take an appropriate regulatory control action to prevent continued egregious inhumane handling and orally notify plant management of an immediate suspension action. Next, the IIC is to immediately notify the District Office (DO) and the DVMS for prompt documentation of the suspension action. The IIC is also to document the facts that serve as the basis of the suspension action on a memorandum of interview (MOI) (see Attachment 1) and promptly provide that information electronically to the DO and the DVMS for their use in documenting the Notice of Suspension. The DO and the DMVS will make an official assessment of the facts supporting the suspension, take any final action with respect to it, and notify the Executive Associate for Regulatory Operations designated for the District.

- Page 22 -- GAO states that 61% of suspensions of inspection related to humane handling "occurred during DVMSs humane handling audit visits." This is incorrect. Of the 97 suspensions related to humane handling violations in CY 2008, 84.5% (82 suspensions) were initiated by in-plant veterinarians or inspection personnel. Only 15.5% (15 suspensions) occurred during DVMS visits.

- Page 25 – In the first full paragraph, discussing the survey results concerning training, GAO states that 57% of IICs reported incorrect answers on "at least one of six possible signs of sensibility." However, footnote 17 on the same page 25 states that when GAO queried the inspection program personnel they "added two [signs] that, alone, do not generally indicate sensibility." It is unclear, therefore, what percentage of respondents in fact gave "incorrect answers." GAO's finding here that inspectors-in-charge "may not have been sufficiently trained" is thus called into question.

- Page 26 – The second bullet concerns a National Academics' Institute of Medicine study recommending "testing and improved training" for inspection program personnel. This

See comment 18.
See comment 19.
See comment 20.

food safety verification. It is unclear how it is applicable to humane handling verification activities.

- Page 31 -- In the first full paragraph, GAO implies that FSIS applies inconsistent amounts of time to humane handling verification in light of differing slaughter volumes at individual establishments. HMSA verification is independent of slaughter volume. Compliance is a function of an establishment's controls and the intensity of verification corresponds to establishment performance over time.

- Pages 33 and 34 – The table and the narrative reference the "total amount specified for FSIS inspection in the agency annual appropriation," and go on to imply that too small a percentage is used for humane handling verification. The referenced funding for "FSIS inspection" included livestock slaughter, poultry slaughter, and processing inspection; egg inspection; import inspection; in-commerce compliance; district office activities; and food safety enforcement activities. Since only the portions of the appropriation related to livestock slaughter inspection would be relevant to humane handling activity, the GAO conclusion that only "slightly above 1 percent of FSIS' total inspection appropriations" is related to humane handling is very misleading.

- Page 40 – The first sentence is contrary to the USDA Office of Inspector General's (OIG) finding concerning the events at Hallmark/Westland. GAO concludes that it is "difficult to know whether the reported incidents of egregious animal handling at the slaughter plants in California and Vermont are isolated cases or indicative of a more widespread problem." OIG found that "the events that occurred at Hallmark were not a systemic failure of the inspection processes/system as designed by FSIS." Given this finding, and the increased scrutiny paid to humane handling compliance by FSIS since Hallmark/Westland, it seems unlikely that there is a significant volume of egregious humane handling violations undetected by FSIS.

Sincerely,

Jerold R. Mande

The following are GAO's comments on the U.S. Department of Agriculture's letter dated January 22, 2010.

GAO Comments

1. Our report acknowledges FSIS's efforts to increase its humane handling enforcement efforts since the events at Westland/Hallmark. However, FSIS did not provide source material for some of the data in its comments, making it difficult to determine the completeness and reliability of the data provided. Therefore we could not include in the report the data that FSIS provides in its comments.

2. We believe our report provides an accurate picture of FSIS's humane handling enforcement activities. However, we have modified text in response to FSIS's technical comments as appropriate or have explained why we disagree with FSIS's comments, as noted below.
3. We revised the report to reflect the agency's comments by deleting the portion of our analysis in our draft report that related to the suspension data that occurred on the days that DVMSs conducted humane handling audits. The report now states that the recods of DVMS audit visits are incomplete and that we were unable to conduct the complete analysis. As a result, we could not fully determine how often DVMSs conducted humane handling audit visits nor whether there is a higher rate of enforcement actions on the days that DVMSs conducted their audits for humane handling. Specifically, our original analysis of the DVMS visits was based on data that FSIS provided to us during the course of our review. Based on the information originally provided to us by FSIS during our audit, these data met all of GAO's data reliability standards. In January 2010, after receiving a draft copy of this chapter for comment, FSIS provided us with revised suspension data and informed us that the original data it had provided were incomplete. However, after reviewing the January 2010 data, we believe the revised data contain incomplete information, and we are therefore unable to corroborate the DVMS humane handling audit visit data.
4. We modified the report to clarify that the FSIS Administrator may file a complaint to withdraw a grant of federal inspection.
5. We modified the report to clarify the difference between a withdrawal of inspectors and a withdrawal of the grant of inspection. We added that only the FSIS Administrator may file a complaint to withdraw a grant of federal inspection. However, the district office can still request such a withdrawal. In 2004, we recommended that FSIS establish additional, clear, specific and consistent criteria for district offices to use when considering whether to take enforcement actions because of repeat violations.[26] We continue to believe that more specific guidance would be valuable to better address situations such as the one at the Bushway Packing plant in Vermont. It is also important to note that inspectors need to be trained to identify what actions may warrant such a request to ensure that FSIS is fully enforcing HMSA.
6. Although we did not state that numerical scoring is not regulatory in nature, we did state that using it to measure compliance would be inconsistent with the HMSA requirement that animals be rendered insensible to pain on the first blow. However, we believe that FSIS, in using its enforcement discretion, should identify some type of objective tool, such as a numerical scoring mechanism, and instruct all inspectors-in-charge at plants to use this measure to assist them in evaluating their plants' HMSA performance and determining what, if any, enforcement actions are necessary in the agency's exercise of its enforcement discretion.
7. We acknowledge in the report FSIS's efforts to strengthen its analysis of humane handling data later this year. Although FSIS officials informed us of plans to implement the Public Health Information System, we found that those plans have experienced delays, and the system has yet to be implemented. For example, Public Health Information System was originally scheduled to be fully functional in the fall 2009—we now understand that the expected date has shifted to the end of 2010.

Without the availability of this system, we analyzed the humane handling data that FSIS made available to us during the course of our review.

8. FSIS questioned whether our survey results provide evidence of systemic inconsistencies in enforcement. Our survey results are based on strict adherence to GAO standards and methodology to ensure the most accurate results possible, as summarized in appendix I of this chapter. From May 2009 through July 2009, we surveyed inspectors-incharge—those responsible for reporting on humane handling enforcement in the plants—from a random sample of inspectors at 257 livestock slaughter plants that were stratified by size—very small, small, and large. We obtained an overall survey response rate of 93 percent.[27]
9. Concerning FSIS's comment on two of our survey questions, our survey results showed that 29 percent of the inspectors reported that they would not take any enforcement action or did not know what enforcement action to take for electrical prodding of most animals. Ten percent of the inspectors reported that they would take no enforcement action or did not know what action to take for electrical prodding in the rectal area. These figures suggest that FSIS may not be fully enforcing HMSA. While FSIS states that HMSA enforcement requires that inspectors make qualitative judgments since each livestock slaughter operation is unique, we found that humane handling experts in academia and industry firmly believe that such judgments need to be based on some type of objective standards, regardless of the size, construction, layout and staffing at the plants. We appreciate FSIS's statement that it plans to examine the GAO survey results as it continues to improve its enforcement training and policies and urge FSIS to fully use the information in the survey results to identify practices that may achieve more consistent enforcement of HMSA.
10. We modified the report to clarify that HMSA exempts ritual slaughter from the requirement we discuss in the sentences immediately preceding the text in that section of the report—that an animal be rendered insensible to pain on the first blow—not to the general HMSA requirements.
11. Our report is correct as stated. FSIS refers to FSIS Directive 6900.2, Rev. 1, section VI (A) but FSIS does not refer to section VI (B), which states that if an inspector determines that "a noncompliance with humane slaughter and handling requirements has occurred and animals are being injured or treated inhumanely," the inspector is to take two specific actions: (1) document the noncompliance on a noncompliance record and (2) take a regulatory control action. FSIS's misapplication of the directive may further illustrate the lack of clarity in FSIS policy on humane handling enforcement, which may contribute to the lack of a clear understanding at the inspector level.
12. Nearly three-quarters of the inspectors-in-charge responding in our survey reported that they were not veterinarians. While 100 percent of the IICs at the large plants that we surveyed were veterinarians, 88 percent of those at very small plants in our representative survey were not veterinarians, and 57 percent of IICs at small plants were not veterinarians. In addition, we modified the text to clarify the responsibility of FSIS veterinarians prior to slaughter.
13. We modified figure 3 to show that patrol veterinarian only applies to some small and very small plants.

14. On page 31 of this chapter, we state that "FSIS began analyzing data across districts from the Humane Activities Tracking System in 2008— 4 years after it developed the system." We also recognize that the Data Analysis Integration Group began "reporting quarterly on HMSA enforcement, including the amount of time inspectors have devoted to HMSA, the number of plants suspended, and the number of noncompliance reports issued in 2009." In reviewing these reports, however, we found no analysis indicating that FSIS used these data to evaluate HSMA enforcement across the districts and plants to identify inconsistent enforcement. Also, FSIS officials acknowledged in our final meeting in November 2009, that it has never conducted any analysis of the noncompliance reports to determine patterns or trends in HMSA enforcement. Furthermore, although FSIS provided us with its monthly minutes of its DVMS conference calls from March through September 2009, these minutes did not identify any FSIS analysis of HMSA enforcement across the districts and possible inconsistent patterns. FSIS did not grant our request to attend the monthly DVMS conference calls in order to better understand the nature of the DVMS discussion and attempt to determine if such analysis was under way.
15. We modified the text to indicate that there is "no clear directive to do so in guidance." Although regulations and policy documents describe when suspensions may take place, the agency has offered no clear directive as to when they should take place.
16. We changed the text to state "six possible signs of sensibility" to clarify, as noted in footnote 17 (now footnote 15), that the list of signs included two that, alone, do not generally indicate sensibility. In addition, we re-checked the coding used in our analysis to ensure that the calculations were correct. We found no discrepancies or errors. Therefore, these results clearly demonstrate that inspectors-in-charge may not have been sufficiently trained.
17. The National Academies' Institute of Medicine study found weaknesses in the noncompliance reports, and as we stated, the institute recommended testing and improved training with special emphasis on the quality and consistency of noncompliance reports for food safety issues. Because FSIS's inspection personnel are responsible for completing noncompliance reports for both food safety and humane handling violations, it is evident that improving training on the quality and consistency of those reports would be useful in supporting FSIS humane handling compliance efforts.
18. Our analysis of similar sized plants with similar slaughter volumes revealed substantial differences in the amount of time devoted to humane handling in different districts. This information might better inform FSIS officials to manage resources and/or training to help improve performance.
19. We disagree. We conducted this analysis in an effort to gain some perspective on the percent of FSIS annual appropriation for inspection devoted to humane handling and estimated that it has been above 1 percent of FSIS's total annual inspection appropriation. FSIS officials informed us that 80 percent of their time should be devoted to food safety and 20 percent to humane handling inspection and other activities. Because FSIS cannot track humane handling funds separately, the agency was unable to provide the amount of funds that it devotes to humane handling activities. To provide context for the reader, we estimated the percentage of the total

annual inspection appropriations dedicated to HMSA enforcement. We modified the text to expand the definition of FSIS inspection fund to include other activities such as livestock slaughter, poultry slaughter, processing inspection, egg inspection, import inspection, in-commerce compliance, district office activities and food safety enforcement activities. However, this clarification does not change the calculation.

20. We disagree. While the OIG report states that "events that occurred at Hallmark were not a systemic failure of the inspection processes/system as designed by FSIS," it is important to note that its scope was based on observations at 10 cull cow (older and weaker) slaughter facilities. Nevertheless, the OIG report presented 25 recommendations to strengthen FSIS activities, and FSIS accepted all of these recommendations. Specifically, OIG recommended that FSIS needs to "reassess the inhumane handling risks associated with cull slaughter establishments and determine if more frequent or in-depth reviews need to be conducted." The report also recommended "that a structured training and development program, with a continuing education component, be developed for both its inspection and management resources." Furthermore, our survey results and analysis of HMSA enforcement data —that inspectors did not consistently identify and take enforcement action for humane handling violations for the period we reviewed—indicate a more widespread problem. Therefore, we continue to believe that it is difficult to know whether these incidents are isolated or not, and the extent of such incidents is difficult to determine because FSIS does not evaluate the narrative in noncompliance reports.

End Notes

[1] GAO, *Humane Methods of Slaughter Act: USDA Has Addressed Some Problems but Still Faces Enforcement Challenges*, GAO-04-247 (Washington, D.C.: Jan. 30, 2004). Also, see GAO, *Humane Methods of Handling and Slaughter: Public Reporting on Violations Can Identify Enforcement Challenges and Enhance Transparency*, GAO-08-686T (Washington, D.C.: Apr. 17, 2008).

[2] U.S. Department of Agriculture, Office of Inspector General, Great Plains Region, *Audit Report: Evaluation of FSIS Management Controls Over Pre-Slaughter Activities*, Report No. 24601-0007KC (November 2008).

[3] All full sample percentage estimates from the survey have margins of error at the 95 percent confidence level of plus or minus 7 percentage points or less, unless otherwise noted. Percentage estimates by plant size have margins of error at the 95 percent confidence level of plus or minus 10 percentage points or less, unless otherwise noted.

[4] Dr. Grandin has served as a consultant to industry and FSIS, written extensively on modern methods of livestock handling, and has designed slaughter facilities that have helped improve animal welfare in the United States.

[5] A captive bolt gun contains a steel bolt—powered by either compressed air or a blank cartridge—that is driven into an animal's brain and then retracted into the gun, which resets the bolt for the next animal. This gun has the same effect as a gun with live bullets but is safer than a firearm.

[6] U.S. Department of Agriculture, Food Safety and Inspection Service, FSIS Notice 12-05, *Documentation of Humane Handling Activities* (Feb. 18, 2005).

[7] Dr. Temple Grandin, testimony before the Domestic Policy Subcommittee, House Committee on Oversight and Government Reform, "*After the Beef Recall: Exploring Greater Transparency in the Meat Industry*" (Washington, D.C: Apr. 17, 2008).

[8] Dr. Temple Grandin, testimony before the Domestic Policy Subcommittee, House Committee on Oversight and Government Reform, "*After the Beef Recall: Exploring Greater Transparency in the Meat Industry*" (Washington, D.C. Apr. 17, 2008).

[9] C.F.R. § 313.2(b).

[10] Electrical stuns must be properly placed on the animal to ensure effective stunning; that is, the current must go through the brain.

[11] See 9 C.F.R. §§ 313.5, 313.15, 313.16, 313.30.

[12] The inspector's report did not indicate whether the original captive bolt stun gun was functioning properly.

[13] These five FSIS districts are Albany, Beltsville, Chicago, Des Moines, and Lawrence.

[14] GAO-04-247.

[15] Our survey presented the four signs of sensibility—natural blinking, lifting head straight up and keeping it up (righting reflex), rhythmic breathing, and vocalizing—and added two that, alone, do not generally indicate sensibility—rear leg(s) kicking and tail moving. In our assessment, if the respondent selected at least one of the two signs that do not indicate sensibility or if he or she indicated that they did not know the answer, the respondent's answer was considered to be incorrect in our calculation.

[16] GAO-04-247.

[17] In addition, we identified a set of principles to help federal agencies improve the effectiveness of their training efforts. See GAO, *Human Capital: A Guide for Assessing Strategic Training and Development Efforts in the Federal Government*, GAO-04-546G (Washington, D.C.: Mar. 1, 2004).

[18] Institute of Medicine of the National Academies, *Review of the Use of Process Control Indicators in the FSIS Public Health Risk-Based Inspection System* (Washington, D.C: Mar. 3, 2009).

[19] U.S. Department of Agriculture, Food Safety and Inspection Service, FSIS Directive 6910.1, Rev. 1, *District Veterinary Medical Specialist Work Methods* (Dec. 7, 2009).

[20] U.S. Department of Agriculture, Office of Inspector General, Great Plains Region, *Evaluation of FSIS Management Controls Over Pre-Slaughter Activities*, Report No. 2460 1-0007KC (November 2008).

[21] Fiscal year 2008 data were the latest available at the time of our review.

[22] An FTE generally consists of one or more employed individuals who collectively complete 2,080 work hours in a given year. Therefore, either one full-time employee or two half-time employees equal one FTE.

[23] GAO, *Veterinarian Workforce: Actions Are Needed to Ensure Sufficient Capacity for Protecting Public and Animal Health*, GAO-09-178 (Washington, D.C.: Feb. 4, 2009).

[24] See GAO, *Agency Performance Plans: Examples of Practices that Can Improve Usefulness to Decisionmakers*, GAO/GGD/AIMD-99-69 (Washington, D.C.: Feb. 26, 1999) and GAO, *Agencies Strategic Plans Under GPRA: Key Questions to Facilitate Congressional Review*, GAO/GGD-10. 1.16 (Washington, D.C.: May 1997).

[25] All full sample percentage estimates from the survey have margins of error at the 95 percent confidence level of plus or minus 7 percentage points or less, unless otherwise noted. Percentage estimates by plant size have margins of error at the 95 percent confidence level of plus or minus 10 percentage points or less, unless otherwise noted.

[26] GAO-04-247.

[27] All full sample percentage estimates from the survey have margins of error at the 95 percent confidence level of +/- 7 percentage points or less, unless otherwise noted. Percentage estimates by plant size have margins of error at the 95 percent confidence level of +/- 10 percentage points or less, unless otherwise noted.

In: Animal Protection: Treatment and Welfare Issues
Editor: Dennis G. Carlton
ISBN: 978-1-61728-353-6

Chapter 4

OPENING STATEMENT OF DENNIS J. KUCINICH, CHAIRMAN, DOMESTIC POLICY SUBCOMMITTEE,OVERIGHT AND GOVERNMENT REFORM COMMITTEE - HEARING ON "CONTINUING PROBLEMS IN USDA'S ENFORCEMENT OF THE HUMANE METHODS OF SLAUGHTER ACT"*

Good afternoon.

About two years ago, an undercover video exposing extreme abuses of downed cattle at a slaughter plant in California shocked the nation. The video depicted scenes of employees at the plant ramming cows with a forklift, poking at their eyes, and repeatedly applying electrical shocks, to make downed cattle regain their footing and walk to the stun box.

Those were apparent violations of the Humane Methods of Slaughter Act. While the USDA acted quickly, at the same time, key department officials disclaimed the extent of the problems depicted. For instance, Dr. Kenneth Petersen, Assistant Administrator for the Office of Field Operations, Food Safety and Inspection Service (FSIS), said, "FSIS believes this to be an isolated incident."

Since that time, this Subcommittee has examined the basis for USDA's espoused confidence. What we found was USDA's belief was not based on actual evidence. In fact in November 2008, the Inspector General found that FSIS had been in the slaughter plant where those scenes of abuse were recorded and found no problems, just months before the video was shot.

The IG also found that in a number of plants similar to the one in California, severe gaps in oversight and enforcement existed. For instance,

- FSIS inspectors "allowed establishment employees to control the required accountability process" at 5 of 10 facilities audited:

* This is an edited, reformatted and augmented edition of a statement/testimony given before the United States Oversight and Government Reform Committee, dated March 4, 2010.

- At one establishment, "the inspector simply re-signed blank pen cards and provided these to establishment personnel for later use";
- At 4 of 10 establishments, inspectors did not inspect the condition of individual animals. Instead, "animals moved past the inspector in rows or groups of 3-4 animals deep, effectively obscuring the observation of potential injuries and abnormalities of each animal";
- At 2 of 10 establishments, "suspect animals were not segregated and slaughtered separately from healthy animals as required"

Then again last October, undercover investigators of the Humane Society caught employees at the Bushway Packing slaughter plant in Vermont on tape committing extreme abuse of veal calves. Scenes like those depicted in the Humane Society undercover video are egregious violations of the Humane Methods of Slaughter Act.

Shortly after this Subcommittee's first hearing on this topic in 2008, I made a request, along with Representative Issa, that GAO conduct an investigation of USDA's oversight of the slaughter industry and update its previous report, published in 2004. Today, GAO will publicly release its new findings.

What GAO has found is significant: Serious management problems at FSIS persist and compromise both the enforcement of HMSA and the ability of the department to change course. Key mechanisms of management oversight of inspection staff are missing. Key guidance to inspection staff making clear to them what constitutes a violation is missing. Consistency in the application of the law and assessing violations is missing: substantial differences exist among the regions. Considerable disagreement exists among the enforcement staff about what kinds of abuses constitute violations, and what enforcement actions need to be taken in response.

The truth of the matter is, we do not know how prevalent are the abuses documented by the Humane Society, and neither does USDA, because of the significant deficiencies in the management of FSIS identified by GAO.

But there is new leadership at the troubled agency, and they are talking about a new commitment to enforce the law. My hope is that today's hearing will give us a clear picture of what the new Administration plans to do to reform FSIS and improve the agency's track record in enforcing humane animal handling laws.

In: Animal Protection: Treatment and Welfare Issues
Editor: Dennis G. Carlton

ISBN: 978-1-61728-353-6

Chapter 5

STATEMENT OF JEROLD R. MANDE, DEPUTY UNDER SECRETARY FOR FOOD SAFETY, DOMESTIC POLICY SUBCOMITTEE, OVERSIGHT AND GOVERNMENT REFORM COMMITTEE - HEARING ON "CONTINUING PROBLEMS IN USDA'S ENFORCEMENT OF THE HUMANE METHODS OF SLAUGHTER ACT"*

Chairman Kucinich, Ranking Member Jordan and members of the Subcommittee, thank you for inviting me to appear before you today at this hearing to review the state of USDA's Food Safety and Inspection Service's (FSIS) enforcement of the Humane Methods of Slaughter Act (HMSA), and a Government Accountability Office (GAO) report requested by the Subcommittee on this matter. I want to assure you that we are deeply committed to the humane handling of livestock and to meeting our obligations to enforce HMSA at federally-inspected establishments. We welcome today's hearing and the GAO report as steps that will help support the mission of ensuring the humane handling of livestock.

I would like to begin my testimony today with a brief description of the mission and an overview of FSIS, and then I will move on to discuss humane handling and FSIS' enforcement of HMSA. Finally, I will close with comments on the GAO report reviewed by FSIS.

MISSION AND OVERVIEW OF FSIS

FSIS is the public health regulatory agency within the U.S. Department of Agriculture. It is responsible for ensuring that the Nation's commercial supply of meat, poultry, and processed egg products is safe, secure, wholesome, and accurately labeled and packaged, whether those products are domestic or imported. We administer and enforce the Federal

---

* This is an edited, reformatted and augmented edition of a statement/testimony given before the United States Oversight and Government Reform Committee, dated March 4, 2010.

Meat Inspection Act, the Poultry Products Inspection Act, the Egg Products Inspection Act, and the Humane Methods of Slaughter Act, which is the topic of our discussion today.

Currently, the Agency employs over 9,500 personnel, including around 7,800 full-time in-plant and other front-line personnel protecting the public health in approximately 6,200 federally-inspected establishments nationwide.

These inspection program personnel are present for all livestock slaughter operations to inspect each animal before slaughter and each carcass after slaughter, as required by our authorizing statutes. FSIS inspection program personnel also inspect each processing establishment at least once per shift. In fiscal year (FY) 2009, FSIS personnel inspected 150 million head of livestock and 9 billion head of poultry.

FSIS' inspection activities are rooted in science and based on data. Through science-based initiatives and continual efforts to strengthen our infrastructure, FSIS works to prevent adulterated food from reaching the consumer. FSIS accomplishes this, in part, through rigorous sampling programs for foodborne pathogens such as *E. coli* O157:H7 in beef products, *Listeria monocytogenes* in ready-to-eat products, and *Salmonella* in raw meat and poultry products. Through the Hazard Analysis and Critical Control Points (HACCP) system, the Agency's responsibility also includes verifying that the establishment has effectively identified hazard points in its system and has deployed steps to prevent and mitigate risks.

FSIS frontline employees inspect and verify that establishments follow their food safety plans and enforce FSIS regulations to prevent contamination from occurring. When outbreaks occur and recalls are issued to protect public health, FSIS personnel are engaged in facilitating rapid response and recovery.

In addition to in-plant personnel in federally-inspected establishments, FSIS employs a number of other field personnel, such as laboratory technicians, veterinarians, and investigators.

FSIS Enforcement of HMSA

As I stated earlier, FSIS enforces HMSA, which provides the Agency with the authority to regulate the handling of livestock prior to slaughter, as well as the method of slaughter at establishments. We take this responsibility very seriously. I want to assure the Subcommittee that enforcing this law is a high priority for FSIS.

When Congress passed HMSA, it found that humane slaughter prevented needless suffering, resulted in safer and better working conditions for employees at slaughter establishments and provided benefits to producers and consumers through better products and improved flow of livestock and livestock products.

FSIS inspectors are in plants every day, and a key duty of these inspectors is to ensure that Congress' intent to assure that humane slaughter at every slaughter plant is carried out properly. FSIS inspectors are tasked with three essential duties: identifying problems, acting on those problems, and documenting the problems.

Documentation is a critical part of enforcement. If a problem is not documented properly, FSIS becomes less able to exercise proper enforcement. For this reason, proper documentation of humane handling violations is a basic part of FSIS inspector training. When

FSIS personnel detect violations, they have the authority to take action by either suspending the establishment or issuing a noncompliance report (NR).

Each of FSIS' 15 District Offices has a District Veterinary Medical Specialist (DVMS) who serves as an expert on humane handling issues. The DVMS in each District Office performs a formal review of each slaughter plant in the district every 12-18 months. In addition, they participate in making decisions about appropriate enforcement actions in response to humane handling violations. For example, the DVMS performs a comprehensive review of a plant 30 days after a suspension has been lifted to determine if proffered corrective actions are effective. They also perform additional follow-up reviews 60 and 90 days following the lifting of a suspension.

FSIS has a rigorous program to train inspection personnel in verifying humane handling at slaughter establishments and ensure that the three essential duties are performed properly. All inspection personnel who might be required to conduct humane handling activities receive humane handling training as part of their basic training. All entry level inspectors receive both classroom instruction and one to two weeks of field training on humane handling. In February 2009, FSIS inspection personnel assigned to livestock slaughter establishments were required to complete refresher training on the Agency's humane handling policies. This training included information on how to determine insensibility, documenting noncompliance, and suspending inspection for egregious situations. FSIS is planning further workforce training activities related to humane handling for FY 2010.

FSIS has a collection of management controls and accountability mechanisms it uses in order to ensure that its personnel are properly enforcing HMSA and its associated regulations. Supervisory personnel at slaughter establishments conduct performance reviews at least twice annually on all aspects of inspection personnel performance, including humane handling. When the DVMS performs the formal review of establishments, corrections with inspection personnel occur at that time, as needed. In addition, FSIS produces a national report on humane handling on a quarterly basis, which compares districts according to humane handling procedures performed, noncompliance records, suspensions, and time spent on specific humane activities, as recorded in the Humane Activities Tracking System (HATS), a nationwide database that provides FSIS with an accurate and complete accounting of the time spent by FSIS inspection program personnel performing HMSA verifying activities in nine specific categories related to humane handling and slaughter. The DVMS reviews noncompliance records and suspension documentation immediately, and other data on a regular basis.

RECENT STEPS

There are a variety of steps that FSIS has recently taken to ensure compliance with HMSA, as well as actions we will be taking in the near future to make our enforcement of HMSA as effective as possible. FSIS continues aggressive hiring and the maximum use of recruitment and retention authorities.

Consistent with directives established in the fiscal year (FY) 2010 Agriculture, Rural Development, Food and Drug Administration, and Related Agencies Appropriations Act,

FSIS devoted approximately 140 full-time equivalent (FTE) staff years to the verification and in-plant enforcement of humane handling requirements at slaughter establishments in 2009.

In addition, FSIS recently added an additional 23 inspection positions, and assigned them to higher-risk establishments in order to boost humane handling oversight and verification inspection activities at those locations. FSIS is also working diligently to fill the newly created position of Humane Handling Enforcement Coordinator. The Coordinator is a headquarters- based position, primarily responsible for providing consistent oversight of the field level humane handling activities. In addition, this individual will play a key role in the various humane handling enforcement and verification activities that I have described in my testimony.

FSIS recently created a new scoring verification tool, called the "Humane Handling and Slaughter Verification Tool" to DVMSs; and on December 7, 2009, included it as part of FSIS Directive 6910.1, Revision 1. While this scoring tool is not used by DVMSs for purposes of regulatory action, it is designed to create an objective system that will facilitate the DVMS' determination of whether there are problems in the establishment's humane handling and slaughter system that the establishment needs to address. The tool allows DVMS to record ante mortem observations, such as the number of times livestock slip and fall while proceeding through the stunning chute area or the number of times an electric prod is used on the animals. Percentages are calculated and compared to minimum acceptable scores as suggested by Dr. Temple Grandin. FSIS conducted training on the scoring tool in August 2009.

Since the events at the Hallmark/Westland establishment in 2008, FSIS has made numerous efforts to strengthen and improve its verification and enforcement related to HMSA. One of the major measures taken since the start of the new Administration was the issuance of a final rule in March 2009 to amend federal meat inspection regulations to require a complete ban on the slaughter of cattle that become non-ambulatory disabled after initial inspection by FSIS personnel. In addition, FSIS issued a notice to its inspection personnel in 2009 that reminds and instructs Public Health Veterinarians (PHVs) and other inspection personnel to conduct humane handling activities randomly throughout their shift. The notice also directs PHVs to encourage establishments to develop and implement a systematic approach to humanely handle livestock. PHVs will regularly verify that establishments are following their plans.

FSIS will significantly strengthen its analysis of humane handling data this year. In an effort to dramatically improve our data collection and analysis, FSIS will launch the Public Health Information System (PHIS) later this year. PHIS will enhance FSIS' data infrastructure through the integration of a variety of relevant data streams, including data collected in HATS. PHIS will allow FSIS to provide ongoing, real-time assessment, analysis and surveillance of public health, food defense, and humane handling data.

In the near future, FSIS intends to issue compliance guidelines to industry for the use of video or other electronic monitoring or recording equipment, in response to USDA's Office of the Inspector General (OIG) recommendations, and will seek public comment on the guidelines. FSIS encourages establishments to consider using such monitoring as part of an overall systematic approach to maintaining humane handling and compliance with regulatory and statutory requirements.

INDUSTRY COMPLIANCE WITH HMSA

As requested by the Chairman, I would like to discuss the industry's compliance with HMSA. It should be noted that only approximately 800, or less than 20 percent, of federally-inspected establishments slaughter livestock and thus are subject to HMSA. As mentioned previously, FSIS personnel have a continuous presence in these establishments, and carry out inspection of all livestock at each federally-inspected slaughter establishment. In addition to the regular ante-mortem inspection of all animals, FSIS inspection program personnel in all livestock slaughter establishments conduct routine daily verification activities in nine categories for plant compliance with humane handling laws and regulations. Examples of the categories include: truck unloading, electric prod use, and stunning effectiveness. Inspectors record the amount of time it takes to conduct these activities into HATS. FSIS projects that in FY 2010, in- plant personnel will spend the equivalent of 140 staff years, or 291,200 person-hours, verifying humane handling activities at livestock slaughter establishments. These activities are in addition to the many hours of time FSIS spends on ante-mortem inspection, when HMSA violations can also be observed and acted on.

When humane handling violations are observed during an inspection, FSIS personnel can initiate one of two regulatory actions at their disposal (suspension, and issuing a noncompliance record), depending on the situation observed. Noncompliance records for humane handling may be issued when the violation observed is less than egregious, such as observation of broken fencing that has the potential for causing injury to penned or driven animals.

In calendar year (CY) 2009, FSIS in-plant personnel conducted 128,417 humane handling verification procedures at federally-inspected livestock slaughter establishments. Only 0.4 percent of these procedures resulted in the issuance of noncompliance records for humane handling violations.

In addition, when FSIS inspection personnel do observe egregious humane handling violations, they take immediate action to issue suspensions. A suspension effectively shuts down all or part of a plant's operations. In CY 2009, inspection personnel issued 87 suspensions for egregious humane handling violations. Of these suspensions, 71 were initial suspensions, and as a result of corrective actions taken by the establishments, did not require suspensions to be reinstated by FSIS.

2008 OIG AUDIT

Following the events that occurred at the Hallmark-Westland establishment in 2008, USDA's OIG conducted an audit to determine what inspection controls and/or processes broke down at Hallmark-Westland including those for humane handling, and whether the events that took place there were isolated or systemic. The OIG found that "the events that occurred at Hallmark were not a systemic failure of the inspection processes/system as designed by FSIS." OIG did determine that FSIS' management controls demonstrate that the sufficiency and competency of its personnel resources were in need of strengthening, and made numerous recommendations.

Although OIG found that the incidents at Hallmark-Westland were not an example of a systemic problem in enforcement, the Agency has nevertheless increased its enforcement of HMSA significantly. Our response to this, I believe, is another demonstration that the Agency takes inhumane handling of livestock very seriously, and is looking for effective ways to strengthen its humane handling program.

FSIS is continuing to complete corrective actions in response to the recommendations made in OIG's audit report. OIG and FSIS are in agreement on all of the corrective actions needed in response to all of the audit recommendations, and we are working to implement these actions. Of the four recommendations related to humane handling issues, three recommendations have been closed, as a result agreed-upon corrective action. These actions include: 1) instructions and additional guidance provided to DVMSs regarding work methods they must use when conducting their humane handling reviews at establishments; 2) analysis of noncompliance rates at establishments that slaughter other market classes of adult cattle; and 3) development of the first quarterly humane handling report for CY 2008. The fourth recommendation asks FSIS to determine whether FSIS-controlled in-plant video monitoring would be beneficial in preventing and detecting animal abuses at cull cow slaughter establishments. We expect it to be closed soon, as a result of the upcoming the publication of an FSIS Directive and a guide for industry regarding video monitoring by establishments to ensure compliance with HMSA requirements.

Similar to its response to OIG's recommendations, I can assure you that FSIS will take the necessary actions to respond to those presented in GAO's most recent audit report. I want to be clear that FSIS appreciates the recommendations from GAO, which builds on the considerable work already being done by FSIS to improve our performance in verifying humane handling at slaughter establishments.

Comments on the GAO HMSA Report

In the fall of 2008, the GAO began a review of FSIS' enforcement of HMSA. Throughout the duration of the review, FSIS worked with the GAO to provide an accurate picture of the Agency's enforcement of HMSA. On behalf of the Agency, I would like to thank the GAO for its efforts to work with us during its investigation and for giving us the opportunity to provide comments on the report.

As can be seen by the above examples of FSIS' enforcement of HMSA, it is clear the Agency is committed to the proper enforcement of HMSA and is constantly improving upon its efforts to ensure that establishments comply with the law and FSIS' humane handling regulations. Thus, the Agency will consider the GAO's findings and recommendations carefully as we strive to improve and evolve. FSIS does recognize the need to improve our inspectors' ability to identify trends in humane handling violations, a weakness that is repeated throughout the report. The Agency will need to work with academia, industry, non-profit organizations, animal health experts, and our workforce to identify practices that will achieve more consistent enforcement of HMSA.

That being said, it should be mentioned that FSIS disagrees with several of the components that were contained in the draft GAO report that FSIS reviewed. We believe that several of these points of disagreement could result in a misleading portrayal of FSIS' enforcement of HMSA. These points are contained in our complete response to the GAO report, which I have included as an addendum to my testimony.

We agree with GAO that FSIS ought to adopt a numerical scoring system for verification of compliance with humane handling requirements. In fact, as I stated earlier, such a verification tool was provided to FSIS DVMSs in December 2009.

As part of its review, the GAO conducted a survey of FSIS inspection program personnel, from which it drew many of its findings and recommendations. Through this survey, the GAO concluded that there are inconsistencies in the enforcement of HMSA, as inspection program personnel answered the survey questions on what regulatory actions they would take for the various examples of HMSA violations very differently.

While we respect GAO's effort to capture a true picture of the knowledge and understanding of humane handling rules by our frontline inspectors, it's important to say that an accurate understanding of HMSA enforcement must consider both the qualitative and quantitative standards that are applied to observations of humane handling practices. The statute and regulations are enforced through the observation of individual events of handling and slaughter practices, which can vary significantly depending on the specifics of an establishment and the situation in question. It can be very difficult to establish definitively which of the two regulatory actions at the disposal of an FSIS inspector (suspension, and issuing a noncompliance record) should be utilized, without knowing the history, context, and situation observed by FSIS inspection personnel.

It is important to note that there was consistency in the survey responses in that FSIS personnel did know that each situation required action. So while inspection program personnel differed on the type of action they would take, they all agreed they would take action. This is a key point that should not be overlooked; FSIS field personnel know when to take action and they do take action.

FSIS has very clear guidance in place on how to implement suspensions for egregious humane handling violations, which carries authority equivalent to an FSIS directive. According to FSIS Notice 21-09, "if the observed inhumane treatment is of an egregious nature, the regulations at 9 CFR 500.3(b) apply. The Notice provides our inspectors 10 examples of egregious situations. For example, "making cuts on or skinning conscious animals, dragging conscious animals, driving animals off semi-trailers over a drop off without providing adequate unloading facilities (animals are falling to the ground), or leaving disabled livestock exposed to adverse climate conditions while awaiting disposition."

The regulations state, "FSIS also may impose a suspension without providing the establishment prior notification because the establishment is handling or slaughtering animals inhumanely." Therefore, the inspector-in-charge (IIC) is to take an appropriate regulatory control action to prevent continued egregious inhumane handling and orally notify plant management of an immediate suspension action.

BUSHWAY PACKING INC.

Before I close, I would like to briefly comment on the abuse of veal cattle at the Bushway Packing Inc., establishment captured by the Humane Society of the United States in a video released on October 30, 2009. Secretary Vilsack, in a statement issued the same day, stated that "The deplorable scenes recorded in the video... are unequivocally unacceptable," and that the "behavior of FSIS and establishment personnel witnessed in the video is inexcusable." The Agency took immediate action in response to the incident. The Secretary called on USDA's Office of Inspector General to conduct a criminal investigation, which remains under way. FSIS suspended operations at the Bushway Packing establishment, which remains in effect today, and subsequently filed formal administrative proceedings regarding the suspension. FSIS also initiated an investigation into the alleged misconduct by Agency personnel and has, to date, terminated one employee. Again, I want to assure the Subcommittee that the Agency takes humane handling violations very seriously, and takes immediate action when violations are observed.

CONCLUSION

Chairman Kucinich, Ranking Member Jordan and members of the Subcommittee, I would like to reiterate that the Agency is committed to ensuring that our livestock are humanely handled, and committed to the enforcement of HMSA at federally-inspected establishments. We must always seek improved performance and we value the opportunity to discuss developments that could enhance our enforcement of the Humane Methods of Slaughter Act.

I would like to thank the GAO for its review of FSIS' enforcement of HMSA, and for giving the Agency an opportunity to comment on its report. The Agency appreciates this review, and considers the GAO's survey results, among other reviews to be essential in our continued efforts to improve HMSA verification and enforcement.

Thank you, Chairman, Ranking Member and members of the Subcommittee for your concern about this important topic and for this opportunity to appear before you today and testify. I look forward to your questions.

In: Animal Protection: Treatment and Welfare Issues
Editor: Dennis G. Carlton
ISBN: 978-1-61728-353-6

Chapter 6

HUMANE METHODS OF SLAUGHTER ACT: WEAKNESSES IN USDA ENFORCEMENT*

Lisa Shames

Mr. Chairman and Members of the Subcommittee:

I am pleased to be here today to discuss our work on the U.S. Department of Agriculture's (USDA) actions to enforce the Humane Methods of Slaughter Act of 1978 (HMSA), as amended, which prohibits the inhumane treatment of livestock in slaughter plants and generally requires that animals be rendered insensible—that is, unable to feel pain—before being slaughtered. USDA's Food Safety and Inspection Service (FSIS) is responsible for enforcing HMSA. Concerns about the humane handling and slaughter of livestock have increased in recent years, particularly after possible HMSA violations were revealed at a slaughter plant in California in 2008 and one in Vermont in 2009.

This statement summarizes our report being released today that (1) evaluates USDA's efforts to enforce HMSA, (2) identifies the extent to which FSIS tracks recent trends in FSIS inspection resources for enforcing HMSA, and (3) evaluates FSIS's efforts to develop a strategy to guide HMSA enforcement.[1] To perform this work we, among other things, conducted a survey of inspectors-in-charge—those responsible for reporting on humane handling enforcement in the plants—from a random sample of inspectors-in-charge at 257 livestock slaughter plants from May 2009 through July 2009. Our sample allowed us to make estimates about the observations and opinions of all inspectors-in-charge at U.S. slaughter plants.[2] We obtained responses from 235 inspectors-in-charge, for an overall survey response rate of 93 percent. We also examined a sample of FSIS noncompliance reports, suspension data, and district veterinary medical specialist reports in all 15 of FSIS's district offices for fiscal years 2005 through 2009.

As detailed in our report, we found the following. First, our survey of inspectors at slaughter plants and analysis of FSIS data suggest that inspectors have not taken consistent actions to enforce HMSA. In responding to our survey, different inspectors indicated they

---

* This is an edited, reformatted and augmented edition of a United States Government Accountability Office Publication, Report #GAO-010-0487T, dated March 4, 2010.

would take different enforcement actions when faced with a violation of humane handling requirements. In addition, our review of noncompliance reports identified incidents in which inspectors did not suspend plant operations or take regulatory actions when they appeared warranted. The lack of consistency in enforcement may be due in part to the lack of clarity in current FSIS guidance and to inadequate training. Second, FSIS cannot fully identify trends in its inspection funding and staffing for HMSA, in part because it cannot track HMSA inspection funds separately from the inspection funds spent on food safety activities. FSIS also does not have a current workforce planning strategy for allocating limited staff to inspection activities, including HMSA enforcement. Last, while FSIS has strategic, operational, and performance plans for its inspection activities, they do not clearly outline goals, needed resources, time frames, or performance metrics. Nor do these plans provide a comprehensive strategy to guide HMSA enforcement. In our report, we recommend, among other things, that FSIS take actions to strengthen its oversight of humane handling and slaughter methods at federally inspected facilities. In commenting on a draft of the report, USDA did not state whether it agreed or disagreed with our findings or recommendations, but it stated that it plans to use them in improving efforts to enforce HMSA.

In preparing this testimony, we relied on our work supporting the accompanying report. That report contains a detailed overview of our scope and methodology. All of our work for this chapter was performed in accordance with generally accepted government auditing standards. Those standards require that we plan and perform the audit to obtain sufficient, appropriate evidence to provide a reasonable basis for our findings and conclusions based on our audit objectives. We believe that the evidence obtained provides a reasonable basis for our findings and conclusions based on our audit objectives.

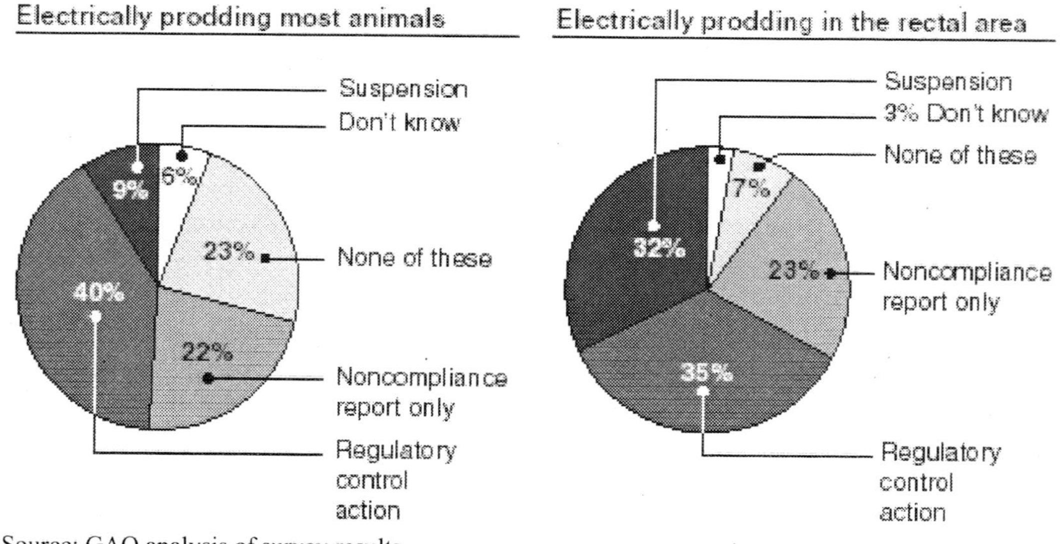

Source: GAO analysis of survey results.

Notes: This figure is based on the following survey question: "Do you believe that each of the following factors alone generally indicates that an establishment's action should result in a (1) suspension, (2) regulatory control action, (3) noncompliance report, or (4) none of these?" These factors included electrically prodding over 50 of 100 animals within acceptable voltage and electrically prodding one animal deliberately in the rectal area.

Figure 1. Percentage of Inspectors Identifying Which Enforcement Action They Would Take for Electrical Prodding

GAO SURVEY RESULTS AND FSIS DATA INDICATE INCONSISTENT FSIS ENFORCEMENT OF HMSA

Our survey results indicate differences in the enforcement actions that inspectors reported they would take when faced with a humane handling violation. For example, in our survey we asked inspectors how they would respond if they observed plant employees electrically prodding more than 50 out of 100 animals—a threshold considered excessive by an industry standard and a leading industry expert, Dr. Temple Grandin. Figure 1 shows that inspectors had varying responses. According to FSIS guidance, when FSIS inspectors observe a violation of HMSA or its implementing regulations and determine that animals are being injured or treated inhumanely, they are to take two actions: (1) issue a noncompliance report, which documents the violations and actions needed to correct the deficiency and (2) issue a regulatory control action, which prohibits the use of a particular piece of equipment or area of the facility until the equipment is made acceptable to the inspector. They also may, but are not required to, initiate an action to suspend plant operations. In addition, according to an FSIS training scenario, electrical prods are never to be used on the anus, eyes, or other sensitive parts of the animal.

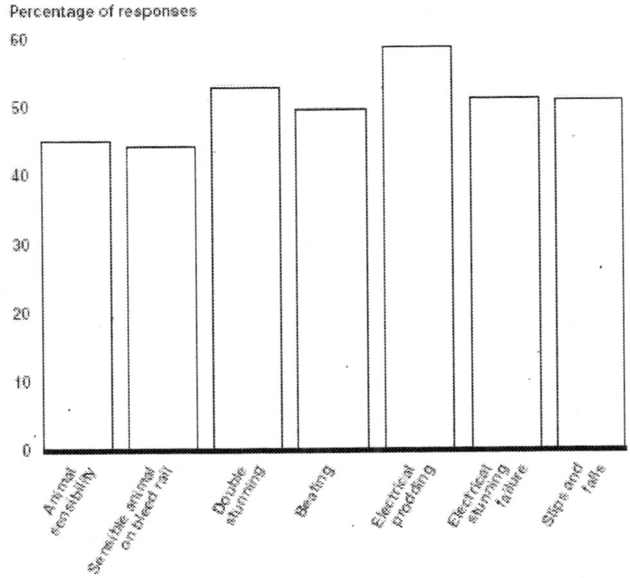

Source: GAO analysis of survey results.

Note: This figure is based on survey question 12: "Would additional guidance and/or training be helpful in the following areas? (1) determining when an animal is sensible or returning to sensibility; (2) determining what, if any, action to take for a sensible animal on the rail; (3) determining what, if any, action to take for double stunning; (4) determining when the use of a driving instrument or tool becomes beating; (5) determining whether a specific incidence of electric prodding requires a suspension, regulatory control action, or noncompliance report; (6) determining whether electrical stunning of an animal fails to render and maintain insensibility; and (7) assessing situations involving slipping and falling."

Figure 2. Inspectors Identified the Need for Additional Guidance and/or Training in Seven Key Areas of Humane Handling Enforcement

Similarly, our analysis of noncompliance reports shows inconsistency in the actions inspectors took in response to excessive beating or prodding. FSIS guidance also states that excessive beating or prodding of ambulatory or nonambulatory disabled animals is egregious abuse—and may therefore warrant suspension of plant operations. From inspectors' noncompliance reports, we identified several specific incidents in which inspectors did not either take a regulatory control action or suspend plant operations.

Incomplete guidance and inadequate training may contribute to the inconsistent enforcement of HMSA. Specifically, according to our survey results, inspectors at the plants we surveyed would like more guidance and training in seven key areas, as figure 2 shows.

Furthermore, inspectors-in-charge at more than half the plants surveyed reported that additional FSIS guidance or training is needed on whether a specific incident of electrical prodding requires an enforcement action. In addition, of the 80 inspectors who provided detailed responses to our survey, 15 noted the need for additional guidance, including clarification on what actions constitute egregious actions. Similarly, 25 of the 80 inspectors who provided written comments identified a need for additional training in several key areas.

In 2004, we recommended that FSIS establish additional clear, specific, and consistent criteria for district offices to use when considering whether to take enforcement actions because of repeat violations.[3] FSIS agreed with this recommendation and delegated to the districts the responsibility for determining how many repeat violations should result in a suspension. However, incidents such as those at the slaughter plants in California and in Vermont suggest that this delegation was not successful. To date, FSIS has not issued additional guidance.

FSIS Cannot Fully Identify Trends in Inspection Resources and Plan Resource Needs for HMSA Enforcement

FSIS cannot fully identify trends in its inspection resources—specifically, funding and staffing—for HMSA enforcement, in part because it cannot track humane handling inspection funds separately from the inspection funds spent on food safety activities. Furthermore, FSIS does not have a current workforce planning strategy to guide its efforts to allocate staff to inspection activities, including humane handling.

According to FSIS officials, funds for humane handling come primarily from two sources: (1) FSIS's general inspection account and (2) the account used to support the Humane Activities Tracking System. The general inspection account supports all FSIS inspection activities, both food safety and other activities, including humane handling enforcement. Because the same inspectors may carry out these tasks concurrently, FSIS cannot track humane handling funds separately, according to FSIS officials.

According to FSIS officials, for the most part, inspectors are to devote 80 percent of their time to food safety inspection activities and 20 percent of their time to humane handling inspection and other activities. However, our analysis of resources shows that this is not the case. We estimated that the percentage of funds dedicated to HMSA enforcement has been about 1 percent of FSIS's total annual inspection appropriation, although it rose slightly in 2008, when FSIS directed the inspectors to increase the amount of time they devoted to humane handling, following the 2008 incident in California.

For fiscal year 2010, FSIS officials told us, they planned to use $2 million of their inspection funds to enhance oversight of humane handling enforcement by hiring 24 inspectors, including both public health veterinarians and inspectors. FSIS officials planned to strategically place these additional inspectors at locations where they are most needed to support humane handling enforcement in addition to their other food safety responsibilities.

While FSIS has increased its hiring, it has not done so in the context of an updated strategic workforce plan. Such a plan would help FSIS align its workforce with its mission and ensure that the agency has the right people in the right place performing the right work to achieve the agency's goals. In February 2009, we reported that the FSIS veterinarian workforce had decreased by nearly 10 percent since fiscal year 2003 and that the agency had not been fully staffed over the past decade.[4] We reported that, as of fiscal year 2008, FSIS had a 15 percent shortage of veterinarians. The majority of these veterinarians work in slaughter plants, and these plants ranged from no vacancy to 35 percent of their veterinarian positions vacant. The FSIS 2007 strategic workforce plan—the most recently available—identifies specific actions to help the agency address some of the gaps in recruiting and retaining these mission-critical occupations over time. However, it does not address specific workforce needs for HMSA enforcement activities.

FSIS officials stated that workforce planning occurs at the district level. According to district officials, they have discretion in deciding where to deploy additional inspectors. Therefore, they can deploy these inspectors at plants that they believe may require more HMSA oversight. However, more than one-third of the inspectors who provided written comments in our survey noted the need for additional staff or the lack of time to perform humane handling activities.

FSIS DOES NOT HAVE A COMPREHENSIVE STRATEGY FOR ENFORCING HMSA

Although FSIS has strategic, operational, and performance plans for its inspection activities, these plans do not specifically address HMSA enforcement. That is, they do not clearly outline the agency's goals for enforcing HMSA, identify expected resource needs, specify time frames, or lay out performance metrics. Specifically, *FSIS Strategic Plan FY 2008 through FY 2013* provides an overview of the agency's major strategic goals and the means to achieve those goals. However, this plan does not clearly articulate or list goals related to HMSA enforcement. Instead, the plan generally addresses agency goals, such as improving data collection and analysis, maintaining information technology infrastructure to support agency programs, and enhancing inspection and enforcement systems overall to protect public health. FSIS Office of Field Operations officials agreed that the plan does not specifically address humane handling, but, they explained, the operational plans and policy performance plans contain the details concerning humane handling performance. However, we did not find that these two plans provide a comprehensive strategy for HMSA enforcement.

In our report, we recommend that FSIS take actions to strengthen its oversight of humane handling and slaughter methods at federally inspected facilities and develop an integrated strategy that clearly defines goals, identifies resources needed, and establishes time frames and performance metrics specifically for enforcing HMSA. We provided USDA with a draft of our report for review and comment. USDA did not state whether it agreed or disagreed with our findings or recommendations. However, it stated that it plans to use them in improving efforts to enforce HMSA. USDA recognized the need to improve the inspectors' ability to identify trends in humane handling violations and work with academia, industry, and others to identify practices that will achieve more consistent HMSA enforcement. USDA also questioned whether the results of our survey of FSIS inspectors provide evidence of systemic inconsistencies in enforcement. We believe they do and would encourage USDA to consider the views of inspectors at the plants who are responsible for daily HMSA enforcement. USDA also provided technical comments, which we incorporated into our report, as appropriate.

Mr. Chairman this concludes my prepared remarks. I would be happy to respond to any questions that you or other Members of the Subcommittee may have.

For questions or further information regarding this statement, please contact Lisa Shames, Director, Natural Resources and Environment at (202) 512-3841 or shamesl@gao.gov. Thomas M. Cook, Assistant Director; Nanette J. Barton; Beverly A. Peterson; Benjamin N. Shouse; and Tyra J. Thompson also made key contributions to this statement. Contact points for our Offices of Congressional Relations and Public Affairs may be found on the last page of this testimony.

End Notes

[1] GAO, *Humane Methods of Slaughter Act: Actions Are Needed to Strengthen Enforcement*, GAO-10-203 (Washington, D.C.: Feb. 19, 2010). See also GAO, *Humane Methods of Handling and Slaughter: Public Reporting on Violations Can Identify Enforcement Challenges and Enhance Transparency*, GAO-08-686T (Washington, D.C.: Apr. 17, 2008).

[2] Full sample percentage estimates from the survey have margins of error at the 95 percent confidence level of plus or minus 7 percentage points or less, unless otherwise noted.

[3] GAO, *Humane Methods of Slaughter Act: USDA Has Addressed Some Problems but Still Faces Enforcement Challenges*, GAO-04-247 (Washington, D.C.: Jan. 30, 2004).

[4] GAO, *Veterinarian Workforce: Actions Are Needed to Ensure Sufficient Capacity for Protecting Public and Animal Health*, GAO-09-178 (Washington, D.C.: Feb. 4, 2009).

In: Animal Protection: Treatment and Welfare Issues
Editor: Dennis G. Carlton

ISBN: 978-1-61728-353-6

Chapter 7

STATEMENT OF DEAN WYATT, FSIS SUPERVISORY PUBLIC HEALTH VETERINARIAN, WILLISTON, VERMONT, BEFORE THE DOMESTIC POLICY SUBCOMMITTEE - HEARING ON "CONTINUING PROBLEMS IN USDA'S ENFORCEMENT OF THE HUMANE METHODS OF SLAUGHTER ACT"*

My name is Dr. Dean Wyatt. I am a supervisory public health veterinarian for the Food Safety and Inspection Service (FSIS) of the USDA. I have served the Agency and the public for over 18 years and have received numerous cash performance awards. I am speaking today in my individual capacity, and not on behalf of USDA. I am very grateful for the opportunity to testify before the subcommittee today, and I am especially grateful to Chairman Kucinich and his staff for their support in my efforts to blow the whistle.

I graduated from the College of Veterinary Medicine at Iowa State University. I have had my own private practice. I ultimately followed in my father's footsteps and became a FSIS Public Health Veterinarian. My father died at a very young age, having contracted cryptococcosis – a highly fatal fungal disease – from a turkey slaughter plant at which he performed inspection services. Public service is in my blood.

People have asked me why I would risk ruining my career by testifying. I would respond by quoting Abraham Lincoln who said "to sin by silence, when one must protest, makes cowards of men." I am not a coward... and I will not be silent. I truly believe that the USDA inspector is the only advocate animals have in slaughter plants. When we turn our backs on the helpless, when we fail to speak on behalf of the voiceless, when we tolerate animal abuse and suffering, then the moral compass of a just and compassionate society is gone.

I must admit that I feel somewhat like Don Quixote here because I have been in the trenches, I have fought the battles, I have the dents in my armor – only the dents in my armor have not come from plant management, they have come from upper-level FSIS management.

* This is an edited, reformatted and augmented edition of a statement/testimony given before the United States Oversight and Government Reform Committee, dated March 4, 2010.

I am a law enforcement officer. The public has entrusted me to enforce the Humane Methods of Slaughter Act and the Federal Meat Inspection Act. The law is in place and regulated establishments must be held accountable when they break the law. When upper-level FSIS management looks the other way as food safety or humane slaughter laws are broken, or, as has been my experience, retaliates against people who are enforcing those laws, then management is just as guilty for breaking those laws as are the establishments. The laws are there. The enforcement of those laws – in my experience – has not been there and, in fact, has been willfully ignored by well-paid public officials. I cannot emphasize this fact enough – public servants like me who take our public trust very seriously and who may even endure personal trauma in order to fulfill that trust are being thwarted in our law enforcement efforts by people who have taken that same public oath to enforce the law. It seems almost unbelievable to me, but I have been ignored by my own people and have suffered physically, emotionally, and financially in the process. More importantly, animal welfare and food safety have suffered as well.

My Experience at Seaboard Farms

In March 2007, I was transferred to Seaboard Farms, a large hog slaughtering and processing establishment located in Guymon, Oklahoma. I was the night shift FSIS supervisor and my job was to oversee the enforcement of food safety and humane slaughter regulations for my shift. From almost the start of my tour there, I found numerous violations of the Humane Slaughter Act by the establishment. As I continued to raise concerns about problems at the plant, Seaboard began appealing my decisions to both my immediate supervisor and to District Office officials in Springdale, Arkansas who had never met me. FSIS officials who were hundreds of miles away simply took company personnel at their word that the egregious events that I personally witnessed did not justify my actions. A high-ranking FSIS official even went so far as to write a letter to Chairman Kucinich claiming that I was "incompetent" when the Congressman's office inquired into allegations I had raised. All the events that I have listed in this testimony are very well documented and I will briefly describe them here:

Event 1

May 23, 2007: I observed conscious pigs on the conveyor belt; some were moving and one was blinking and breathing regularly. As I stopped by the leg shackle station, a plant employee pointed at the blinking pig, indicating that he knew the pig was conscious, yet the pig was shackled and its neck was slit while it was awake. I suspended inspection operations and documented the event on a non-compliance report (NR). The plant did not appeal this NR to the FSIS district office.[1]

decision, Dr. Ganzel asked me what I expected the plant to do about the slipping and falling. I stated the obvious – that, per regulations, the pigs should not be slipping and falling (proper flooring and sanitation are supposed to prevent this), and the plant employee should not continue to drive other pigs around the fallen animals.[4] I wrote an NR to document the event and asked Dr. Ganzel if it was acceptable. He approved it for submission.

District Office Response

The following day, I was again chastised by the District Manager and told that they would not support my NR. I was told to drastically cut back on the amount of time that I was spending on humane handling enforcement. I was also notified that I would be demoted to a non-supervisory position for two weeks, a move meant to break my spirit and resolve to enforce regulations.

These were traumatic times for me, but even after these retaliatory incidents, I still felt it was my duty to identify infractions of the law and address them.

Event 6

On April 25, 2008, Seaboard was operating under a suspension held in abeyance because of two egregious humane slaughter violations that had occurred shortly before my shift. I was observing pigs being unloaded.[5] Again, the pigs were being unloaded too fast, with pigs falling down and others being driven on top of them. I informed the plant official, and he replied "I don't think that they are being unloaded too fast," and did nothing. After a few more minutes of observing this and seeing no corrective action taken, I went to another plant employee and told him that the problem must be corrected. He was responsive and took action. I documented this sequence of events in an email and sent it to the inspector-in-charge (IIC), Dr. Evan Sumner. Dr. Sumner told me to inform the frontline supervisor, Dr. Kevin Ehlers, about the unloading problem. Dr. Ehlers told me that I needed to document the event on a non-compliance report and to call the District Veterinary Medical Specialist – Dr. David Ganzel, which I did. Dr. Ganzel also agreed that a non compliance report should be written.

District Office Response

Regardless of the fact that my immediate supervisors had approved the filing of an NR concerning the unloading incident, I was informed by Dr. Sumner the following Monday that I was to call Dr. Endersby, the District Office manager. With her on the call were the two assistant District Managers, the Frontline Supervisor, and the District Veterinary Medical Specialist. Dr. Endersby told me that there was no way I could have seen what I did indeed see during the truck unloading. She berated me for several minutes. Dr. Endersby then told me that I either had to transfer or I would be terminated. I was told that I would have to transfer to a graveyard shift at a poultry plant in Batesville, Arkansas. I was to leave the plant immediately and to never come back.

These episodes at Seaboard served to greatly undermine the authority and effectiveness of all inspection personnel, not only in that plant but throughout the district. Field inspectors could see what had happened to me simply because I was doing my job. They did not want the same thing to happen to them... .Why would they risk their jobs by writing too many non-compliance reports?

It also served to embolden plant management. They knew that they could greatly push the line in the areas of humane slaughter enforcement and food safety and get away with it. After the District Office failed to support my NRs, the plant foreman snickered and laughed when I walked by. At one point, I took over to give a line inspector a break at the rail inspection station; a plant foreman came up beside me and told the meat trimmer in a loud voice so that I could hear, "This guy doesn't know anything. Don't trim what he tells you, just trim what you see."

MY EXPERIENCE AT BUSHWAY

Because of my long tenure in FSIS, I was able to avoid being forced to transfer immediately to the graveyard shift at a location selected unilaterally by the District Office. I eventually transferred to Western Vermont, believing that there would be no way that I would see the same sort of violations as at Seaboard. However, I soon encountered inhumane handling practices at Bushway Packing and other slaughter plants, and experienced the same lack of support from FSIS management in yet another District Office.

Rifle stunning is commonly used in New England. FSIS regulations require *immediate* unconsciousness with a single bullet.[6] Yet, I have seen cows shot multiple times in the head, thereby enduring unrelieved and needless suffering while plant management looked on until finally a properly placed bullet brought about death. After witnessing just such an event – a cow was shot once near her eye, again in her nose, and was still standing, fully conscious, and obviously suffering – I notified plant management that they were under suspension for an egregious humane slaughter violation. I called the District Office and my immediate supervisor. I was told by FSIS management to only document the event on a weekly meeting letter and not to even write an NR on the issue.

At Bushway, a calf slaughtering facility in Vermont, newborn male calves are typically brought in at one to seven days old. They are often trucked from long distances away, ten or twelve hours or more, and they often arrive injured, weak and dehydrated. As a result, calves may arrive "downed" and unable to get up.

I have suspended government inspection operations three times at Bushway for egregious humane handling events. And each time the district office allowed the plant to re-open and to continue operations. I witnessed animal handlers at Bushway grab a downed calf by a hind leg and drag him down an unloading ramp. Another calf was dragged through the holding pens. Dragging any non-ambulatory animal is against regulations. During another delivery, a handler swore at a downed calf and threw him off the second tier of the hauling trailer like a football. I wrote MOIs for all three of these inhumane handling events.[7] In the case of the calf thrown to the lower level of the truck, the district office softened and diluted my written report of what happened, changing the significant word "thrown" to "dropped."[8] The District Office even deleted the fact that the calf handler was cursing angrily at the animal that could not rise. Cursing angrily at newborn animals that are in a weakened condition is something that could and should be addressed. Often animals are mishandled because of misdirected anger and frustrations and these impulses need to be controlled in a job where humane handling is required.

On another occasion, the District DVMS came to the calf plant and noted that the stunning pen was too large and that there was a risk of mis-stunning the calves, as the person operating the large stunning device would often have to pursue moving calves while trying to make contact with their skulls. The size of the stunning floor also allowed too many calves to be stunned at one time, increasing the likelihood that the last calves to be shackled could regain consciousness. The DVMS told the plant manager that he had to reduce the size of the stunning area. The plant owner became very angry and said he would not do it. In response, the DVMS told us to disregard the size of the stunning area and to not enforce that regulation.

Calves arriving at Bushway after slaughter hours were destined to spend yet another 12-18 hours without food, when already they had been deprived of sustenance for perhaps days, since they were usually removed from their mothers immediately after birth. Sometimes calves are held overnight and it always broke my heart that employees would carry the bodies of these dead baby calves out of the pen because they died of dehydration and starvation. This should be considered inhumane handling.

Most likely through someone in my own agency, the plant manager at Bushway Packing in Grand Isle Vermont found out about my experience at Oklahoma and wanted me kicked out of his plant. In the middle of all the humane handling suspension actions at Bushway that I've mentioned above, the owner filed formal complaints against me implying that I was harassing him, when I was only doing my job. Suddenly, I was ordered by my FSIS supervisors to go to training for *new* Public Health Veterinarians, which took me out of the plant for three weeks. Again – an effort at retaliation for doing my job. I strenuously objected to this ridiculous order that was not only an insult but a waste of taxpayer money.

The turning point for me was when The Humane Society of the United States (HSUS), unbeknownst to me, hired an undercover investigator to look into my allegations of wrong doing at Bushway Packing. The video documentation produced by this investigation confirmed the gruesome humane handling violations that I was witnessing and documenting by way of noncompliance reports at Bushway. In fact, the video showed even more egregious events than I had been aware of and, in fact, showed footage of one of my subordinates telling plant personnel to only engage in violations when I was not present because otherwise "Doc (referring to me) would shut the plant down."

As a result of the HSUS undercover investigation, I have had conversations with high-level USDA officials who listened to my concerns and have expressed a willingness to make changes in the current system. Operations at Bushway have been suspended and USDA officials are working with law enforcement officials to investigate the misconduct seen on the video. I am glad that after a long struggle, my disclosures have finally been corroborated. However, I am the exception. Food integrity and humane handling whistleblowers should not have to rely on an undercover video investigation in order for USDA supervisors to take their disclosures seriously.

As a result of my contacting advocacy groups, I am closer to achieving my dual goals of shedding light on humane handling issues and assuring that Public Health Veterinarians and inspectors are given the necessary support they need to adequately enforce the provisions of the Humane Slaughter Act. I am sincerely grateful for the opportunity to speak before

Congress as both an advocate for animals and as an advocate for PHV's and inspectors who are charged with enforcing the Humane Slaughter Act. I would like to use this opportunity to propose several recommendations that will allow FSIS personnel to better protect our food integrity and to prevent the types of egregious humane handling violations that I saw at Bushway and Seaboard from happening again.

RECOMMENDATIONS

Staffing

It is essential that FSIS is adequately staffed in order to allow USDA to ensure the integrity of our food supply, including humane handling. FSIS employees in the field have a very difficult job. Their main focus in slaughter plants is on performing livestock carcass inspection procedures, and they keep receiving additional duties – more testing, more reporting, more record keeping, more record reviews, more meetings with plant management, etc. FSIS staffing is such that field employees simply do not have adequate time to ensure proper humane handling along with all their other important responsibilities. This was a big problem at Bushway Packing. The inspector spent ninety-nine percent of his time doing carcass inspections and was unable to do his humane slaughter and other duties properly. The plant management loved this. The inspector told me once, "Frank Perretta [the plant manager] loves the fact that I am on the line all the time – I don't have time to snoop around!"

Even when FSIS employees do manage to spend a small amount of time on humane slaughter enforcement, the plant management always knows when the inspector is doing humane handling inspections because the slaughter line is stopped. Plant management knows what is proper and not proper. With the exception of the Bushway plant, managers will usually refrain from violating regulations when they know the FSIS inspector is watching. This points to the need for an FSIS inspector who is devoted to humane handling inspections.

There are other problems relevant to staffing that need to be addressed. New veterinarians are hired using recruitment bonuses, which has caused some frustration with established PHVs. New veterinarians are being hired with the understanding that a substantial percentage of their student loans will be paid back; in addition, a large bonus will be paid to them over a four year period. Established veterinarians who have spent their whole lives in public service receive nothing along these lines.

Also related to salary disparity – each district office has several Enforcement Investigative Analysis Officers (EIAOs). These officers do food safety assessments in plants – basically reviewing written plant records to check for compliance with regulations – and they also help with recall actions. EIAOs have no supervisory duties and most have never been a supervisor. The only qualifications are that they have a high school diploma and thirty online credit hours in a science-related course. Sometimes, these EIAO officers are asked to write humane slaughter verification plans when they have had no humane slaughter enforcement experience. Public Health Veterinarians have a doctorate degree and they have extensive supervisory duties, they conduct critical post-mortem examinations on often dozens of animals each day and make food safety disposition decisions. PHVs also deal with Labor-Management issues, supervise complex HACCP (Hazard Analysis and Critical Control Point) programs in slaughter plants, and perform extensive humane slaughter enforcement duties. Yet PHVs receive the same amount of pay as the EIAOs. This has been a big source of frustration in the field – experienced PHVs feel under- appreciated and under-valued.

I would also like to suggest that plant management should be required to go through accredited humane handling training.

Whistleblower Protection

FSIS personnel need to know that they will not lose their jobs or suffer retaliation if they report misconduct, abuse of power or illegal activity. Whistleblower laws need to be strengthened, and agency officials must do everything possible to support personnel who report such problems, as it is in the interests of the agency and the public to know and address these problems.

Ombudsman

There is a disconnect between upper-level FSIS management and field inspection personnel. In all my years of service, I have never seen a Washington official or a district manager or deputy district manager visit a plant in the field. Personally, although I have been to the District Office five times, I have not met the district manager or two deputy district managers. These interactions are important to build camaraderie and support.

An ombudsman's office should be established so field inspectors have a place to go where they can report problems when they are not being supported by their supervisors. They need someone who will really listen to them, care about what they are saying, and actually try to have problems rectified. Such a position would be extremely valuable not only in terms of humane slaughter enforcement, but also for public health and food safety. Bushway Packing had serious food safety issues in addition to its humane handling problems – the two often go hand-in-hand.

MOI and NR

FSIS staff are required to record and document violations of any regulation on a non-compliance report (NR). The daily tasks are displayed on the computer and if there is a non-compliance, then it is entered into the computer system (PBIS) and inspectors in other plants can access these NRs. Also, each NR has to have corrective actions documented by plant management. These are permanently put into place and the plants are held accountable for implementing and enforcing them. In addition, NRs are accessible to the public through FOIA requests.

Ironically, egregious violations are *not* documented through the transparent NR system. After the Westland/Hallmark episode in California, the Agency started documenting egregious humane handling events only on a Memorandum of Interview (MOI) system. These are not documented as being a non-compliance in the establishment's PBIS system; the computer shows that everything is ok when in reality it is not. These MOI's cannot be accessed by other inspectors in other plants. Moreover, with the MOIs, the plant's corrective actions are documented on a verification plan system. The verification plan corrective actions are required to be performed during the time the suspension held in abeyance is in place but, contrary to a NR, they can be dropped once the suspension is lifted. For example, if there was a problem with truck unloading and the plant's verification plan required a plant monitor to monitor truck unloading, with the NR, that would always have to be in place; with an MOI, immediately after the suspension is lifted, they would not have to have a monitor and could go back to the same system as they had before. In other words, only the most serious violations do not lead to permanent corrective actions, and only the most serious violations are unavailable to other inspectors and kept from being readily accessible to the public.

Concern about Suspensions

Sometimes the effects of a plant suspension action by the FSIS can be just as bad or worse in terms of animal suffering as the action that caused the suspension. This is true especially in larger plants. An example would be if an employee was observed dragging a downed pig across a pen, and the plant was placed under suspension. Animals are often trucked from very far distances – sometimes several states – and the result of this suspension could be that pigs that arrive at the suspended plant would have to remain for very long periods of time in trailers without water in extreme heat or cold. My suggestion would be to allow the plant to continue to operate – only at a reduced line speed so that an FSIS inspector would be free to observe humane handling operations on the part of the plant. Stiff fines could be levied upon the plant as a deterrent against future humane handling violations.

Conclusion

Businesses are held accountable by their customers, their employees are held accountable by their bosses, Congress and the President are held accountable by their constituents and the media...yet, the supervisors in the FSIS are held accountable to no one. The FSIS is like a chain. There are many strong links but there are weak links also. When these weak links break, the whole system is affected and the public's health is at risk. This administration, many District and Washington level officials, and this committee all are committed to proper and strong humane handling enforcement. I know these officials have so many issues that they deal with on a daily basis, so many crises and so many "fires" to put out. Unfortunately, though, they did not know that there was a "fire" in the field. It took HSUS, GAP and the GAO to actually reveal the raging fire that was burning out of control in the area of humane slaughter enforcement.

I have outlined several remedies to help keep these problems from flaring up into another fire storm of humane handling and food safety violations. Ensuring transparency and permanent corrective action for egregious violations will improve the integrity of the system. Passage of the whistleblower legislation will provide conscientious employees with the legal protection they need to speak out about violations of food safety and humane handling rules.

An ombudsman's office will provide employees with a safe and direct avenue to reveal these "fires" to the highest levels of USDA without having their concerns trapped under layers of bureaucratic inefficiency and industry interference. Stiff fines and slower line speeds could provide useful deterrents against inhumane treatment, while avoiding unintended consequences from plant suspensions. Most importantly, we must encourage the change in the culture of USDA that I hope is already underway, so that FSIS treats the consumer as its client, not industry, and that FSIS employees are valued and supported for protecting the integrity of our food.

Respectfully submitted,
Dean C. Wyatt D.V.M., SPHV

End Notes

[1] FSIS Notice 12-05: VI. EGREGIOUS NONCOMPLIANCE: Noncompliances involving injury or inhumane treatment of an egregious nature warrant immediate enforcement in accordance with 9 CFR 500.2 and 500.3, including suspension of inspection. As stated in FSIS Directive 6900.2, Revision 1, if there is an egregious situation of inhumane handling or slaughter, the Inspector-in-Charge (IIC) is to immediately suspend inspection in accordance with 9 CFR 500.3(b) and orally notify plant management of the suspension. In such situations, the IIC is to immediately notify the District Office (DO) for prompt documentation of the suspension action. An egregious situation is any act that is cruel to animals or a condition that is ignored and leads to the harm of animals such as: making cuts on or skinning conscious animals)

[2] *Id.*

[3] FSIS Notice 12-05: Category II - Truck Unloading: Inspection program personnel must record their verification of the establishment's humane handling procedures while unloading livestock. An example of verification procedures include observing that the proper positioning of vehicles and unloading ramps permits the unloading of animals without injury [9 CFR 313.1(b)].

[4] FSIS Notice 12-05 Category VII - Observations for Slips and Falls: Under this category, inspection program personnel record time spent observing whether any animals are slipping and falling. The observance of animals slipping or falling necessitates inspection program personnel to verify the following: presence of flooring that provides adequate footing [9 CFR 313.1 (b)]

[5] FSIS Notice 12-05 Category II - Truck Unloading: Under this category, inspection program personnel record their verification of the establishment's humane handling procedures while unloading livestock.

[6] FSIS Notice 12-05 Category VIII - Stunning Effectiveness: Under this category, inspection program personnel record their verification of the establishment's procedures to appropriately and effectively administer stunning methods that produce unconsciousness in the animal before the animal is shackled, hoisted, thrown, cast, or cut (9 CFR 313.2 (f). In the case of cattle, calves, horses, mules, sheep, goats, swine and other livestock, all animals are to be rendered insensible to pain by a single blow or gun shot or an electrical, chemical, or other means that is rapid and effective. Failure to properly stun animals is a serious violation of the Humane Methods of Slaughter Act (HMSA) and represents a deficiency in training, equipment design, maintenance, or application.

[7] *Id.* at 1 (An egregious situation is any act that is cruel to animals or a condition that is ignored and leads to the harm of animals such as: dragging conscious animals).

[8] *Id.* at 1 (An egregious situation is any act that is cruel to animals or a condition that is ignored and leads to the harm of animals such as: driving animals off semi-trailers over a drop off without providing adequate unloading facilities (animals are falling to the ground).

In: Animal Protection: Treatment and Welfare Issues
Editor: Dennis G. Carlton
ISBN: 978-1-61728-353-6

Chapter 8

TESTIMONY OF STAN PAINTER, CHAIRMAN, NATIONAL JOINT COUNCIL OF FOOD INSPECTION LOCAL UNIONS, AMERICAN FEDERATION OF GOVERNMENT EMPLOYEES, AFL-CIO, BEFORE THE DOMESTIC POLICY SUBCOMMITTEE - HEARING ON "CONTINUING PROBLEMS IN USDA'S ENFORCEMENT OF THE HUMAN METHODS OF SLAUGHTER ACT"*

Chairman Kucinich, Ranking Member Jordan and Members of the Subcommittee, my name is Stan Painter and I am Chairman of the National Joint Council of Food Inspection Local Unions (NJC) which is affiliated with the American Federation of Government Employees, AFL-CIO. I have served in that capacity for over six years, and I have served as an inspector for USDA's Food Safety and Inspection Service (FSIS) for over 24 years. The NJC represents some 6500 non-supervisory meat, poultry and egg products inspectors who work for FSIS. We provide continuous inspection of some 6300 domestic food establishments and 130 import establishments to ensure the safety and wholesomeness of products covered by the Federal Meat Inspection, Poultry Products Inspection, and Egg Products Inspection Acts. In FY 2009, we oversaw the slaughter and processing of 112.5 million domestic head of livestock, 6.7 billion domestic poultry animals, and inspected nearly 3.8 billion pounds of imported meat and poultry products. We also performed some 8.5 million verification procedures to determine whether meat and poultry processors were following their Hazard Analysis and Critical Control Points (HACCP) plans.[1]

* This is an edited, reformatted and augmented edition of a statement/testimony given before the United States Oversight and Government Reform Committee, dated March 4, 2010.

HUMANE METHODS OF SLAUGHTER ACT

Our responsibilities also include enforcement of the Humane Methods of Slaughter Act (HMSA) of 1958 (7 U.S.C. 1901-1907) that was further amended in 1978 and 2002. I would like to thank you for inviting us to participate in the hearing that you are holding today because it is a very important issue and this proceeding is very timely. My union strongly supports the enforcement of this law. We take our responsibilities under this statute very seriously, but occasionally there are lapses. As you are undoubtedly aware, there was a recent incident at Bushway Packing -- a small slaughter facility in Vermont -- that was captured on video tape by the Humane Society of the United States. I am not going to go into detail about that situation as it is still under investigation, but we do not condone the actions depicted in the video.

As you know, the HMSA requires that the employees of slaughter facilities and USDA employees not to abuse livestock during the slaughter process. Specifically, the statute states the following:

> No method of slaughtering or handling in connection with slaughtering shall be deemed to comply with the public policy of the United States unless it is humane. Either of the following two methods of slaughtering and handling are hereby found to be humane:
>
> (a) in the case of cattle, calves, horses, mules, sheep, swine, and other livestock, all animals are rendered insensible to pain by a single blow o r gunshot or an electrical, chemical or other means that is rapid and effective, before being shackled, hoisted, thrown, cast, or cut; or
>
> (b) by slaughtering in accordance with the ritual requirements of the Jewish faith or any other religious faith that prescribes a method of slaughter whereby the animal suffers loss of consciousness by anemia of the brain caused by the simultaneous and instantaneous severance of the carotid arteries with a sharp instrument and handling in connection with such slaughtering. (7 U.S.C. 1902)

In addition, there are implementing regulations (9 CFR 313) and FSIS has issued a specific directive (FSIS Directive 6900.2) and a notice (FSIS Notice 21-09) to inspection personnel that further explain what the policy is. I have attached the Directive and Notice as part of my testimony for your reference.

PROBLEMS ENFORCING HMSA

So, why are there problems with enforcing this Act? I think that the problems lie in three basic areas:

1. There is not a priority being made by the agency to enforce this statute
2. There is inadequate staffing to enforce all of the statutes and regulations for which we are responsible
3. There is confusion as to what latitude my members have to enforce the rovisions of the provisions of the HMSA.

FSIS Does Not Make Enforcement of HMSA a Priority

The basic training that inspectors receive to carry out their responsibilities does not make enforcement of the HMSA a priority. I can speak from direct experience to this point since just this past July, I took the Food Safety Regulatory Essentials training that the agency offers to all inspectors. This is the basic training that all FSIS inspectors are required to receive. The instructor spent a few minutes out of the 13 working days of training explaining the HMSA.

When the Hallmark/Westland scandal broke in 2008, the agency promised Congress that FSIS inspectors would receive additional training to enforce the provisions of the HMSA. All we received was an on-line training module that we could access on the internet to refresh our responsibilities under the Act. There was no follow-up by the agency management to emphasize the importance of enforcing the provisions of the Act.

As a direct result of the Bushway incident in Vermont, the Northeast regional president of our union requested to agency management that additional training be made available in his region on the enforcement of HMSA because of the changing nature of slaughter processes in the industry. The agency has told our regional president that training is a management right and that the agency is under no obligation to honor the union's request.

There Are Too Few Eyes Looking at Too Many Animals Going to Slaughter

There are just not enough inspection personnel to keep up with the volume of livestock going to slaughter to enforce all of the food safety laws and regulations. We are still experiencing staffing shortages in various parts of the country. I do not have access to the staffing numbers for FY 2009, but through a Freedom of Information Act filed by the consumer group Food & Water Watch, I have attached to my testimony a chart of the FY 2008 staffing pattern. You will note that some FSIS regions are still experiencing double-digit vacancy rates – especially the Albany District that covers Connecticut, Maine, Massachusetts, New Hampshire, New York, Rhode Island, Vermont. The agency has worked in recent years to close the vacancy gap; but they are experiencing problems with keeping up with large numbers of retiring FSIS inspectors who need to be replaced in addition to closing the chronic staffing shortages from which that region has suffered in recent years.

But even if we had 100 percent staffing, I am not sure if we would still be able to enforce all of our food safety laws the way they should be. The agency claimed that there was a full complement of staffing at Hallmark/Westland when that situation came to light, yet the facility management was able to game the system and abused animals in order to squeeze every last penny for the bottom line. There are some slaughter facilities in this country that are processing cattle at 390 head per hour and hogs at 1106 head per hour. At that rate of production, we would need to increase the number of inspectors assigned to be able to enforce all of laws and regulations adequately.

How Much Latitude Do FSIS Inspectors Have to Enforce the HMSA?

As result of concern expressed by Congress in 2001 about the enforcement of the HMSA and armed with additional appropriations to enforce it, the agency hired District Veterinary Medical Specialists (DVMS) who are responsible for acting as a resource to inspection personnel in each of the 15 FSIS districts on the HMSA. While that was a positive step, in reality, we rarely see these district veterinary medical specialists visiting plants. They are rarely in the field.

We are also hamstrung by our supervisors who are either not qualified to do their jobs, unwilling to let us do our jobs, or who are not committed to making animal welfare a priority – either in FSIS-regulated facilities or in their private lives.

Let me give you some recent examples of each. On February 10, 2010, WSB-TV in Atlanta broke a story exposing that the agency had hired the DMVS in the Atlanta District who was not a veterinarian. He worked for the agency for four years in that capacity before it came to light that he was a fraud. That person was responsible for the enforcement of the HMSA in the Atlanta District. That individual has since resigned his position with FSIS and he is now under criminal investigation by USDA's Office of Inspector General. I have attached a transcript of the WSB-TV story for your information.

In early 2009, one of my members in Utah informed his supervisor that cattle were being abused in a slaughter facility holding pen. When he was rebuffed, my member took pictures of the cattle with his cell-phone camera and transmitted the photographs to his wife. When the agency found out about what he had done, both he and his wife were told to destroy the pictures. My member tried to do the right thing, but he was admonished for taking action.

In 2006, an FSIS veterinarian, Lori Gabri, was found guilty of neglecting 13 horses on the horse farm she owned in West Virginia. If our own supervisors cannot practice what they preach, then what do you think they will do when it comes time to enforce the HMSA in an FSIS-regulated slaughter facility? I have attached a copy of a news article describing that incident for your information.

Summary

The NJC believes that the enforcement of the HMSA is an important part of our jobs as inspectors. We need to have a clear commitment from our management that is also important to them. The way they can show that commitment is by giving us the authority to take action when we see violations of the law; give us the training so that we can do our jobs properly; hire competent veterinarians; either lower the line speeds of high production slaughter facilities or set realistic staffing patterns so that we can adequately enforce all of the laws and regulations for which we are responsible.

I will be happy to answer any questions that you might have.

End Notes

[1]United States Department of Agriculture Food Safety and Inspection Service, Quarterly Enforcement Report, July 1, 2009 through September 30, 2009, see http://originwww.fsis.usda.gov/regulations #records)

In: Animal Protection: Treatment and Welfare Issues ISBN: 978-1-61728-353-6
Editor: Dennis G. Carlton

Chapter 9

FSIS DIRECTIVE: HUMAN HANDLING AND SLAUGHTER OF LIVESTOCK*

United States Department of Agriculture

Monthly Employment and Vacancy Data
February - September, FY 2008

Inplant Inspection Employment (Chart 1)

District	Month							
	Feb '08	Mar '08	Apr '08	May '08	Jun '08	Jul '08	Aug '08	Sept '08
Alameda	410	415	412	412	417	418	420	421
Denver	415	417	421	424	430	436	434	436
Minneapolis	295	297	296	297	304	301	298	300
Des Moines	589	592	597	595	594	600	599	602
Lawrence	515	512	502	508	501	499	507	509
Springdale	686	688	685	687	687	690	684	684
Dallas	502	503	511	507	511	507	507	509
Madison	233	238	238	237	236	236	235	239
Chicago	388	387	389	390	391	392	392	388
Philadelphia	370	376	378	375	378	380	377	377
Albany	220	218	217	220	221	223	220	226
Beltsville	397	396	403	406	406	412	417	420
Raleigh	689	689	690	691	687	685	683	678
Atlanta	753	756	759	752	745	750	752	754
Jackson	835	841	843	847	847	845	840	833
Total	7297	7325	7341	7348	7355	7374	7365	7376

* This is an edited, reformatted and augmented version of a U. S. Department of Agriculture publication dated March 2010.

Inplant Inspection Vacancy Rate (Chart 2)

District	Month							
	Feb '08	Mar '08	Apr '08	May '08	Jun '08	Jul '08	Aug '08	Sept '08
Alameda	10.68%	9.78%	9.05%	9.05%	7.74%	7.93%	7.49%	7.27%
Denver	15.65%	15.07%	13.37%	12.94%	11.89%	9.92%	10.14%	8.21%
Minneapolis	10.06%	9.73%	9.48%	8.33%	6.17%	7.10%	6.29%	5.66%
Des Moines	10.35%	10.44%	10.63%	10.93%	11.08%	10.18%	10.06%	11.47%
Lawrence	7.37%	3.58%	5.82%	5.40%	6.88%	7.25%	5.76%	5.74%
Springdale	11.37%	12.13%	10.92%	10.55%	9.61%	8.97%	9.04%	6.30%
Dallas	13.89%	13.57%	13.24%	12.74%	11.74%	12.28%	11.83%	11.48%
Madison	6.43%	4.80%	4.80%	4.44%	4.84%	4.84%	5.62%	4.02%
Chicago	9.35%	9.79%	10.37%	10.34%	10.53%	10.09%	10.30%	11.62%
Philadelphia	8.19%	6.47%	4.06%	4.34%	3.82%	3.31%	4.07%	4.31%
Albany	17.60%	18.66%	19.63%	18.22%	18.15%	17.41%	18.52%	16.30%
Beltsville	9.36%	9.59%	8.20%	7.09%	7.31%	6.15%	5.44%	6.04%
Raleigh	9.10%	9.10%	7.75%	7.74%	7.41%	7.68%	6.95%	7.25%
Atlanta	10.14%	9.79%	8.55%	9.40%	10.24%	9.64%	9.29%	8.27%
Jackson	6.07%	5.29%	5.92%	5.89%	3.86%	4.84%	7.49%	3.59%
Total	10.12%	9.66%	9.21%	9.04%	8.61%	8.40%	8.48%	7.66%

Data does not include T/A positions

Note: Employment derived from NFC Bi-weekly reports, Excludes OTP

PART I - GENERAL

I. Purpose

This directive informs inspection program personnel of the requirements, verification activities, and enforcement actions for ensuring that the handling and slaughter of livestock, including the slaughter of livestock by religious ritual methods, is humane. This directive explains how inspection program personnel should approach these activities.

II. Cancellation

FSIS Directive 6900.2, dated 10/7/03

III. Reason for Reissuance

FSIS is reissuing this directive to provide additional clarification to the instructions in Part V, Ritual Slaughter of Livestock.

IV. References

9 CFR parts 313 and 500, the Humane Methods of Slaughter Act - 7 U.S.C. 1901, 1902, and 1906, and FSIS Directive 6900.1 – Humane Handling of Disabled Livestock.

V. Background

a. The Humane Methods of Slaughter Act of 1978 (HMSA) (Section 1901, 1902 and 1906, *Attachment 1*) states that the slaughtering and handling of livestock are to be carried out only by humane methods. In that Act, Congress determined (among other things) that the use of humane methods of handling and slaughtering livestock prevents needless suffering of animals and results in safer and better working conditions for employees in slaughter establishments.
b. Once a vehicle carrying livestock enters an official slaughter establishment's premises, the vehicle is considered to be a part of that establishment's premises. The animals within that vehicle are to be handled in accordance with 313.2.

PART II -- VERIFICATION OF THE LIVESTOCK PENS, DRIVEWAYS, AND RAMPS

A. What are the regulations related to livestock pens, driveways and ramps?

Section 313.1 states:

(a) Livestock pens, driveways and ramps shall be maintained in good repair. They shall be free from sharp or protruding objects which may, in the opinion of the inspector, cause injury or pain to the animals. Loose boards, splintered or broken planking and unnecessary openings where the head, feet, or legs of an animal may be injured shall be repaired.

(b) Floors of livestock pens, ramps, and driveways shall be constructed and maintained so as to provide good footing for livestock. Slip resistant or waffled floor surfaces, cleated ramps and the use of sand, as appropriate, during winter months are examples of acceptable construction and maintenance.

(d) Livestock pens and driveways shall be so arranged that sharp corners and direction reversal of driven animals are minimized.

NOTE: Verification of compliance with 9 CFR 313.1(c) is addressed in FSIS Directive 6900.1, Humane Handling of Disabled Livestock.

B. How do Inspection Program Personnel Verify Compliance with this Regulation?

When verifying compliance with 9 CFR 313.1(a), (b), and (d), inspection program personnel should determine whether the pens, driveways, and ramps are designed and maintained to prevent injury or pain to the animals. To do this, inspection program personnel need to seek answers to questions such as:

1. Are pens free of loose boards or openings, so that the head, feet or legs of an animal will not be injured?
2. Are the floors of pens, ramps, and driveways constructed so that an animal is not likely to fall (e.g., cleated, waffled, use of sand)?
3. Are driveways arranged so that sharp turns or sudden reversals of direction are minimized, so that they are not likely to cause injury to the animals?

These questions are examples and are not an all-inclusive list.

C. What Actions do Inspection Program Personnel Take if There is a Noncompliance with 9 CFR 313.1?

If inspection program personnel observe a noncompliance with 9 CFR 313.1, they are to determine whether the situation does or will immediately lead to animal injury or inhumane treatment. If the noncompliance is such that it will not immediately lead to injury (e.g., a few loose boards), inspection program personnel are to take action as set out in Part VI A. If the noncompliance is such that an animal has been injured (e.g., an animal's leg falls in between boards), inspection program personnel are to take action as set out in Part VI B.

PART III – VERIFICATION OF HUMANE HANDLING OF LIVESTOCK

A. What is the Regulation Related to Handling of Livestock?

Section 313.2 states:

(a) *Driving of livestock from the unloading ramps to the holding pens and from the holding pens to the stunning area shall be done with a minimum of excitement and discomfort to the animals. Livestock shall not be forced to move faster than a normal walking speed.*

(b) *Electric prods, canvas slappers, or other implements employed to drive animals shall be used as little as possible in order to minimize excitement and injury. Any use of such implements which, in the opinion of the inspector, is excessive, is prohibited. Electrical prods attached to AC house current shall be reduced by a transformer to the lowest effective voltage not to exceed 50 volts AC.*

(c) *Pipes, sharp or pointed objects, and other items which, in the opinion of the inspector, would cause injury or unnecessary pain to the animal shall not be used to drive livestock.*

(d) *Disabled livestock and other animals unable to move.* (Also refer to FSIS Directive 6900.1, Humane Handling of Disabled Livestock).

   (1) *Disabled animals and other animals unable to move shall be separated from normal ambulatory animals and placed in the covered pen provided for in section 313.1(c).*

   (2) *The dragging of disabled animals and other animals unable to move, while conscious, is prohibited. Stunned animals may, however, be dragged.*

   (3) *Disabled animals and other animals unable to move may be moved, while conscious, on equipment suitable for such purposes; e.g., stone boats.*

(e) *Animals shall have access to water in all holding pens and, if held longer than 24 hours, access to feed. There shall be sufficient room in the holding pen for animals held overnight to lie down.*

(f) *Stunning methods approved in section313.30 shall be effectively applied to animals prior to their being shackled, hoisted, thrown, cast or cut.*

B. How do Inspection Program Personnel Verify Compliance with These Regulations?

When verifying compliance with 9 CFR 313.2, inspection program personnel should determine whether the handling of livestock is being done with a minimum of excitement and discomfort to the animals. Inspection program personnel will verify the moving of livestock, the availability of water and the handling of disabled livestock in the establishment. To do this, inspection program personnel need to seek answers to questions such as:

1. Are animals driven from the unloading ramps to the holding pens with a minimum of excitement and not at a running pace?
2. Are electric prods and other implements used as little as possible to move animals within the establishment?
3. Are animals driven by using an object that would not cause unnecessary pain (e.g., not using a sharp object or pipe)?
4. Are disabled animals separated from ambulatory animals and placed in a covered pen?
5. Do the animals have access to water?
6. Is there sufficient room in the holding pens for animals that are held over night?

The above questions are examples and are not an all-inclusive list.

NOTE: Verification of compliance with 9 CFR 313.2(d) that deals specifically with disabled livestock, is also addressed in FSIS Directive 6900.1, Humane Handling of Disabled Livestock.

C. What Actions do Inspection Program Personnel Take if There is a Noncompliance with 9 CFR 313.2?

If inspection program personnel observe a noncompliance with 9 CFR 313.2, they are to determine whether the situation does or will immediately lead to animal injury or inhumane treatment. If the noncompliance can be immediately remedied (e.g., providing water to penned animals), inspection program personnel are to take the action as set out in Part VI A 1 and 2. If an immediate remedy is not forthcoming (e.g., the establishment fails to provide water immediately after being notified that animals do not have water available), inspection program personnel are to take the action as set out in Part VI A 3. If the noncompliance is resulting in the injury or inhumane treatment of animals (e.g., the dragging of disabled animals), inspection program personnel are to take action as set out in Part VI B.

PART IV – STUNNING METHODS

Appropriate stunning methods are required for an establishment to be in compliance with the HMSA. When stunning is done correctly, animals feel no pain, are rendered instantly unconscious, and remain unconscious until slaughtered. There are four methods of stunning approved for livestock. A summary of these approved stunning methods appear below (refer to 9 CFR sections 313.5, 313.15, 313.16 and 313.30).

A. What Are the General Regulatory Requirements Related to Approved Stunning Methods?Chemical; Carbon Dioxide

Regulatory requirements for the use of carbon dioxide as a humane method of slaughter are specified in section 313.5 and include, among other things, the following:

1. Carbon dioxide gas may be used to slaughter and handle sheep, calves and swine.
2. The carbon dioxide gas shall be administered in a chamber so as to produce surgical anesthesia (a state where an animal feels no painful sensation) before the animal is shackled, hoisted, thrown, cast, or cut. Animals shall be exposed to the carbon dioxide gas in a way that will accomplish the anesthesia quickly and calmly.
3. Gas concentrations and exposure times shall be graphically recorded throughout each day's operation.
4. It is necessary that the operator be skilled, attentive, and aware of his or her responsibility.

Mechanical; captive bolt

Regulatory requirements for the use of captive bolt stunners as a humane method of slaughter are specified in section 313.15 and include, among other things, the following:

1. Captive bolt stunners may be used to slaughter and handle sheep, swine, goats, calves, cattle, horses, mules, and other equines.

2. The captive bolt stunners shall be applied to livestock so as to produce immediate unconsciousness in the animals before they are shackled, hoisted, thrown, cast, or cut.
3. The stunning operation is an exacting procedure and requires a well-trained and experienced operator who must use the correct detonating charge with regard to kind, breed, size, age, and sex of the animal to produce the desired results.
4. Stunning instruments must be maintained in good repair.

Mechanical; gunshot

Regulatory requirements for the use of gunshot as a humane method of slaughter are specified in section 313.16 and include, among other things, the following:

1. Shooting by firearms may be used to slaughter and handle cattle, calves, sheep, swine, goats, horses, mules, and other equines.
2. A single shot delivery of a bullet or projectile into the animal is to produce immediate unconsciousness in the animal before it is shackled, hoisted, thrown, cast or cut.
3. Firearms must be maintained in good repair.
4. The shooting operation is an exacting procedure and requires a well-trained and experienced operator who must be able to accurately direct the projectile to produce immediate unconsciousness.
5. The operator must use the correct caliber firearm, powder charge and type of ammunition to produce instant unconsciousness in the animal.

Electrical; stunning or slaughtering with electric current

Regulatory requirements for the use of electric current as a humane method of slaughter are specified in section 313.30 and include, among other things, the following:

1. Electric current may be used to slaughter and handle swine, sheep, calves, cattle, and goats.
2. The animal shall be exposed to the electric current in a way that will accomplish surgical anesthesia (a state where an animal feels no painful sensation) quickly and effectively before they are shackled, hoisted, thrown, cast, or cut.
3. It is necessary that the operator of electric current application equipment be skilled, attentive, and aware of his or her responsibility.
4. Suitable timing, voltage and current control devices shall be used to ensure that each animal receives the necessary electrical charge to produce immediate unconsciousness.

B. How do Inspection Program Personnel Verify Compliance with These Regulations?

When verifying compliance with 9 CFR 313.5, 313.15, 313.16, and 313.30, inspection program personnel should assess the stunning method used for its effectiveness in rendering animals immediately unconscious and verify that animals are being properly stunned at the knocking box before hoisting. To do this, inspection program personnel need to seek answers to questions such as:

1. During stunning operations, is the establishment consistently rendering animals unconscious with a single application of the stunning methodology?
2. Is stunning equipment in good repair?
3. Are carbon dioxide gas concentrations graphically recorded throughout each day's stunning operation so that the correct amount of gas is used to adequately anesthetize an animal?
    1. Is the captive bolt stunner accurately placed so that after it is applied the animal is immediately unconscious?
    2. Is the correct caliber firearm being used to produce quick and complete unconsciousness in an animal?
    3. Is the proper voltage of electric current being used so that the animal is quickly rendered unconscious?

NOTE: The above questions are examples and are not an all-inclusive list.

C. What Actions do Inspection Program Personnel Take if There is a Noncompliance with 9 CFR 313.5, 313.15, 313.16, or 313.30?

If inspection program personnel observe a noncompliance with 9 CFR 313.5, 313.15, 313.16, or 313.30, they are to determine whether the situation does or will immediately lead to animal injury or inhumane treatment. If the noncompliance is such that animals will not be injured or treated inhumanely (e.g., the gas concentration was not graphically recorded, but the establishment showed that the proper concentration was administered), inspection program personnel are to take an action as set out in Part VI A. If the noncompliance is resulting in the injury or inhumane treatment of animals (e.g., an animal is not properly rendered unconscious) inspection program personnel are to take action as set out in Part VI B.

PART V -- RITUAL SLAUGHTER OF LIVESTOCK

A. General Requirement

Section 1902 (b) of the Humane Methods of Slaughter Act of 1978 provides that "slaughtering in accordance with the ritual requirements of the Jewish faith or any other religious faith that prescribes a method of slaughter whereby the animal suffers loss of consciousness by anemia of the brain caused by the simultaneous and instantaneous severance of the carotid arteries with a sharp instrument and handling in connection with such slaughtering" is humane. Section 1906 of the Act further provides that, "Nothing in this chapter shall be construed to prohibit, abridge, or in any way hinder the religious freedom of any person or group. Notwithstanding any other provision of this chapter, in order to protect freedom of religion, ritual slaughter and the handling or other preparation of livestock for ritual slaughter are exempted from the terms of this chapter. For the purposes of this section the term 'ritual slaughter' means slaughter in accordance with section 1902(b) of this title."

B. What are the Responsibilities of Inspection Program Personnel in Establishments Where There is Ritual Slaughter?

1. In an establishment that performs ritual slaughter, inspection program personnel are to request the plant manager to inform them about what type of ritual slaughter (e.g., Kosher, Halal) will be performed, when it will be performed, and who will perform the ritual slaughter.
2. Inspection program personnel are to verify that the humane handling of animals prior to preparation of the animal for ritual slaughter is consistent with parts II and III of this directive, with the exception of the discussion of stunning (9 CFR 313.2(f)) in part III of this directive. Examples of verification activities may include confirming the availability of water, checking the condition of pens and ramps, and verifying that there is no excessive use of electric prods.
3. Inspection program personnel are to verify that after the ritual slaughter cut and any additional cut to facilitate bleeding, no dressing procedure (e.g., head skinning, leg removal, ear removal, horn removal, opening hide patterns), is performed until the animal is insensible.

C. What Actions do Inspection Program Personnel Take if They Have Concerns with HumaneHandling Prior to the Handling and Preparation of the Animals for Ritual Slaughter or Concerns with Dressing Procedures Performed After Ritual Slaughter Prior to the Animal Becoming Insensible?

1. Inspection program personnel are not to interfere in any manner with the preparation of the animal for ritual slaughter, including the positioning of the animal, or the ritual slaughter cut and any additional cut to facilitate bleeding.
2. If inspection program personnel have concerns while verifying part V. paragraph B., they are to call the DO through supervisory channels.

PART VI – ENFORCEMENT AND DOCUMENTATION

A. What do Inspection Program Personnel do When They Have Determined That a Noncompliancewith the Humane Slaughter and Handling Requirements Has Occurred That is not Immediately Causing Injury or Inhumane Treatment of Animals?

1. Inspection program personnel are to document the noncompliance on an FSIS Form 5400-4, Noncompliance Record (NR), under the Inspection System Procedure (ISP) code 04C02 using the "Protocol" trend indicator. Inspection program personnel are to specify the regulation or statutory provision that pertains to the incident, provide a concise description of the noncompliance and provide any other evidence that supports the determination that a noncompliance has occurred.
2. Inspection program personnel are to verify that the establishment takes the necessary immediate and further preventive actions.
3. If an establishment fails to adequately respond to an NR or fails to take its immediate and further preventive actions, inspection program personnel are to take a control action (i.e., apply a U.S. Reject Tag) as set out in 9 CFR 500.2 (a)(4), *inhumane handling or slaughter of livestock*. The control action will remain in place until the establishment implements the appropriate immediate and further preventive actions that ensure compliance with the appropriate section of 9 CFR part 313.

B. What do Inspection Program Personnel do When They Have Determined That a Noncompliance with the Humane Slaughter and Handling Requirements Has Occurred and Animals Are Being Injured or Treated Inhumanely?

1. Inspection program personnel are to document the noncompliance on an NR, under the ISP code 04C02 using the "Protocol" trend indicator. Inspection program personnel are to specify the regulation or statutory provision that pertains to the incident, provide a concise description of the noncompliance and provide any other evidence that supports the determination that a noncompliance has occurred.
2. Inspection program personnel are to take a control action (i.e., apply a tag) as set out in 9 CFR 500.2 (a)(4), *inhumane handling or slaughter of livestock*. The control action will remain in place until the establishment implements the appropriate immediate and further preventive actions that ensure compliance with the appropriate section of 9 CFR part 313.

C. How do Inspection Program Personnel Determine Whether There is a Trend of a Noncompliance with the Humane Slaughter and Handling Requirements?

To determine whether a noncompliance trend exists, inspection program personnel will need to decide whether they can link NRs. Inspection program personnel should only link NRs when the noncompliances are from the same cause.

To make a determination as to whether a trend exists, inspection program personnel are to seek answer to the following questions:

1. How much time has lapsed since the previous NR was written?
2. Was this noncompliance from the same cause as the previous NR?
3. Were the establishment's further planned actions implemented?
4. Were the establishment's further planned actions effective in reducing the frequency of these noncompliances?
5. Is the establishment implementing additional planned actions that reduce the possibility of recurrence?

Inspection program personnel should be discussing any linkages with plant management during the weekly meetings. Inspection program personnel should also include in Block 10 of the NR that these discussions were held. Inspection program personnel should also include a statement in Block 10 of the NR stating that continued failure to meet regulatory requirements can lead to the enforcement actions described in 9 CFR 500.3(b).

Inspection program personnel should continue to link NRs together that derive from the same or a related cause until he or she determines that an enforcement action is necessary to bring the establishment into compliance with the regulations.

When inspection program personnel determine that an enforcement action (i.e., suspension as described in 9 CFR 500.3(b)) is necessary, they should contact the District Office (DO) and provide support for this determination.

The DO will determine whether inspection should be suspended as set out in 9 CFR 500.3(b). As provided in 9 CFR 500.3(b), FSIS may impose a suspension without providing the establishment prior notification if the establishment is handling or slaughtering animals inhumanely.

D. When May the Inspector-in-Charge (IIC) Immediately Suspend Inspection Because the Establishment is Handling or Slaughtering Animal Inhumanely?

If there is an egregious situation of inhumane handling or slaughter, the IIC may immediately suspend inspection in accordance with 9 CFR 500.3(b) of the regulations. The IIC verbally notifies plant management of the suspension. In such situations, the IIC is to immediately notify the DO for prompt documentation of the suspension action.

PART VII – INFORMATION FOR THE DISTRICT VETERINARY MEDICAL SPECIALISTS (DVMS)

What do inspection program personnel provide to the DO to document noncompliance findings with the humane handling and slaughter requirements?

When noncompliances occur, inspection program personnel are to send copies of the NRs to the DVMS (or to the Deputy District Manager if there is no DVMS in a District). These NRs should be kept on file in the DO. When necessary, the DVMS or the Deputy District Managers will follow-up on issues of concern and will correlate resolutions.

/s/ Philip S. Derfler
Assistant Administrator
Office of Policy and Program Development

DISTRIBUTION: Inspection Offices; T/A Inspectors; Plant Mgt; T/A Plant Mgt; TRA; ABB; TSC; Import Offices **OPI: OPPD**

Sec. 1901. - Findings and declaration of policy

The Congress finds that the use of humane methods in the slaughter of livestock prevents needless suffering; results in safer and better working conditions for persons engaged in the slaughtering industry; brings about improvement of products and economies in slaughtering operations; and produces other benefits for producers, processors, and consumers which tend to expedite an orderly flow of livestock and livestock products in interstate and foreign commerce. It is therefore declared to be the policy of the United States that the slaughtering of livestock and the handling of livestock in connection with slaughter shall be carried out only by humane methods.

Sec. 1902. - Humane methods

No method of slaughtering or handling in connection with slaughtering shall be deemed to comply with the public policy of the United States unless it is humane. Either of the following two methods of slaughtering and handling are hereby found to be humane:

(a) in the case of cattle, calves, horses, mules, sheep, swine, and other livestock, all animals are rendered insensible to pain by a single blow or gunshot or an electrical, chemical or other means that is rapid and effective, before being shackled, hoisted, thrown, cast, or cut; or

(b) by slaughtering in accordance with the ritual requirements of the Jewish faith or any other religious faith that prescribes a method of slaughter whereby the animal suffers loss of consciousness by anemia of the brain caused by the simultaneous and instantaneous severance of the carotid arteries with a sharp instrument and handling in connection with such slaughtering.

Section 1906 – Exemption of ritual slaughter

Nothing in this chapter (Humane Methods of Slaughter Act of 1978 – Title 7 of the U.S. Code, Chapter 48) shall be construed to prohibit, abridge, or in any way hinder the religious freedom of any person or group. Not withstanding any other provision of this chapter, in order to protect freedom of religion, ritual slaughter and the handling or other preparation of livestock for ritual slaughter are exempted from the terms of this chapter. For the purposes of this section the term "ritual slaughter" means slaughter in accordance with section 1902(b) of this title.

13 horses seized from veterinarian
Roane, WV (US)
Incident Date: Friday, Jul 28, 2006
County: Roane
Disposition: Dismissed (Conditional)
Person of Interest: Lori Gabri, DVM
Case Updates: 2 update(s) available

More than a dozen horses are seized from a Roane County Farm after the State Veterinarian says to remove them.

"Right now some people from the animal shelter and some private citizens have agreed to help us haul them," said Chief Deputy Jeff Smith with the Roane County Sheriff's Department. Saturday he served Lori Gabri, the horses' owner, with a search warrant allowing the horses to be removed. Neighbors had been complaining for months that the close to 20 horses Gabri owner were not being fed properly.

Deputies came to the farm on July 28 with State Veterinarian Dr. Joe Starcher to inspect the horses and the property.

"The state vet recommended that the horses be removed," said Chief Deputy Smith. The horses were taken to a stock yard in Spencer where they will be housed temporarily.

No official charges have been filed against Gabri but she has been suspended from her job as a veterinarian in Kanawha County.

Connie Lupardus is a member of the West Virginia Horse Council. She helped transport the horses Saturday. "We domesticate them. We bring them onto our farms and lock them in stalls. We pen them up and we put them behind barbed wire and electric fence," said Lupardus. "They are dependent on us to take care of them and when we fail that we should be held responsible."

Neighbors calledlocal newsafter trying for months to get authorities to help the horses. Lupardus says the state needs to do a better job of training the people who respond to abuse calls like this one.

"The lesson to be learned is there has got to be some education done with the officials who handle these situations," Lupardus said.

But for now the horses seized from the farm are getting a second chance thanksto the efforts of a few people willing to speak up.

"You just have to be one or two persons that stand up for what you think is right," Lupardus said.

Lori Gabri gave five horses away before the vet came to inspect the farm.

The people caring for those horses need your help.. .specifically whole oats and grass hay. You can call them at (304) 988-3901.

For information on how to help the other horses call the Roane County Sheriff's Department at (304) 927-3410.

Case Updates

The Roane prosecutor says it was the best way to resolve the case. The local humane society says it's the result of lack of funding for animal issues. A national animal rights group called it "disgusting."

Authorities seized the horses from Charleston veterinarian Lori Gabri after neighbors complained that the animals weren't being fed. According to a humane officer who visited Gabri's 6-acre farm on Abbott Road, you could see the backbones and ribs of the horses because of weight loss.

In her agreement with Prosecutor Mark Sergant last month, she will get her horses back when she gets some more land on which they can graze. For the time being, they're being kept at a horse sanctuary in Leon. Meanwhile, Gabri's veterinary license is under review.

Source: Charleston Daily Mail - Sept 25, 2006

Update posted on Sep 28, 2006 - 11:08PM

Back to Top

A West Virginia state veterinarian has paid a visit to that farm.

Earlier this week we spoke with neighbors who were outraged about the condition of some horses in Roane County.

They say the owner, Lori Gabri, has been starving nearly 20 horses in her care, including one that had to be put down on Tuesday.

Many of you were surprised to find out that Gabri works as a vet in Kanawha county.

"I was asked to come up here by the sheriff's department and the humane society in Roane county to look at the horses." said Dr. Joe Starcher, the WestVirginia state veterinarian.

Friday Starcher, a Roane county sheriff's deputy and the Roane county humane officer inspected the horses and the property.

"I can't say much the investigation is ongoing." Starcher said.

Right now no officials charges have been filed.

Sources tell us that since our story aired on Tuesday, Lori Gabri has been suspended from her job.

Gabri says one of the horses was stolen from the pasture Thursday night, and five other horses have been given away.

Late Friday afternoon there were still several horses in the pasture.

The people caring for the five horses that Gabri agreed to give away need help with feed and hay and other supplies.

They specifically need whole oats and grass hay.

For information on how to help call (304) 988-3901.

Source: WOWK - July 28, 2006

Update posted on Sep 28, 2006 - 2:09PM

Fake Veterinarian Caught By Channel 2

Posted: 6:49 pm EST February 10, 2010

Updated: 9:53 am EST February 11,2010

ATLANTA -- At first glance, Tim Holt looks like the average college student on the campus of Athens Tech. He's studying anatomy andmicrobiology. But those intro level courses do look strange for someone who already claims to be a veterinarian.

David Cantrell is a close friend of Holt's. He says he knows his friend isn't a vet, and started asking questions about Holt's job.

"I picked up on a few lies, not made to cover up anything, but they were just kind of compulsive lies."

For the last four years, Holt worked as a veterinarian for the U.S. Department of Agriculture. Your tax dollars paid for him to supervisedozens of employees, and inspect food processing plants around Georgia to make sure the animals were healthy and the food supply safe.

"He's never been to vet schools, he's read book and gone to some seminars and listened," Cantrell said. "I don't know that you would feel safe if Iwere inspecting your food supply, and I'm just as qualified as he is."

Ken Berkholtz recruits veterinarians for companies around the country. He got Tim Holt's first resume for a job back in 2004. We asked him how many items on that resume were untrue. "The majority. Out of maybe 10 items, he probably lied on 8 of them."

The company hired Tim, but fired him after three months saying his skills didn't back his credentials. His resume claims a D.V.M. and a Ph.D. from Auburn University. He had even named himself Georgia Veterinarian of the Year.

"They confronted him and he didn't deny anything, so they just terminated him," Berkholtz said.

Then in 2009, Tim sent Ken his most recent resume. Ken remembered the name and checked the files.

"He changed his resume considerably. (He) no longer had gotten his degree from Auburn. It was Missouri now."

Someone named Tim Holt did graduate from the University of Missouri Veterinarian School, but that was before this Tim Holt was born.

We confronted Holt on the campus of Athens Tech. He wouldn't answer any of our repeated questions.

David Cantrell also found a University of Georgia letterhead, addressed to Dr. Timothy Holt, Class of 2002. The fax number listed to verify his education, rings in Tim's home office in Athens.

Cantrell called the USDA several times, but says no one wanted to hear the truth. So he called Channel 2. We shared his records with a criminal investigator. Now the federal agency won't show us Holt's job application, saying it would jeopardize their investigation.

"Once is a wake up call, oh my gosh I shouldn't do this," Cantrell said. "Twice is just brazen. Then to continue doing it? There's no question he's going to do it again."

In: Animal Protection: Treatment and Welfare Issues
Editor: Dennis G. Carlton ISBN: 978-1-61728-353-6

Chapter 10

TESTIMONY OF MR. BEV EGGLESTON, BEFORE THE DOMESTIC POLICY SUBCOMMITTEE - HEARING ON "CONTINUING PROBLEMS IN USDA'S ENFORCEMENT OF THE HUMANE METHODS OF SLAUGHTER ACT"*

Good Afternoon, Chairman Kucinich, Ranking Member Issa, and Members of the Domestic Policy Subcommittee. I appreciate the opportunity to share with you my testimony in this hearing, "Continuing Problems in USDA's Enforcement of the Humane Methods of Slaughter Act," regarding the enforcement of the Humane Slaughter Act.

I am Bev Eggleston, founder and president of Eco-Friendly Foods, LLC, loacted in Moneta, Va. For the last 7 years, our company has operated a USDA-inspected, small-scale, multi-species slaughter plant serving dozens of farmers and livestock producers throughout Virginia and the greater Mid- Atlantic Region, and it is in that capacity that I appear before this subcommittee today.

1. ISSUES AND PROBLEMS

As you are well aware, the past decade has seen a continuing consolidation of packing capacity within the beef, pork, and chicken sectors. Not only are a handful of the largest companies now able to dominate the slaughter and processing of cattle and hogs, but numerous small-scale and regional packers have been bought up, shut down or sold out, due to their inability to compete with the economies of scale of the largest meat companies.

This consolidation raises several important issues for this oversight hearing, and should serve as the basis for congressional action going forward.

First, there are significant concerns for the safety of our meat supply, given the scale and the speed at which the largest beef and pork packaging operate. When hundreds of animals an

* This is an edited, reformatted and augmented edition of a statement/testimony given before the United States Oversight and Government Reform Committee, dated March 4, 2010.

hour are being processed, it is extremely challenging, to say the least, for operators—and federal inspectors—to ensure that the meat products produced in these plants do not enter commerce contaminated with potentially deadly microbial pathogens. The size, frequency and public health impact of the numerous product recalls and food-borne illness outbreaks traced to products from the nation's largest packing operations is testimony to the problems associated with high-speed, industrial-scale meatpacking.

Second, there are serious animal welfare issues associated with the disappearance of so many regional packing plants. No matter how humanely livestock are raised on farms and ranches, and no matter how conscientiously they are off-loaded and handled at the packing plants, too many animals must be transported thousands of miles to one of the steadily decreasing number of large packing plants—often spending over 24 hours aboard trucks until they reach their destination.

That is a serious concern for most American consumers, who are increasingly sensitive to and insistent upon higher standards of welfare for the nation's food animals. Without the availability of regional and local packing plants, farmers and ranchers are increasingly forced to subject their livestock to lengthy transport under less-than optimum conditions, a problem that cannot be addressed even with tougher regulations or stepped-up scrutiny of the part of federal inspection personnel.

2. Remedies

There is, however, a solution that not only mitigates the food-safety problems inherent in our high-volume, industrialized meatpacking system, but that also addresses the humane handling challenges mentioned above. Futhermore, this remedy will also provide significant additional benefits, including:

- Financial stimulus for our country's hardest-hit rural economies
- Strong support for the U.S. Department of Agriculture's stated goal of maintaining and enhancing agricultural diversity
- Reduction in the overall carbon footprint of the U.S. food production system
- Preservation of our country's limited natural resources
- Additional healthy food choices for American consumers

Here is what I believe can be Congress' role in addressing the concerns related our overly consolidated, highly concentrated meatpacking system. First, there should be direct and immediate aid and assistance provided to small-scale, regional packing plant operations that service local farmers, ranchers and livestock producers. At the same time as we are witnessing phenomenal growth in the sales of organically grown, locally raised, humanely certified meat products both at retail and foodservice, we are allowing a potentially devastating bottleneck to develop: access to slaughter plants.

Without the availability of regional packing plants equipped and designed to service small growers and specialty producers in every state and region in this country, we not only exacerbate the problems endemic to larger plants, we eventually force smaller producers out of production, and that ultimately means fewer choices for consumers and a greater reliance on imported foodstuffs.

At Eco-Friendly Foods, for example, we purchase livestock from over forty small, diversified farmers and producers throughout Virginia and the greater Mid-Atlantic Region. Few—if any—of them would be able to continue in the livestock business if they did not have access to our plant and instead had to ship their animals hundreds of miles away for processing. In fact, without the income generated by the sales—at a premium—of the humanely certified, locally grown, specialty breeds most of them raise, their entire farming operations would be in serious jeopardy of becoming economically unsustainable.

We need Congress to direct the USDA to provide financial assistance in the form of low-cost loans and grants for small-scale processing facilities and also to educate their inspectors on the realities of small-scale meatpacking operations, such as slower production rates, multiple species, and often irregular working hours.

3. Results and Benefits

Ideally, there should be several, if not dozens, of small, locally operated slaughter facilities available to farmers, ranchers and livestock producers in every state and region. This would sustain the current growth in specialty livestock raising and encourage a new generation of farmer-growers to become producing members of our agricultural sector.

The economic benefits to rural America of such an investment would be substantial. Our total gross sales during the implementation of our model thus far (7 years) are \$3.1 million, half of which (roughly \$1.5 million) has gone directly into the pockets of our producers. This directly stimulates rural economic development, because our plant makes the business of raising livestock on a small-scale economically viable for Virginia farmers who otherwise would not be able to be profitable. That enhances agricultural diversity, rather than continuing to move toward a system of increasingly larger farms dedicated to monoculture of a limited number of commodity crops.

Such a trend jeopardizes our national food security, forces greater dependence on imported foods, raises, not reduces, food production's carbon footprint and potentially devastates the economic viability rural America as we look ahead too the next generation or two in the farm community.

For these reasons, I urge this subcommittee to take seriously the need to sustain and enlarge access to slaughter plant facilities for the tens of thousands of small livestock growers and producers by directing USDA to prioritize its support and assistance for the dwindling number of small plant operators serving the needs of farmer-producers across America.

Thank you very much.
Sincerely,
Beverly P. Eggleston, IV

In: Animal Protection: Treatment and Welfare Issues
Editor: Dennis G. Carlton
ISBN: 978-1-61728-353-6

Chapter 11

STATEMENT OF WAYNE PACELLE, PRESIDENT AND CEO OF THE HUMANE SOCIETY OF THE UNITED STATES, BEFORE THE DOMESTIC POLICY SUBCOMMITTEE - HEARING ON "CONTINUING PROBLEMS IN USDA'S ENFORCEMENT OF THE HUMANE METHODS OF SLAUGHTER ACT"*

Mr. Chairman and Members of the Subcommittee, thank you for the opportunity to testify about enforcement of the Humane Methods of Slaughter Act. The Humane Society of the United States (HSUS) is the nation's largest animal protection organization with 11 million supporters nationwide, and I serve as president and CEO of the organization. Our organization worked hard to get this law enacted more than 50 years ago, and we have continued to press for reforms and agency resources to improve enforcement over the subsequent decades.

We deeply appreciate Chairman Kucinich's leadership in calling this hearing and requesting the GAO's study and report, which we look forward to reading. This is a follow-up to a hearing the Chairman held in 2008 at which I also had the privilege to testify. That hearing came after an undercover investigation our organization conducted at the Hallmark/Westland Meat Packing Company in Chino, Calif. revealed horrendous abuse of downed cows too sick and injured even to stand and walk. The Hallmark footage showed workers ramming cows with the blades of a forklift, jabbing them in the eyes, applying painful electrical shocks often in sensitive areas, dragging them with chains pulled by heavy machinery, and torturing them with a high-pressure water hose to simulate drowning as they attempted to force these animals to walk to slaughter. The USDA shut down that plant – which we discovered after our investigation had been the second largest ground beef supplier to the National School Lunch Program and had been honored by the agency as "supplier of the year" in 2004-2005 – and the largest beef recall in U.S. history resulted.

* This is an edited, reformatted and augmented edition of a statement/testimony given before the United States Oversight and Government Reform Committee, dated March 4, 2010.

Subsequently, in April and May of 2008, we conducted additional undercover investigations at several livestock auctions in Texas, Pennsylvania, New Mexico, and Maryland. At each of these facilities, we found egregious humane handling violations of downer cows. Incidents included a downer forced to crawl on her front knees by workers who repeatedly shocked her, a blind cow being shocked and struck, another downer being dragged by a tractor attached to a chain around her severely hyper-extended leg, calves kicked repeatedly in the head, and downers left to languish and die after being abandoned.

Bushway Packing Investigation

Then in August and September of 2009, we conducted an undercover investigation at Bushway Packing, Inc. of Grand Isle, Vermont, a plant that specialized in "bob veal" – that is, the slaughter of baby calves, typically less than a week old. We undertook this investigation acting on concerns that had been flagged to us by Dr. Dean Wyatt, who had been in private contact with our organization since the Hallmark case became public. Dr. Wyatt was not aware of our undercover investigation at Bushway while it was going on – he did not learn about it until we brought it to the attention of USDA officials.

Approximately 15% of the 700,000 veal calves slaughtered in the U.S. annually are sold for bob veal. These newborns are taken from their mothers and, only hours or days old, may be deprived of any nourishment during the long transit to the slaughter plant. Current federal law allows them to be transported for up to 28 hours without food, water, or even enough space to lie down. Consequently, once they reach the slaughter plant, they are often too weak, exhausted, and malnourished to stand.

Our investigator, who worked as a floor cleaner at the plant, gathered hidden-camera evidence showing many cruelties. Video footage revealed workers repeatedly shocking calves with electric prods and kicking them in an attempt to force them to stand. Some calves were shocked more than 30 times, and, in at least one case, water was splashed on a calf to intensify the effect of the electric current. The slaughter plant's co-owner, who later claimed in press reports that he had no knowledge of cruel treatment at his facility, was captured on film shocking downed calves with electric prods, and saying to one, "There ain't nothing wrong with you, sh*t box." The infant animal, covered in his own diarrhea, then staggered and fell hard into the side of the trailer. At another point, the co-owner joked that one of the staggering calves "looks like you on a Friday night," referring to the USDA inspector, who laughed at the co-owner's joke.

The investigator videotaped calves crowded together and improperly stunned as a group, rather than restrained individually to allow accurate placement of the stun gun. Federal law requires that animals be rendered insensible to pain before being bled out and dismembered, but the footage shows movements and breathing not characteristic of post-mortem reflexes. In one case, a shackled calf whose head had been half-way removed vocalized at a point when he should have been unconscious, leading animal science experts Dr. Temple Grandin and Kurt Vogel, who reviewed the footage, to comment that the calf was "definitely sensible." In another case, a worker is seen having to move away from a calf who kicked after having one of his feet cut off. The Grandin/Vogel review also concluded that "electric prods were commonly used in an abusive manner to force nonambulatory calves to rise. This is unacceptable and should not continue. It is unacceptable to allow workers to kick calves to make them rise as was observed... .This is a definite act of abuse."

Perhaps most troubling, the hidden camera revealed a USDA inspector failing to act when confronted with clear evidence of serious violations. In one scene, a worker attempted to skin a calf who was still alive, directly in front of this inspector. The government official told the worker that if another USDA inspector (referring to Dr. Wyatt, who shared duties at the plant) saw this, the plant would be shut down, but he allowed the abuse to continue. Further, he told the HSUS investigator on video not to tell him if a live calf was in the pile of dead animals because, "I'm not supposed to know. I could shut them down for that."

Pattern of Abuse and Denial of a Broader Problem

So, as with the case at Hallmark and the various livestock auctions, our undercover investigation at Bushway uncovered terrible abuse. And again, as has been the case each time the HSUS and other organizations have called attention to investigative findings of inhumane treatment in the slaughter process, the general response by those in the animal agriculture business was to suggest that the events at Bushway were an aberration – a case of a "bad apple" obviously not conforming to industry's high standards of animal welfare.

The logic of this escapes me. Every time we've done an undercover investigation at a slaughter plant or a livestock auction, we've found horrendous mistreatment. Without having conducted investigations at the thousands of slaughter plants in the U.S., we can't know how frequently this sort of abuse occurs. But for those in industry to say that it simply doesn't occur elsewhere implies that they are vigilantly watching for it. That would mean they were watching at Hallmark and Bushway and the other sites where undercover investigations found abuse, and they didn't stop it. Or they weren't watching at those particular sites, but we are supposed to believe that they do watch vigilantly everywhere else.

It would be refreshing if, instead of rushing to label these as mere bad apples, industry leaders took revelations of abuse as a wake-up call – a challenge to address systemic concerns and bring about meaningful changes that would improve the treatment of animals and meet consumer concerns. Not only is humane handling at slaughter plants important for animal welfare, it also plays a significant role in ensuring food safety. For our part, we at the HSUS would like nothing more than to undertake investigations in the future and find that animals are being treated humanely and that there are no egregious abuses to report.

A New Opportunity for Reform

We believe there is a real moment now – an opportunity to make significant reforms to strengthen oversight of slaughter processes. We've been heartened by the new Administration's willingness to take humane concerns seriously. Within his first 50 days in office, President Obama personally announced that the USDA would close the downer cattle loophole and ban slaughter of all downed cattle. The USDA's final rule published on March 18, 2009 made clear that the decision to close the loophole was strongly motivated by humane handling concerns that were highlighted by the Hallmark investigation. This was a reform we had been seeking for many years, with increased urgency as "mad cow disease" concerns emerged in the U.S. and then as the Hallmark/Westland case demonstrated how allowing some downers to be slaughtered creates a financial incentive for workers to use unimaginably cruel tactics to try to get downed animals on their feet for slaughter.

When we brought the Bushway video footage to Agriculture Secretary Vilsack's attention, he took decisive action, immediately suspending operations at the plant and initiating an agency investigation. We've also appreciated the opportunity to meet with his staff and other USDA officials to discuss a range of reforms that could strengthen protections for animals and agency oversight of humane handling rules.

While we are heartened by the direction that top agency officials seem headed, we know that much work remains to be done. It's like turning a battleship around. It will take significant effort to overcome the habits built up over so many years, in which inspectors have been made to feel that they shouldn't rock the boat and that their clients essentially are the companies they inspect, not the public or the animals entrusted to their care. The culture throughout FSIS must shift to acknowledge that humane treatment is a core, ongoing responsibility, not just something to address when an undercover investigation shines a spotlight on the issue.

As Dr. Wyatt has testified, some of the most serious problems have involved high-level supervisors putting pressure on inspectors below them to not rigorously enforce humane standards – discouraging them from reporting violations, rewriting and watering down their reports, second- guessing their first-hand observations, insisting that actions comport with humane standards even when they run contrary to the guidelines of Dr. Grandin (whose expertise is well-respected by industry), and reprimanding and punishing them for taking enforcement actions. Even some District Veterinary Medical Specialists – the very positions funded by Congress to focus on ensuring compliance with the Humane Methods of Slaughter Act – have engaged in this undermining of inspectors, as Dr. Wyatt explained. For the humane slaughter law to be properly enforced, it is imperative that personnel at all levels – and certainly those in the supervisory ranks – take this mission seriously. It is simply outrageous that some DVMSs have themselves been corrupting the system.

Specific Changes Proposed

1. Staffing and Resources

We were encouraged to learn that the USDA is creating a new position in its Washington headquarters, a Humane Handling Enforcement Coordinator who will oversee the work of the DVMSs. That could provide accountability, greater consistency, and enhanced enforcement efforts across regions if the person hired truly embraces the goals of the Humane Methods of Slaughter Act and is knowledgeable on issues such as specific indicators of animal suffering and distress, and problematic slaughter plant designs and practices.

In addition, we urge the establishment of an ombudsman to provide inspectors with an avenue to take their concerns and grievances, and help ensure that they are able to carry out their responsibilities – both food safety and humane slaughter – without undue interference. Ideally, this ombudsman would be independent from F SIS, reporting directly to the Under

Secretary for Food Safety, or alternatively could perhaps be in the Office of Program Evaluation, Enforcement & Review (OPEER) that helps ensure the effectiveness of FSIS.

We also recommend that a mobile review team be hired to conduct unscheduled audits and undercover surveillance focused on assessing compliance with humane handling rules of live animals as they arrive and are offloaded and handled in pens, chutes, and stunning areas. Knowing that a member of this team might make a surprise visit at any time, and might even be engaged in undercover work, could help keep plant personnel and inspectors on their toes. Audits and reports produced by this team should be accessible to other inspectors and the public, and the team should be allowed to devote its primary attention to evaluating treatment of live animals.

The agency should fire any inspectors who flout their obligations to report clear animal abuse. As we understand it, the inspector caught on video at Bushway was indeed fired, but that was only possible because he was still on probationary status as a new hire with less than one year on the job.

Ultimately, we believe that an inspector should be stationed at all times at each stunning area and another inspector (or more, depending on the facility's size) should be present at all times and able to observe live animals as they arrive, and are moved from trucks and through pens and chutes to the stunning area. Recognizing the current budget constraints, though, we feel the new positions described above would help in the short term to improve the effectiveness of FSIS staff across-the- board with respect to humane handling enforcement.

We are also encouraged about the FSIS's planned transition to a more integrated computer system which, as we understand it, will accommodate both Non Compliance Reports (NR) and Memoranda of Interview (MOI) in one comprehensive profile for each slaughter plant, so that egregious humane handling violations will be readily apparent to inspectors and the public. Under the current system, the egregious cases fall outside the computerized data tracking system to which inspectors have access.

2. Policy Reforms

The Bushway case highlighted two reforms urgently needed specifically for veal calves: First, the USDA must close the downer calf loophole, which allows downer calves to be set aside and reevaluated for possible slaughter. That loophole perpetuates the economic incentives for workers to mistreat calves in cruel attempts to get them on their feet so they can be approved for slaughter. While the Obama Administration did close the downer cattle loophole in March 2009, a move we applauded, it has not yet addressed an exemption for veal calves that remains from a July 2007 regulation under the Bush Administration. 9 C.F.R. § 309.13(b).

Second, the USDA should also end the transport of baby calves to slaughter, similar to existing regulations in the European Union. Calves less than 10 days old should not be considered fit for transport, since they are ill-equipped to handle the trauma of transport to slaughter plants. Those who survive the trip arrive weak, malnourished and often unable to stand, leading to increased rates of disease and death and leaving them more vulnerable to abuse. We note that bob veal calves generally sell for just $ 10-20 each, according to figures provided by FSIS Administrator Al Almanza.

In addition, the USDA should stop excluding chickens, turkeys, and other poultry – who constitute approximately 95% of all farm animals slaughtered for food in the U.S. (9 billion birds per year) – from the modest protections of the Humane Methods of Slaughter Act. Chickens and turkeys at slaughter plants are typically collected manually by workers at an intense pace (up to 180 birds a minute) and shackled upside down by their legs on a fast-moving mechanized line. Still conscious, they are dragged through an electrified water tank designed to immobilize them, passed through a neck-slicer, and dropped into scalding water to loosen their feathers. Due to the speed of the assembly line and their own desperate motions, millions of birds – according to USDA statistics – evade both the immobilization tank and the neck-slicer and literally drown in tanks of scalding water. The agency should require and help guide an industry transition to Controlled Atmosphere Killing methods that, when done using a proper mix of gases, can provide a more humane end and also yield higher productivity (e.g., fewer broken bones) and fewer worker injuries from repetitive stress.

The USDA should also require that when gas is used to stun pigs, more humane gas mixtures be utilized. Use of CO_2 alone – as is the current practice – is highly aversive and causes unacceptable suffering, as pigs suffocate rather than first losing consciousness.

Over the past year, we have shared with the USDA and GAO a more detailed set of policy and oversight recommendations, which I am attaching as an addendum to this testimony. We look forward to further discussions, as we seek to work together to strengthen enforcement of the Humane Methods of Slaughter Act.

Thank you again for the opportunity to testify here today on this crucial issue.

ADDENDUM: HUMANE SLAUGHTER – NEEDED REFORMS

1. Oversight Reforms

USDA should immediately develop a significantly improved oversight system to ensure that USDA inspectors are observing live animals when they first arrive at slaughter facilities and as they are offloaded and handled in pens and chutes, and that the inspectors are acting to avert violations of the Humane Methods of Slaughter Act and regulations pursuant to that law, as well as regulations regarding nonambulatory animals. To meet these goals, the following combination of reforms should be implemented:

A. More inspectors are needed to directly observe live animals. In particular, we recommend that one inspector be stationed at all times at the stunning area and another inspector (or more, depending on the facility's size) be present and able to observe at all times live animals as they arrive, are offloaded, held in pens, and moved through chutes;

B. All inspectors must be trained and directed to monitor the treatment of live animals to ensure that they are handled humanely. Inspectors must understand that their oversight responsibilities begin at the moment animals arrive at slaughter premises, including when the animals are on trucks at slaughter facilities. Inspectors should also be trained to consider the animals and the public, rather than the slaughter facilities, as their "clients." Inspectors must receive adequate in-person, on-theground training so they can properly assess and score the conditions and treatment of animals, as well as receive regular subsequent in-person, on-the-ground training to refresh and hone their skills;

C. Inspectors must be encouraged to report violations, rather than being discouraged from and even reprimanded for doing so by their superiors; superiors must support inspectors in their observations, rather than second-guessing and rewriting and/or watering down their reports;

D. An ombudsman office should be created to provide inspectors with an avenue to take their concerns and grievances, and help ensure that they are able to carry out their responsibilities – both food safety and humane slaughter – without undue interference;

E. Egregious humane handling violations must be noted through Noncompliance Reports (as they had been until agency changes* were instituted following the Hallmark case), so that documentation of these serious violations will become part of the computerized data base, accessible through the PBIS system to other inspectors, USDA's Office of Food Safety, the media, the public, Congress, and others evaluating HMSA compliance and analyzing trends, and will require permanent corrective action (*following the Hallmark case, FSIS instructed inspectors to report egregious humane handling violations only via faxed Memoranda of Interview that are not readily reviewable and involve just temporary corrective action no longer required after a suspension is lifted);

F. Permanent corrective actions must be required by the agency. Under the current system, plants placed under "suspension in abeyance" have their suspension lifted and are not required to continue corrective action after a set period of 60 or 90 days;

G. Inspections and DVMS visits must be unannounced and not on a predictable schedule (except for 3C below);

H. In-person inspections could be supplemented with video surveillance to allow for agency oversight of all animal handling, from the time each animal arrives at the slaughter premises through the time of death. But it is critical to note that while video surveillance could be an important supplemental tool, it does not negate the need for greater real-time in-person inspector observation. Video footage should be preserved for forensic purposes so that it is possible to go back and look at particular scenes to determine if violations occurred;

I. Inspectors should be rotated to ensure that they do not develop inappropriate relationships with plant personnel that could jeopardize their objectivity;

J. Whistleblower reforms (as envisioned in pending Whistleblower Protection Act bills – H.R. 1507/S. 372) must be enacted to enable inspectors to report abuses without fear of retribution;

K. Undercover investigations at slaughter facilities should be conducted by USDA personnel – under the OIG or otherwise – to provide a significant deterrent against violations and expand on the capacity of private nonprofit organizations to carry out such investigations;

L. "Objective scoring" standards, if used to enhance enforcement, should not trump an inspector's expertise in witnessing inhumane treatment, and such standards must be overseen with real-time inspector observation to be useful (just having standards on paper that no one oversees will not be helpful).

2. Recognition That Poultry Must Have Protection under Humane Methods of Slaughter Act

USDA should stop excluding chickens, turkeys, and other poultry – who constitute approximately 95% of all land animals slaughtered for food in the U.S. (9 billion birds per year) – from this basic law that is supposed to protect animals from cruel and abusive treatment in their final moments. USDA should require and help guide industry transition to Controlled Atmosphere Killing methods that, when done using a proper mix of gases, can provide a more humane end and also yield higher productivity (e.g., fewer broken bones) and less worker injuries.

3. Actions Regarding Calves

A. Close loophole that allows slaughter of downer calves (as noted in 4A below);
B. End transport of live baby calves to slaughter plants (prior to 10 days of age, as in EU regulations);

4. Actions Regarding Downed Animals

A. Extension of the downer cattle ban to auctions, markets, stockyards, and livestock haulers, and to other species, as well as to calves;
B. Prohibition of specific egregious practices on any disabled or injured animal, such as forcefully striking the animal with an object, dragging the animal, ramming or otherwise attempting to get the animal to stand using heavy machinery, or using electric shock, water pressure, or other extreme methods;
C. A requirement for immediate and humane euthanasia – by personnel trained to use either a captive bolt gun (followed by exsanguination), firearm (using appropriate caliber), or euthanasia solution – of all nonambulatory animals at auctions, markets, stockyards, and slaughter facilities, and on livestock trucks, regardless of the reason(s) the animal is nonambulatory. An inspector meeting each truck when it arrives on the premises should order the immediate humane euthanasia and condemnation of any animal who is nonambulatory;
D. A requirement that nonambulatory animals be first rendered unconscious if they must be moved prior to euthanasia, and the use of suitable equipment for such movement by trained personnel;
E. A requirement of confirmation of clinical death prior to disposal of the carcass. Confirmation of death should include all three of the following, each absent for more than 5 minutes:
    - Lack of heartbeat (determined with stethoscope, not pulse)
    - Lack of respiration
    - Lack of corneal reflex (touching surface of eyeball)

    (Visible rigor mortis can also serve to confirm death, when observed over a longer period, but the three indicators above should have already been checked);

5. Requirement That More Humane Gas Mixtures Be Used to Stun Pigs

Use of CO_2 alone is highly aversive and causes unacceptable suffering, as pigs suffocate rather than first losing consciousness.

In: Animal Protection: Treatment and Welfare Issues
Editor: Dennis G. Carlton
ISBN: 978-1-61728-353-6

Chapter 12

BRIEF SUMMARIES OF FEDERAL ANIMAL PROTECTION STATUTES*

Vivian S. Chu

SUMMARY

This chapter contains brief summaries of federal animal protection statutes, listed alphabetically. It includes statutes enacted to implement certain treaties, but it does not include treaties. Additionally, this chapter includes statutes that concern animals but that are not necessarily animal protection statutes. For example, it discusses a statute authorizing the eradication of predators, because one of the statute's purposes is to protect domestic and "game" animals; and it includes statutes to conserve fish even though the ultimate purpose of such statutes may not be for the benefit of the fish. This chapter also includes statutes that allow the disabled to use service animals and statutes aimed at acts of animal rights advocates—i.e., the Animal Enterprise Protection Act of 1992, and the Recreational Hunting Safety and Preservation Act of 1994.

ADOPTION OF MILITARY ANIMALS, 10 U.S.C. § 2583

This statute provides, in part: "The Secretary of the military department concerned may make a military animal of such military department available for adoption ... under circumstances as follows: (1) At the end of the animal's useful life. (2) Before the end of the animal's useful life, if such Secretary ... determines that unusual or extraordinary circumstances justify [it]. (3) When the animal is otherwise excess to the needs of such military department." The statute defines "military animal" as "[a] military working dog" or "[a] horse owned by the Department of Defense." When this statute was first enacted in 2000,

* This is an edited, reformatted and augmented version of a CRS Report for Congress publication, Report #94-731, dated February 1,2010.

it applied only to military working dogs; prior to then, under Department of Defense policy, such dogs were caged, sometimes for as long as a year, and then euthanized. See 146 Cong. Rec. H 9599 (daily ed. October 10, 2000). The statute was amended to cover horses in 2006.[1]

AFRICAN ELEPHANT CONSERVATION ACT,16 U.S.C. §§ 4201-4245

This statute establishes an African Elephant Conservation Fund, from which the Secretary of the Interior may provide financial assistance "for approved projects for research, conservation, management, or protection of African elephants." It requires the Secretary to establish a moratorium on the importation of raw and worked ivory from an ivory producing country that does not meet specified criteria, including being a party to CITES and adhering to the CITES Ivory Control System. ("CITES" is the Convention on the International Trade in Endangered Species of Wild Fauna and Flora.)

The act imposes civil and criminal penalties on any person who, among other things, imports raw ivory from any country other than an ivory producing country, or from a country for which a moratorium is in effect, or who exports raw ivory from the United States. A person who furnishes information that leads to a civil penalty or a criminal conviction under the act may be rewarded up to one-half of any criminal or civil penalty or fine, or $25,000, whichever is less.

AGRICULTURE APPROPRIATIONS ACT, 2006, P.L. 109-97(2005), AND SUBSEQUENT APPROPRIATIONS ACTS

Section 794 of P.L. 109-97 (2005) provides:

> Effective 120 days after the date of enactment of this act, none of the funds made available by this act may be used to pay the salaries or expenses of personnel to inspect horses under section 3 of the Federal Meat Inspection Act (21 U.S.C. 603) or under guidelines issued under section 903 [of] the Federal Agriculture Improvement and Reform Act of 1996 (7 U.S.C. 1901 note; P.L. 104-127).[2]

Because the Federal Meat Inspection Act, 21 U.S.C. § 603, requires horses (and specified other mammals) to be inspected before they may be slaughtered for human consumption, § 794 of P.L. 109-97, by precluding appropriated funds from being used to pay inspectors' salaries and expenses to inspect horses, would have effectively prohibited the slaughter of horses for human consumption from March 10, 2006, until September 30, 2006. The Department of Agriculture, however, on February 8, 2006, issued a regulation allowing slaughter plants to pay for inspections by the Department of Agriculture's Food Safety and Inspection Service so that horses could continue to be slaughtered for human consumption. 9 C.F.R. § 352. 19.[3]

The 110th Congress prevented the Department of Agriculture from continuing to charge slaughter plants for inspections, and it thereby effectively prohibited the slaughter of horses for human consumption. It accomplished this by prohibiting appropriated funds from being used not only, as in P.L. 109-97, to pay salaries and expenses under the Federal Meat Inspection Act and the Federal Agriculture Improvement and Reform Act of 1996, but also from being used to implement or enforce 9 C.F.R. § 352.19, under which the Department of Agriculture allowed slaughter plants to pay for inspections. P.L. 110-161, § 741, 121 Stat. 1881 (2007); P.L. 110-329, Div. A, § 101, 122 Stat. 3574-3575 (2008) (incorporating provisions of P.L. 110-161).

AIRBORNE HUNTING ACT, 16 U.S.C. § 742J-1

This statute makes it a crime (1) while in an aircraft, to shoot any bird, fish, or other animal, or (2) to use an aircraft to harass any bird, fish, or other animal. These prohibitions do not apply to persons employed by or licensed by a state or the federal government to administer or protect "land, water, wildlife, domesticated animals, human life, or crops."

ALASKA NATIONAL INTEREST LANDS CONSERVATION ACT

Sections 1313-1314 of this act, 16 U.S.C. §§ 3201-3202, authorize the Secretary of the Interior to designate zones within national preserves in Alaska "where and when no hunting, fishing, trapping, or entry may be permitted," and prohibits "the taking of fish and wildlife" in national parks or national park system monuments in Alaska, except as specified in the act.

Section 1005 of the act, as amended in 1990, 16 U.S.C. § 3145, provides that the Secretary of the Interior

> shall work closely with the State of Alaska and Native Village and Regional Corporations in evaluating the impact of oil and gas exploration, development, production, and transportation and other human activities on the wildlife resources of these lands, including impacts on the Arctic and Porcupine caribou herds, polar bears, muskox, grizzly bear, wolf, wolverine, seabirds, shorebirds, and migratory waterfowl.

AMERICANS WITH DISABILITIES ACT, 42 U.S.C. §§ 12101-12213

This statute (together with the Rehabilitation Act of 1973, 29 U.S.C. § § 791-794) prohibits discrimination against people with disabilities in employment, public services, and public accommodations.[4] Discrimination includes refusing to make reasonable accommodations for individuals with disabilities, and a reasonable accommodation generally includes permitting the use of service animals, such as seeing eye dogs. See, e.g., 28 C.F.R. § 36.302(c). See also, "Fair Housing Act, 42 U.S.C. § 3604," discussed below.

ANADROMOUS FISH CONSERVATION ACT,16 U.S.C. §§ 757A-757F

This statute authorizes the Secretary of Commerce to take various actions for the protection of fishery resources.

ANIMAL DAMAGE CONTROL ACT, 7 U.S.C. §§ 426-426C

This statute directs the Secretary of Agriculture:

> to conduct investigations, experiments, and tests as he may deem necessary in order to determine, demonstrate, and promulgate the best methods of eradication, suppression, or bringing under control on national forests and other areas of the public domain as well as on State, Territory, or privately owned lands of mountain lions, wolves, bobcats, prairie dogs, gophers, ground squirrels, jack rabbits, brown tree snakes, and other animals injurious to agriculture, horticulture, forestry, animal husbandry, wild game animals, fur-bearing animals, and birds.

This statute was enacted in 1931 (though "brown tree snakes" were added in 1991). The functions of the Secretary of Agriculture under it were transferred to the Secretary of Interior in 1939, and back to Agriculture in 1985.[5] In 1987, P.L. 100-202, 101 Stat. 1329-33 1, added the following provision to the act:

> The Secretary of Agriculture is authorized, except for urban rodent control, to conduct activities and enter into agreements with States, local jurisdictions, individuals, and public and private agencies, organizations, and institutions in the control of nuisance mammals and birds and those mammal and bird species that are reservoirs for zoonotic diseases, and to deposit any money collected under any such agreement into the appropriation accounts that incur the costs to be available immediately and to remain available until expended for Animal Damage Control activities.

ANIMAL DISEASE RISK ASSESSMENT, PREVENTION, ANDCONTROL ACT OF 2001, P.L. 107-9 (2001)

This statute requires the Department of Agriculture to submit to the House and Senate agriculture committees a preliminary report by June 23, 2001, and a final report by October 20, 2001, concerning foot-and-mouth disease, bovine spongiform encephalopathy, and related diseases.

ANIMAL ENTERPRISE TERRORISM ACT, 18 U.S.C. § 43

This statute, which replaced the Animal Enterprise Protection Act of 1992, makes it a crime to "travel[ ] in interstate or foreign commerce, or use[ ] ... the mail or any facility in interstate or foreign commerce—(1) for the purpose of damaging or interfering with the operations of an animal enterprise; and (2) in connection with such purpose—(A) intentionally damag[ing] or caus[ing] the loss of any real or personal property ... [or] (B) intentionally plac[ing] a person in reasonable fear of the death of, or serious bodily injury to that person, a member of the immediate family ... of that person, or a spouse or intimate partner of that person. ..." The statute defines "animal enterprise" as:

> (A) a commercial or academic enterprise that uses or sells animals or animal products for profit, food or fiber production, agriculture, education, research, or testing;
> (B) a zoo, aquarium, animal shelter, pet store, breeder, furrier, circus, rodeo, or other lawful competitive animal event; or
> (C) any fair or similar event intended to advance agricultural arts and sciences.

ANIMAL HEALTH PROTECTION ACT, 7 U.S.C. §§ 8301-8321

This statute authorizes the Secretary of Agriculture, if he determines it to be necessary to prevent the introduction into or dissemination with the United States of any pest or disease of livestock, to prohibit or restrict, among other things, the importation or exportation of any animal into or from the United States, the movement in interstate commerce of any animal, or the use of any means of conveyance in connection with the importation or entry of livestock. The statute also authorizes the Secretary, if it is necessary for the above purpose, to order the destruction or removal from the United States of any animal, or to seize, quarantine, or dispose of any animal.

ANIMAL WELFARE ACT, 7 U.S.C. §§ 2131-2159

The AWA authorizes the Secretary of Agriculture to "promulgate standards to govern the humane handling, care, treatment, and transportation of animals by dealers, research facilities, and exhibitors."[6] 7 U.S.C. § 2143(a)(1). Such standards must include requirements "for animal care, treatment, and practices in experimental procedures to ensure that animal pain and distress are minimized. ..." 7 U.S.C. § 2143(a)(3)(A). The act also requires the Secretary to "promulgate standards to govern the transportation in commerce, and the handling, care, and treatment in connection therewith, by intermediate handlers, air carriers, or other carriers, of animals consigned by any ... person ... for transportation in commerce." 7 U.S.C. § 2143(a)(4).

The AWA's definition of "animal" makes the act applicable to any warmblooded animal used "for research, testing, experimentation, or exhibition purposes, or as a pet; but such term excludes (1) birds, rats of the genus Rattus, and mice of the genus Mus, bred for use in research, (2) horses not used for research purposes, and (3) other farm animals. ..." 7 U.S.C. § 2132(g). Prior to this provision's amendment by P.L. 107-171 (2002), § 10301, it did not exclude birds, rats, or mice. Nevertheless, the Secretary had promulgated regulations that excluded birds, and rats and mice bred for use in research, from coverage under the act. A federal court found this exclusion to violate the act, but the decision was overturned on appeal on the ground that the plaintiffs lacked standing to bring the suit.[7] Subsequently, in a case unrelated to the birds, rats, and mice question, the en banc D.C. Circuit held that a plaintiff who "suffered [injuries] to his aesthetic interest in observing animals living under humane conditions" had standing to sue the Secretary of Agriculture to enforce the act.[8]

Subsequently, another suit was brought to challenge the exclusion of birds, rats, and mice, and a federal district court, citing the D.C. Circuit case, denied the Department of Agriculture's motion to dismiss for lack of standing.[9] As a result, the Department of Agriculture settled the case by agreeing to revise its regulations to include birds, rats, and mice. Then Congress intervened, and, in the Department of Agriculture appropriations for FY2001 (P.L. 106-387, § 772), prohibited FY2001 funds from being used to "modify the definition of 'animal' in existing regulations pursuant to the Animal Welfare Act." The FY2002 appropriations contained the same prohibition (P.L. 107-76, § 732), and then P.L. 107-171, § 10301, amended the statute to exclude birds, rats, and mice bred for research. Section 10304 of the statute, however, directs the National Research Council, by May 13, 2003, to submit to the House and Senate Agriculture Committees "a report on the implications of including rats, mice, and birds within the definition of animal under the regulations promulgated under the Animal Welfare Act (7 U.S.C. 2131 et seq.)." No report appears to have been written.

The AWA requires every research facility to establish an Institutional Animal Committee of at least three members, at least one of whom shall not be affiliated in any way with the facility and who is intended to represent "general community interests in the proper care and treatment of animals." The Committee's responsibilities include to review practices involving pain to animals and to file a report with the Secretary. 7 U.S.C. § 2143(b).

The AWA also provides for the licensing of dealers and exhibitors (7 U.S.C. § 2133) and prohibits research facilities from purchasing dogs or cats from unlicensed dealers or exhibitors (7 U.S.C. § 2137). The act defines "dealer" in part as a person who, for compensation, transports, buys, or sells any animal "for research, teaching, exhibition, or use as a pet," but it excludes from the definition a retail pet store that does not sell "animals to a research facility, an exhibitor, or a dealer" (7 U.S.C. § 2132(f)). The act defines "exhibitor" to include carnivals, circuses, and zoos, but to exclude retail pet stores, state and country fairs, livestock shows, rodeos, and purebred dog and cat shows (7 U.S.C. § 2 132(h)).

The AWA also prohibits dealers and exhibitors from selling or otherwise disposing of any dog or cat within five business days after they acquire it, except that this requirement does not apply to operators of auction sales. 7 U.S.C. § 2135. A 1990 amendment requires public and private pounds and shelters, and research facilities licensed by the Department of Agriculture, to "hold and care for" any dog or cat they acquire "for a period of not less than five days to enable such dog or cat to be recovered by its original owner or adopted by other individuals before such entity sells such dog or cat to a dealer."[10] 7 U.S.C. § 2158(a). Does this provision prohibit a pound, shelter, or research facility from euthanizing a dog or cat before five days? Perhaps not on its face, but that appears to be its intent, as to read it otherwise would seem to defeat its purpose.[11]

Another 1990 amendment authorized the Attorney General to seek, and federal courts to issue, injunctions against dealing in stolen animals or placing the health of an animal in serious danger in violation of the act. 7 U.S.C. § 2159.

P.L. 110-234, § 14210 (2008)[12] added a new section to the AWA (7 U.S.C. § 2148) that prohibits any person from importing a dog into the United States for purposes of resale unless the Secretary determines that the dog is in good health, has received all necessary vaccinations, and is at least six months old. This section does not apply, however, if a dog is imported for research purposes or veterinary treatment, or if it is imported into Hawaii from the British Isles, Australia, Guam, or New Zealand, if the dog is not transported out of Hawaii for purposes of resale at less than six months of age. P.L. 110-234, § 14214, also amended the AWA (7 U.S.C. § 2149(b)) to increase, from $2,500 to $10,000, the civil penalty that the Secretary of Agriculture may assess for any violation of any provision of the act, or of any rule, regulation, or standard promulgated by the Secretary.

Animal Fighting, 7 U.S.C. § 2156, 18 U.S.C. § 49

The Animal Welfare Act, as amended, most recently by P.L. 110-234, § 14207 (2008) prohibits any person "to knowingly sponsor or exhibit an animal in an animal fighting venture," or "to knowingly sell, buy, possess, train, transport, deliver, or receive any animal for the purposes of having the animal participate in an animal fighting venture." However,

> [w]ith respect to fighting ventures involving live birds in a State where it would not be a violation of the law, it shall be unlawful under this subsection for a person to sponsor or exhibit a bird in a fighting venture only if the person knew that any bird in the fighting venture was knowingly bought, sold, delivered, transported, or received in interstate commerce for the purpose of participation in the fighting venture.[13]

On August 15, 2008, a Louisiana statute (14:102.23) took effect that made it the 50th state (plus the District of Columbia) to outlaw cockfighting, thereby essentially rendering moot this exception in the AWA.

P.L. 110-22 (2007) made it "unlawful for any person to knowingly sell, buy, transport, or deliver in interstate or foreign commerce a knife, a gaff, or any other sharp instrument attached, or designed or intended to be attached, to the leg of a bird for use in an animal fighting venture." P.L. 110-22 also increased the penalty for violations of the animal fighting ventures section from a misdemeanor to a felony, with a maximum penalty of a fine and three years' imprisonment per violation. P.L. 110-234, § 14207(b) (2008) then increased the maximum penalty to a fine and five years' imprisonment per violation.

The animal fighting section of the AWA also prohibits knowingly using the mail or any instrumentality of interstate commerce to advertise an animal, or a sharp instrument, for use in an animal fighting venture, or to promote or further an animal fighting venture, except that this prohibition applies "to fighting ventures involving live birds only if the fight is to take place in a State where it would be in violation of the laws thereof."

ANTARCTIC CONSERVATION ACT OF 1978,16 U.S.C. §§ 2401-2412

This statute makes it unlawful for any United States citizen, unless authorized by the Director of the National Science Foundation, to engage in commerce in any native animal or native bird taken in Antarctica.

ANTARCTIC MARINE LIVING RESOURCES CONVENTION ACTOF 1984, 16 U.S.C. §§ 2431-2444

This statute implements the Convention on the Conservation of Antarctic Marine Living Resources, and makes it unlawful to harvest, or knowingly to engage in commerce in any Antarctic marine living resource harvested in violation of the Convention.

ASIAN ELEPHANT CONSERVATION ACT OF 1997,16 U.S.C. §§ 4261-4266

This statute establishes the Asian Elephant Conservation Fund and directs the Secretary of the Interior to use amounts in the Fund for projects for the conservation of Asian elephants.

ATLANTIC COASTAL FISHERIES COOPERATIVE MANAGEMENTACT, 16 U.S.C. §§ 5101-5108

The statute requires the Secretary of Commerce, in cooperation with the Secretary of the Interior, to develop and implement a program to support the interstate fishery management efforts of the Atlantic States Marine Fisheries Commission.

ATLANTIC SALMON CONVENTION ACT OF 1982,16 U.S.C. §§ 3601-3608

This statute limits salmon fishing pursuant to the Convention for the Conservation of Salmon in the North Atlantic Ocean.

ATLANTIC STRIPED BASS CONSERVATION ACT,16 U.S.C. §§ 5151-5158

This statute directs the Secretary of Commerce and the Secretary of the Interior to jointly declare a moratorium on fishing for Atlantic striped bass within the coastal waters of any state that does not comply with the plan for managing Atlantic striped bass that is adopted by the Atlantic States Marine Fisheries Commission.

ATLANTIC TUNAS CONVENTION ACT OF 1975,16 U.S.C. §§ 971-971K

This statute authorizes the Secretary of Commerce to promulgate regulations to "limit the size of the fish and the quantity of the catch which may be taken from each area ... [and] limit or prohibit the incidental catch of a regulated species. ..."

BALD AND GOLDEN EAGLE PROTECTION ACT,16 U.S.C. §§ 668-668D

This statute makes it a crime to possess, buy, sell, or transport any bald or golden eagle, alive or dead, or any part, nest, or egg thereof. The Secretary of the Interior may issue regulations authorizing exceptions "for the scientific or exhibition purposes of public museums, scientific societies, and zoological parks, or for the religious purposes of Indian tribes, or ... for the protection of wildlife or of agricultural or other interests in any particular locality. ..."

CAPTIVE WILDLIFE SAFETY ACT: SEE LACEY ACTAMENDMENTS OF 1981

CHIMPANZEE HEALTH IMPROVEMENT, MAINTENANCE,AND PROTECTION ACT, 42 U.S.C. § 287A-3A

The CHIMP Act, P.L. 106-55 1 (2000), as amended by P.L. 110-170 (2007), added § 481C to the Public Health Service Act. It requires the Secretary of Health and Human Services (HHS) to "provide for the establishment and operation ... of a [sanctuary] system to provide for the lifetime care of chimpanzees that have been used, or were bred or purchased for use, in research conducted or supported by the National Institutes of Health, the Food and Drug Administration, or other agencies of the Federal Government," when such "surplus chimpanzees" are not needed for such research. Non-federal chimpanzees may also be accepted into the system. Chimpanzees in the system may not be used in research except as specified in the statute, and must be cared for in accordance with the Animal Welfare Act.

The sanctuary system shall be operated by a nonprofit private entity under a contract awarded by the Secretary of HHS. The nonprofit private entity shall have a board of directors composed of not more than 13 voting members, who shall include individuals with expertise and experience in various fields, including primate veterinary care, animal protection, behavioral primatology, management of nonprofit organizations, laboratory animal medicine, and biohazards.

COMMERCIAL TRANSPORTATION OF EQUINE FOR SLAUGHTER,7 U.S.C. § 1901 NOTE

This statute, enacted as part of P.L. 104-127, 110 Stat. 1184 (1996), provides that "the Secretary of Agriculture may issue guidelines for the regulation of the commercial transportation of equine for slaughter by persons regularly engaged in that activity within the United States." Specifically, "the Secretary of Agriculture shall review the food, water, and rest provided to equine for slaughter in transit, the segregation of stallions from other equine during transit, and such other issues as the Secretary considers appropriate." The Secretary's regulations implementing this statute were issued in 2001 and are published at 9 C.F.R. Part 88.[14]

DEPARTMENT OF DEFENSE APPROPRIATIONS ACTS

P.L. 101-511, § 8019 (1990) provides:

> None of the funds appropriated by this Act or hereafter shall be used to purchase dogs or cats or otherwise fund the use of dogs or cats for the purpose of training Department of Defense students or other personnel in surgical or other medical treatment of wounds produced by any type of weapon: *Provided*, That the standards of such training with respect to the treatment of animals shall adhere to the Federal Animal Welfare Law and to those prevailing in the civilian medical community.

This provision, without the words "or hereafter," had been included in Department of Defense appropriations statutes since P.L. 98-212, § 791 (1984). However, because of the words "or hereafter" in the language quoted above, this prohibition on the use of funds continues to operate unless it is repealed.

Other Department of Defense appropriations statutes use the phrase "this Act or any other Act" instead of "this Act or hereafter." The Comptroller General has "held that the words 'or any other act' do not indicate futurity, but merely extend the effect of the provisions to other appropriations available in that fiscal year." 65 Comp. Gen. 588, 589 (1986). The following example of the use of this phrase in connection with the use of animals in research appeared in P.L. 103-139, § 8044 (1993), and P.L. 104-61, § 8034 (1995):

> None of the funds provided in this Act or any other Act shall be available to conduct bone trauma research at any Army Research Laboratory until the Secretary of the Army certifies that the synthetic compound to be used in the experiments is of such a type that its use will result in a significant medical finding, the research has military application, the research will be conducted in accordance with the standards set by an animal care and use committee, and the research does not duplicate research already conducted by a manufacturer or any other research organization.[15]

Finally, some limitations on the use of Department of Defense funds for animal research have applied only to a particular appropriations statute. For example, P.L. 103-139 § 8043 (1993), and P.L. 104-61, § 8032 (1995), provide:

> None of the funds appropriated by this Act shall be available for payments under the Department of Defense contract with the Louisiana State University Medical Center involving the use of cats for Brain Missile Wound Research. ...

DEPARTMENTS OF LABOR, HEALTH AND HUMAN SERVICES,AND EDUCATION, AND RELATED AGENCIESAPPROPRIATIONS ACT FOR THE FISCAL YEAR ENDING SEPTEMBER 30, 1993

P.L. 102-394, § 213 (1992) provides:

> No funds appropriated under this Act or subsequent Departments of Labor, Health and Human Services, and Education, and Related Agencies Appropriations Acts shall be used by the National Institutes of Health, or any other Federal agency, or recipient of Federal funds on any project that entails the capture or procurement of chimpanzees obtained from the wild. For purposes of this section, the term "recipient of Federal funds" includes private citizens, corporations, or other research institutions located outside the United States that are recipients of Federal funds.

This provision had previously appeared, without the reference to subsequent acts, in P.L. 101-166, § 214 (1989), P.L. 101-517, § 211 (1990), and P.L. 102-170, § 213 (1991).

DEPICTIONS OF ANIMAL CRUELTY, 18 U.S.C. § 48

This statute, enacted as P.L. 106-152 (1999), makes it a crime knowingly to create, sell, or possess any visual or audio "depiction of animal cruelty with the intention of placing that depiction in interstate or foreign commerce for commercial gain." It provides an exception for "any depiction that has serious religious, political, scientific, educational, journalistic, historical, or artistic value." The statute was aimed at outlawing "crush video" films, in which small animals are crushed to death. A federal court of appeals has held that the statute violates the First Amendment's guarantee of freedom of speech, and the Supreme Court has agreed to review the case. *United States v. Stevens*, 533 F.3d 218 (3d Cir. 2008) (en banc), *cert. granted*, No. 08-769 (Apr. 20, 2009).

DINGELL-JOHNSON SPORT FISH RESTORATION ACT,16 U.S.C. §§ 777-777*L*

This statute is also known as the "Federal Aid in Fish Restoration Act" and the "Fish Restoration and Management Projects Act." It directs the Secretary of the Interior "to cooperate with the States through their respective State fish and game departments in fish restoration and management projects." It includes the New England Fishery Resources Restoration Act of 1990, 16 U.S.C. § 777e- 1. This statute was amended by the Wildlife and Sport Fish Restoration Programs Improvement Act of 2000, discussed below.

DISPOSITION OF UNFIT HORSES AND MULES,40 U.S.C. § 1308

This statute provides, in full:

> Subject to applicable regulations under this subtitle and title III of the Federal Property and Administrative Services Act of 1949 (41 U.S.C. 251 et seq.), horses and mules belonging to the Federal Government that have become unfit for service may be destroyed or put out to pasture, either on pastures belonging to the Government or those belonging to financially sound and reputable humane organizations whose facilities permit them to care for the horses and mules during the remainder of their natural lives, at no cost to the Government.

DOG AND CAT PROTECTION ACT OF 2000, 19 U.S.C. § 1308

This statute, P.L. 106-476, §§ 1441-1443 (2000), makes it unlawful to import into, or export from, the United States any dog or cat fur product; or to engage in interstate commerce in any dog or cat fur product.

DOLPHIN PROTECTION CONSUMER INFORMATION ACT, 16 U.S.C. § 1385

This statute, as amended by § 5 of the International Dolphin Conservation Program Act, P.L. 105- 42 (1997), makes it a violation of § 5 of the Federal Trade Commission Act, 15 U.S.C. § 45,

> for any producer, importer, exporter, distributor, or seller of any tuna product that is exported from or offered for sale in the United States to include on the label of that product the term "dolphin safe" or any other term or symbol that falsely claims or suggests that the tuna contained in the product were harvested using a method of fishing that is not harmful to dolphins if the product contains tuna harvested—
>
> (A) on the high seas by a vessel engaged in driftnet fishing; or
>
> (B) outside the eastern tropical Pacific Ocean by a vessel using purse seine nets ...
>
> (C) in the eastern tropical Pacific Ocean by a vessel using a purse seine net unless the tuna meet the requirements for being considered dolphin safe under paragraph (2). ...

Violators are subject to a civil penalty of up to $100,000.

DRIFTNET IMPACT MONITORING, ASSESSMENT, ANDCONTROL ACT OF 1987, 16 U.S.C. § 1822 NOTE

This statute finds that "the use of long plastic driftnets is a fishing technique that may result in the entanglement and death of enormous numbers of target and nontarget marine resources in the waters of the North Pacific Ocean, including the Bering Sea." It therefore provides that the Secretary of Commerce, through the Secretary of State, shall negotiate with foreign governments to monitor driftnet fishing, and shall evaluate the feasibility of various methods of reducing the number of driftnets discarded or lost at sea.

The Driftnet Act Amendments of 1990, 16 U.S.C. § 1826, incorporate and expand upon provisions of the Driftnet Impact Monitoring, Assessment, and Control Act of 1987.

Eastern Pacific Tuna Licensing Act of 1984, 16 U.S.C. §§ 972-972h

This statute makes it unlawful to fish for designated species of tuna within the "Area Agreement" specified in the act without a license, or in contravention of regulations promulgated by the Secretary of Commerce.

Endangered Species Act, 16 U.S.C. §§ 1531-1544

This statute authorizes the Secretary of the Interior (the Secretary of Commerce in the case of marine mammals) to promulgate lists of species which are endangered or threatened (defined as "likely to become ... endangered") and to designate critical habitats of such species. Among other things, the act prohibits any person or private or governmental entity from importing, exporting, taking, possessing, selling, or transporting any endangered species. 16 U.S.C. § 1538. It prohibits federal agencies, unless granted an exemption, from taking action "likely to jeopardize the continued existence of any endangered species or threatened species or result in the destruction or adverse modification of [critical] habitat of such species." 16 U.S.C. § 1 536(a)(2). (No similar prohibition applies to entities other than federal agencies.) The act also requires the Secretary to develop and implement recovery plans for the conservation and survival of endangered and threatened species. 16 U.S.C. § 1533(f).

In 1988, P.L. 100-478 amended the act to require the Secretary to develop and implement recovery plans for the conservation and survival of endangered species and threatened species, and to implement a system in cooperation with the states to monitor the status of recovered species. It also directed the Secretary of Commerce to contract for an independent review, by the National Academy of Sciences, of scientific information pertaining to the conservation of sea turtles.

Fair Housing Act, 42 U.S.C. § 3604

This statute, as interpreted by the Department of Housing and Urban Development (HUD), requires that all public and private housing (except as exempted in 42 U.S.C. §§ 3603(b) and § 3607) allow seeing eye dogs, even if they otherwise have a "no pets" policy. 24 C.F.R. § 100.204. The act prohibits discrimination "in the terms, conditions, or privileges of sale or rental of a dwelling, or in the provision of services or facilities in connection" with such a dwelling, because of a race, color, religion, sex, familial status (living with children), national origin, or handicap. One form of discrimination based on handicap is "a refusal to make reasonable accommodations in rules, policies, practices, or services, when such accommodations may to necessary to afford [a handicapped] person equal opportunity to use and enjoy a dwelling." HUD has determined that allowing seeing eye dogs is a reasonable accommodation.

FEDERAL HAZARDOUS SUBSTANCES ACT,15 U.S.C. §§ 1261-1275

The Consumer Product Safety Commission, which administers this statute, adopted a policy statement on animal testing "intended to minimize the number of animals tested and to reduce the pain associated with such tests." The statement notes "that neither the FHSA nor the Commission's regulations require any firm to perform animal tests," although it adds that "animal testing may be necessary in some cases." 49 *Fed. Reg.* 22522 (May 30, 1984).

FEDERAL LAW ENFORCEMENT ANIMAL PROTECTION ACTOF 2000, 18 U.S.C. § 1368

This statute makes it a crime "willfully and maliciously" to harm a dog or horse used by a federal agency in law enforcement.

FISH AND WILDLIFE CONSERVATION ACT,16 U.S.C. §§ 2901-2912

This statute authorizes the Secretary of the Interior to approve state conservation plans for "nongame fish and wildlife," which are defined as "wild vertebrate animals that are in an unconfined state and that—(A) are not ordinarily taken for sport, fur, or food ...; (B) are not listed as endangered species or threatened species ... and (C) are not marine mammals. ..." A 1988 amendment (adding 16 U.S.C. § 2912) requires the Secretary to undertake research and conservation activities concerning population trends of, and the effects of environmental changes and human activities on, "migratory nongame birds."

FISH AND WILDLIFE COORDINATION ACT,16 U.S.C. §§ 661-667D

This statute authorizes the Secretary of the Interior:

> to provide assistance to, and cooperate with, Federal, State, and public or private agencies and organizations in the development, protection, rearing, and stocking of all species of wildlife, resources thereof, and their habitat, and in controlling losses of the same from disease or other causes, in minimizing damages from overabundant species, in providing public shooting and fishing areas. ...

FISHERY CONSERVATION AMENDMENTS OF 1990,P.L. 101-627

In addition to containing numerous amendments of the Magnuson Fishery Conservation and Management Act and the Atlantic Tunas Convention Act of 1975, this statute includes the Dolphin Protection Consumer Information Act, which this chapter summarizes separately.

FOOD, AGRICULTURE, CONSERVATION, AND TRADE ACTOF 1990, 7 U.S.C. § 5801(A)(5)

This statute funds "research designed to increase our knowledge concerning agricultural production systems that" serve six specified purposes, one of which is to "promote the well being of animals."

FUR SEAL ACT OF 1966, 16 U.S.C. §§ 1151-1175

This statute prohibits the "taking" (defined as to "harass, hunt, capture, or kill") of fur seals in the North Pacific Ocean or on any lands or waters under the jurisdiction of the United States, or to engage in commerce in fur seals' skins taken contrary to the act or the Interim Convention on the Conservation of North Pacific Fur Seals.

The act contains an exception allowing taking by "Indians, Aleuts, and Eskimos who dwell on the coasts of the North Pacific Ocean," and authorizes the Secretary of Commerce to permit taking for "educational, scientific, or exhibition purposes." The act also directs the Secretary to administer the fur seal rookeries on the Pribilof Islands to "ensure that activities on such Islands are consistent with the purposes of conserving, managing, and protecting the North Pacific fur seals and other wildlife. ..." The 1983 amendments to the act repealed the Protection of Sea Otters on the High Seas Act, formerly 16 U.S.C. §§ 1171-1172, as unnecessary because of the enactment of the Marine Mammal Protection Act of 1972.

GREAT APE CONSERVATION ACT OF 2000,16 U.S.C. §§ 6301-6305

This statute "established in the Multinational Species Conservation Fund a separate account to be known as the 'Great Ape Conservation Fund.'" The Secretary of the Interior shall use the fund for projects that he approves for the conservation of great apes.

HIGH SEAS FISHING COMPLIANCE ACT OF 1995 ,16 U.S.C. §§ 5501-5509

The purpose of this statute is "(1) to implement the Agreement to Promote Compliance with International Conservation and Management Measures by Fishing Vessels on the High

Seas ... , and (2) to establish a system of permitting, reporting, and regulation for vessels of the United States fishing on the high seas."

HORSE PROTECTION ACT, 15 U.S.C. §§ 1821-1831

This statute makes it a crime to exhibit, or transport for the purpose of exhibition, any "sore" horse, which is a horse whose feet have been injured in order to alter the horse's gait. The Secretary of Agriculture is authorized to enforce the act.

The Horse Protection Act also provides that "no horse may be exported by sea from the United States, or any of its territories or possessions, unless such horse is part of a consignment of horses with respect to which a waiver has been granted" by the Secretary of Commerce. Such waivers may be granted only "if the Secretary of Commerce, in consultation with the Secretary of Agriculture, determines that no horse in that consignment is being exported for purposes of slaughter."[16]

HUMANE SLAUGHTER ACT, 7 U.S.C. §§ 1901-1906

The central provision of the Humane Slaughter Act (HSA) reads:

> No method of slaughter or handling in connection with slaughtering shall be deemed to comply with the public policy of the United States unless it is humane. Either of the following two methods of slaughtering and handling are hereby found to be humane:
>
> (a) in the case of cattle, calves, horses, mules, sheep, swine, and other livestock, all animals are rendered insensible to pain by a single blow or gunshot or an electrical, chemical or other means that is rapid and effective, before being shackled, hoisted, thrown, cast, or cut; or
>
> (b) by slaughtering in accordance with the ritual requirements of the Jewish faith or any other religious faith that prescribes a method of slaughter whereby the animal suffers loss of consciousness by anemia of the brain caused by the simultaneous and instantaneous severance of the carotid arteries with a sharp instrument and handling in connection with such slaughtering.

The Humane Slaughter Act is enforced by the Secretary of Agriculture under provisions of the Federal Meat Inspection Act, 21 U.S.C. §§ 603(b), 610(b), 620(a). The HSA does not apply to chickens or other birds.[17] In 2002, P.L. 107-171, § 10815, 7 U.S.C. § 1907, added a section to the HSA directing the Secretary of Agriculture to submit a report to Congress on practices involving nonambulatory livestock (commonly known as "downed animals"). It also authorized the Secretary, based on the findings of the report, to promulgate regulations to provide for the humane treatment of such animals.[18]

ICCVAM AUTHORIZATION ACT OF 2000, 42 U.S.C. §§ 285*L* - 285*L*-6

This statute provides that the Interagency Coordinating Committee on the Validation of Alternative Methods (ICCVAM) shall, among other things, "[r]eview and evaluate new or revised or alternative test methods," and "[f]acilitate appropriate interagency and international harmonization of acute or chronic toxicological test protocols that encourage the reduction, refinement, or replacement of animal test methods."

The ICCVAM was established by the Director of the National Institute of Environmental Health Sciences pursuant to section 463A(b) of the Public Health Services Act (NIEHS), 42 U.S.C. § 285*l*-1(b). The ICCVAM Authorization Act of 2000 requires the Director of the NIEHS to designate the ICC VAM "as a permanent interagency coordinating committee of the Institute [the NIEHS] under the National Toxicology Program Interagency Center for the Evaluation of Alternative Toxicological Methods." The new act also provides that the ICCVAM shall be composed of the heads (or their designees) of 15 named federal agencies plus "[a]ny other agency that develops, or employs tests or test data using animals, or regulates on the basis of the use of animals in toxicity testing."

INTERNATIONAL DOLPHIN CONSERVATION ACT OF 1992, P.L.102-523

This statute amended the Marine Mammal Protection Act of 1972, the Tuna Conventions Act of 1950, and the South Pacific Tuna Act of 1988, all of which are discussed in this chapter.

INTERNATIONAL DOLPHIN CONSERVATION PROGRAM ACT, P.L. 105-42 (1997)

This statute amended the Marine Mammal Protection Act of 1972, the Dolphin Protection Consumer Information Act, and the Tuna Conventions Act of 1950, all of which are discussed in this chapter.[19]

LACEY ACT, 18 U.S.C. §§ 41-48 (SEE ALSOANIMAL ENTERPRISE PROTECTION ACT OF 1992 AND DEPICTIONS OF ANIMAL CRUELTY)[20]

This statute makes it a crime to (1) willfully disturb or kill any bird, fish, or wild animal, or take or destroy the eggs or nest of any bird or fish, on any lands or waters set apart or reserved under federal law as sanctuaries, refuges, or breeding grounds for such birds, fish, or animals (18 U.S.C. § 41); (2) import species of wild animals, wild birds, fish (including mollusks and crustacea), amphibians, reptiles, or the offspring or eggs or any of the foregoing which the Secretary of the Interior prescribes by regulation to be injurious to human beings or to the interests of agriculture, horticulture, forestry, or wildlife, except that the Secretary may permit importation for zoological, education, medical, or scientific purposes (18 U.S.C. § 42); or (3) use an aircraft or a motor vehicle to hunt, or to pollute a watering hole of, any wild unbranded horse, mare, colt, or burro running at large on any public land or ranges (18 U.S.C. § 47).[21] P.L. 110-161, § 109, 121 Stat. 2119 (2007), contains an exception to this last provision. It permits the Secretary of the Interior to use "helicopters or motor vehicles on the Sheldon and Hart National Wildlife Refuge for the purpose of capturing and transporting horses and burros," but "[s]uch use shall be in accordance with humane procedures prescribed by the Secretary."

LACEY ACT AMENDMENTS OF 1981,16 U.S.C. §§ 3371-3378

This statute, as amended in 1988, makes it unlawful to engage in commerce in any fish or wildlife or plant taken, possessed, transported, or sold in violation of any treaty, or any federal or state law or regulation, or any Indian tribal law. This statute was amended by the Captive Wildlife Safety Act, P.L. 108-191 (2003), to cover "prohibited wildlife species," which it defines as "any live species of lion, tiger, leopard, cheetah, jaguar, or cougar or any hybrid of such species." The Captive Wildlife Safety Act, however, "does not apply to any licensed, registered, and federally inspected exhibitor (zoos, circuses, etc.) or research facility. It also exempts sanctuaries, humane societies, animal shelters, or societies for the prevention of cruelty to animals that meet specified criteria."[22]

MAGNUSON-STEVENS FISHERY CONSERVATION ANDMANAGEMENT ACT, 16 U.S.C. §§ 1801-1891D

This statute, which was amended by the Magnuson-Stevens Fishery Conservation and Management Reauthorization Act of 2006, P.L. 109-479, provides that, except with respect to highly migratory species of fish, "the United States claims, and will exercise in the manner provided for in this act, sovereign rights and exclusive fishery management authority over all fish, and all Continental Shelf fishery resources. ..." 16 U.S.C. § 1811(a). See also, "Shark Finning Prohibition Act."

MARINE MAMMAL PROTECTION ACT OF 1972,16 U.S.C. §§ 1361-1423H

This statute imposes a moratorium on the taking ("take" means "harass, hunt, capture, or kill") and importation of all marine mammals or their products, except that the Secretary of Commerce or Interior (depending on the type of animal) may grant permits to allow taking and importation (1) for scientific research and public display, (2) incidentally, in the course of commercial fishing, and (3) "in accord with sound principles of resource protection and conservation." The act also makes it unlawful, except pursuant to a permit for scientific research, to import a marine mammal that is (1) pregnant, (2) nursing or less than eight months old, (3) taken from a species or population stock designated by the Secretary as depleted, or (4) taken in a manner deemed inhumane by the Secretary.

The act also establishes a Marine Mammal Commission whose duties include undertaking studies and making recommendations as to the protection and conservation of marine mammals. 16 U.S.C. §§ 1401-1402.

An exception to the Marine Mammal Protection Act of 1972 authorizes the Secretary of Defense to "authorize the taking of not more than 25 marine mammals [not a member of an endangered or threatened species] each year for national defense purposes. Any such authorization may be made only with the concurrence of the Secretary of Commerce after consultation with the Marine Mammal Commission. ..." 10 U.S.C. § 7524.

In 1988, P.L. 100-711 added "a number of provisions to the act for the specific purpose of reducing the morality [sic] of porpoise in the course of fishing for yellowfin tuna in the ETP [Eastern Tropical Pacific]."[23]

In 1992, Congress added two new laws to the Marine Mammal Protection Act of 1972. P.L. 102- 523 added the International Dolphin Conservation Act of 1992, "to prohibit certain tuna harvesting practices." P.L. 102-587, Title III, added the Marine Mammal Health and Stranding Response Act, which directed the establishment of the Marine Mammal Health and Stranding Response Program, the purpose of which is to collect data on marine mammal health and to coordinate effective responses to unusual mortality events by establishing a process in the Department of Commerce.

The Marine Mammal Protection Act Amendments of 1994, P.L. 103-238, was intended "to improve the program to reduce the incidental taking of marine mammals during the course of commercial fishing operations, and for other purposes. ..." S.Rept. 103-220, 103rd Cong., 2nd sess. (1994). The 1994 statute, among other things, amended 16 U.S.C. § 1374 to authorize the Secretary of Commerce to issue permits "for the importation of polar bear parts (other than internal organs) taken in sport hunts in Canada," but required the Secretary to "undertake a scientific review of the impact of [such] permits ... on the polar bear population stocks in Canada within 2 years. ..." 108 Stat. 539 (1994).

The 1994 statute also amended 16 U.S.C. § 1374 to provide that the Secretary of Commerce may issue permits "to take or import a marine mammal for the purpose of public display only to a person which the Secretary determines ... is registered or holds a license issued under" the Animal Welfare Act. The effect of this provision apparently is that the Department of Agriculture rather than the National Marine Fisheries Service is authorized to regulate such marine mammals once they are held in captivity. 108 Stat. 537 (1994).[24]

In 1997, the International Dolphin Conservation Program Act, P.L. 105-42, amended various provisions of the Marine Mammal Protection Act of 1972. In 2007, title IX of the Magnuson- Stevens Fishery Conservation and Management Reauthorization Act of 2006, P.L. 109-479, added the United States-Russia Polar Bear Conservation and Management Act of 2006 to the Marine Mammal Protection Act of 1972.

MARINE PLASTIC POLLUTION RESEARCH AND CONTROL ACTOF 1987, P.L. 100-220, TITLE II

This statute amended the act to Prevent Pollution from Ships, 33 U.S.C. §§ 1901-1915, to, among other things, direct the Environmental Protection Agency, in consultation with the Secretary of Commerce, to study "improper disposal practices and associated specific plastic articles that occur in the environment with sufficient frequency to cause death or injury to fish or wildlife."

MARINE PROTECTION, RESEARCH, AND SANCTUARIES ACTOF 1972, 16 U.S.C. §§ 1431-1445B

This statute authorizes the Secretary of Commerce to designate national marine sanctuaries.

MARINE TURTLE CONSERVATION ACT OF 2004,16 U.S.C. §§ 6601-6607

This statute states that its purpose "is to assist in the conservation of marine turtles and the nesting habitats of marine turtles in foreign countries by supporting and providing financial resources for projects to converse the nesting habitats, conserve marine turtles in those habitats, and address other threats to the survival of marine turtles."

MIGRATORY BIRD CONSERVATION ACT,16 U.S.C. §§ 715-715S

This statute authorizes the Secretary of the Interior to purchase or rent such areas as have been approved for purchase or rental by the Migratory Bird Conservation Commission "which he determines to be suitable for use as an inviolate sanctuary, or for any other management purpose, for migratory birds."

MULTINATIONAL SPECIES CONSERVATION FUND,16 U.S.C. § 4246

This fund was created in 1998 to carry out the African Elephant Conservation Act, the Asian Elephant Conservation Act, and the Rhinoceros and Tiger Conservation Act. Separate accounts in the fund were established as the Neotropical Migratory Bird Conservation Account, and the Great Ape Conservation Fund.

National Agricultural Research, Extension, and Teaching Policy Act of 1977, 7 U.S.C. §§ 3191-3202

This statute is designed to promote "the improved health and productivity of domestic livestock, poultry, aquatic animals, and other income-producing animals that are essential to food supply of the United States and the welfare of producers and consumers of animal products." 7 U.S.C. § 3191, as amended by P.L. 104-127 (1996), § 810. It was amended in 1990 to require the Secretary of Agriculture to commission the National Academy of Sciences "to conduct a study of the delivery system utilized to provide farmers ... and ranchers with animal care and veterinary medical services, including animal drugs." The study shall assess opportunities to, among other things, "advance the well-being and treatment of farm animals." 7 U.S.C. § 3193.[25]

P.L. 104-127 (1996), § 812, amended 7 U.S.C. § 3196(c) to provide:

> In order to establish a rational allocation of funds appropriated under this section, the Secretary shall establish annual priority lists of animal health and disease, food safety, and animal well-being problems of national or regional significance. ... In establishing such priorities, the Secretary, the Joint Council, the Advisory Board, and the Board shall consider the following factors: ... (3) issues of animal well-being related to production methods that will improve the housing and management of animals to improve the well-being of livestock production species.

National Fish and Wildlife Foundation Establishment Act, 16 U.S.C. §§ 3701-3710

This statute created the National Fish and Wildlife Foundation as a nonprofit corporation to, among other things, "encourage, accept and administer private gifts of property for the benefit of, or in connection with, the activities and services of the United States Fish and Wildlife Service. ..."

National Housing Act, 12 U.S.C. § 1701r-1

A 1983 amendment to this statute prohibits owners or managers of federally assisted rental housing for the elderly or handicapped to (1) as a condition of tenancy or otherwise, prohibit, or prevent tenants from keeping "common household pets," or (2) restrict or discriminate against any person in connection with admission to, or continued occupancy of, such housing by reason of the presence of such pets. The Secretary of Housing and Urban Development and the Secretary of Agriculture are authorized to issue regulations establishing guidelines under which housing owners or managers may prescribe reasonable rules for the keeping of pets, including restricting pet size and types of pets.[26] Owners or managers may require the removal of pets "duly determined" to constitute a nuisance or a threat to health or safety.

P.L. 105-276, § 526 (1998), added a new § 31 to the United States Housing Act of 1937, 42 U.S.C. § 1437z-3, which extended the right to keep common household pets to residents of all public housing, not only to residents of public housing designated for the elderly or handicapped. (The right to keep pets in federally assisted rental housing for the elderly or handicapped remains under the National Housing Act.) The new provision took effect August 9, 2000. 24 C.F.R. Part 960.

NATIONAL WILDLIFE REFUGE SYSTEM ADMINISTRATION ACT OF 1966, 16 U.S.C. §§ 668DD-668EE

This statute established the National Wildlife Refuge System, which is administered by the Secretary of the Interior through the United States Fish and Wildlife Service. The purpose of the System is to "consolidat[e] the authorities relating to the various categories of areas that are administered by the Secretary of the Interior for the conservation of fish and wildlife. ..."

NEOTROPICAL MIGRATORY BIRD CONSERVATION ACT, 16 U.S.C. §§ 6101-6109

This statute "established in the Multinational Species Conservation Fund of the Treasury a separate account to be known as the 'Neotropical Migratory Bird Conservation Account.'" The fund is to be used for a program, established by the Secretary of the Interior, "to provide financial assistance for projects to promote the conservation of neotropical migratory birds."

NONINDIGENOUS AQUATIC NUISANCE PREVENTION AND CONTROL ACT OF 1990, 16 U.S.C. §§ 4701-4751

This statute is intended "to prevent unintentional introduction and dispersal of nonindigenous species into waters of the United States through ballast water management and other requirements." The statute finds that nonindigenous species, such as the zebra mussel, if left uncontrolled, would disrupt the economy and "the diversity and abundance of native fish."

NORTH PACIFIC ANADROMOUS STOCKS ACT OF 1992, 16 U.S.C. §§ 5001-5012

This statute authorizes the Secretary of Commerce to enforce the Convention for the Conservation of Anadromous Stocks in the North Pacific Ocean.

NORTHERN PACIFIC HALIBUT ACT OF 1982, 16 U.S.C. §§ 773-773K

This statute authorizes the Secretary of Commerce to enforce the Convention between the United States of America and Canada for the preservation of the Halibut Fishery of the Northern Pacific Ocean and Bering Sea.

NORTHWEST ATLANTIC FISHERIES CONVENTION ACT OF 1995, 16 U.S.C. §§ 5601-5612

This statute implements the Northwest Atlantic Fisheries Convention.

PACIFIC SALMON TREATY ACT OF 1985, 16 U.S.C. §§ 3631-3645

This statute implements a treaty between the United States and Canada, the purposes of which were to "prevent overfishing and provide for optimum production" and to "provide for each Party to receive benefits equivalent to the production of salmon originating in its waters." The act repealed the Sockeye Salmon or Pink Salmon Fishing Act of 1947, formerly 16 U.S.C. §§ 776- 776f.

PACIFIC WHITING ACT OF 2006, 16 U.S.C. §§ 7001-7010

This statute requires the Secretary of Commerce to

> establish the United States catch level for Pacific whiting according to the standards and procedures of the Agreement [between the Government of the United States and the Government of Canada on Pacific Hake/Whiting] and this [statute] ... rather than under the standards and procedures of the Magnuson-Stevens Fishery Conservation and Management Act (16 U.S.C. 1801 et seq.), except to the extent necessary to address the rebuilding needs of other species.

PARTNERSHIPS FOR WILDLIFE ACT, 16 U.S.C. §§ 3741-3744

"The purposes of this title are to establish a partnership among the United States Fish and Wildlife Service, designated State agencies, and private organizations and individuals—(1) to carry out wildlife conservation and appreciation projects. ..." 16 U.S.C. § 3742.

PETS EVACUATION AND TRANSPORTATION STANDARDS ACT OF 2006, 42 U.S.C. §§5170B(A)(3)(J), 5196(E)(4), 5196(J)(2), 5196B(G)

This statute (P.L. 109-308) amended the Robert T. Stafford Disaster and Emergency Assistance Act to authorize federal disaster assistance in the "rescue, care, shelter, and essential needs" of "household pets and service animals"; to authorize the Director of the Federal Emergency Management Agency (FEMA) to develop "plans that take into account the needs of individuals with pets and service animals prior to, during, and following a major disaster or emergency"; to authorize the Director of FEMA to "make financial contributions ... to the States and local authorities for animal emergency preparedness purposes, including the procurement, construction, leasing, or renovating of emergency shelter facilities ..."; and to require the Director of FEMA, "[i]n approving standards for State and local emergency preparedness operational plans ... , [to] ensure that such plans take into account the needs of individuals with household pets and service animals prior to, during, and following a major disaster or emergency."

PITTMAN-ROBERTSON WILDLIFE RESTORATION ACT, 16 U.S.C. §§ 669-669K

Also known as the "Federal Aid in Wildlife Restoration Act," this statute authorizes the Secretary of the Interior to coöperate with the states, through their respective fish and game departments, in wildlife restoration projects, which are defined as the "selection, restoration, rehabilitation, and improvement of areas of land or water adaptable as feeding, resting, or breeding places for wildlife." This statute was amended by the Wildlife and Sport Fish Restoration Programs Improvement Act of 2000, discussed below.

PUBLIC HEALTH SERVICE ACT, 42 U.S.C. §§ 283E, 289D

Section 404C of this statute, 42 U.S.C. § 283e, directs the Director of the National Institutes of Health (NIH), by October 1, 1993, to prepare a plan for the NIH to conduct or support research into methods of biomedical research and experimentation that do not require the use of animals, that reduce the number of animals used, that produce less pain and distress in animals used, and that involve the use of marine life other than marine mammals.

Section 495 of this statute, 42 U.S.C. § 289d, directs the Secretary of Health and Human Services, acting through the Director of the NIH, to establish guidelines for research facilities as to the proper care and treatment of animals, including the appropriate use of tranquilizers, analgesics, and the like; but such guidelines may not prescribe methods of research. Entities that conduct biomedical and behavioral research with NIH funds must establish animal care committees which must conduct reviews at least semi-annually and report to the Director of NIH at least annually. If the Director determines that an entity has not been following the guidelines, he must give it an opportunity to take corrective action, and, if it does not, suspend or revoke its grant or contract.[27]

Recreational Hunting Safety and Preservation Act of 1994, 16 U.S.C. §§ 5201-5207

This statute makes it a violation, subject to a civil penalty of up to $10,000, "intentionally to engage in any physical conduct that significantly hinders a lawful hunt ... on Federal lands." The conference report states that, to be a violation, "the conduct must be intentional, and must be done with the intention of significantly hindering a lawful hunt."[28] The statute also authorizes injunctive relief against violations.

The conference report gives examples of violations of the statute, including "using visual, aural, olfactory, or physical stimuli to affect wildlife behavior." Ibid. This suggests the possibility that a court could construe mere words addressed to a hunter as "physical conduct," if such words affected wildlife behavior (or a hunter's concentration) so as significantly to hinder a hunt. This apparently would not violate the First Amendment's guarantee of freedom of speech, provided that the statute's civil penalty were imposed on the speaker for the effect of the *sound* of his words and not for their content. The statute states that "[t]he term 'conduct' does not include speech protected by the first article of amendment to the Constitution" (the statute does not otherwise define "conduct" or "physical conduct"), but this of course would go without saying, as Congress cannot punish speech that is protected by the First Amendment.

Rehabilitation Act of 1973: See Americans with Disabilities Act

Rhinoceros and Tiger Conservation Act of 1994, 16 U.S.C. §§ 5301-5306

This statute created the Rhinoceros and Tiger Conservation Fund "to provide financial assistance for projects for the conservation of rhinoceros and tigers."

Salmon and Steelhead Conservation and Enhancement Act of 1980, 16 U.S.C. §§ 3301-3345

This statute authorizes the establishment of a cooperative program involving the United States, the States of Washington and Oregon, and Indian Tribes, to "encourage stability in and promote the economic well being" of commercial fishing through "coordinated research, enhancement, and management of salmon and steelhead resources and habitat."

Shark Finning Prohibition Act, 16 U.S.C. § 1822 note

This statute amended the Magnuson-Stevens Fishery Conservation and Management Act by adding 16 U.S.C. § 1857(1)(P) to make it unlawful "to remove any of the fins of a shark (including the tail) and discard the carcass of the shark at sea." It also requires the Secretary of Commerce, acting through the Secretary of State, to, among other things, "initiate discussions as soon as possible for the purpose of developing bilateral or multilateral agreements with other nations for the prohibition of shark-finning."

SIKES ACT, 16 U.S.C. §§ 670A-670O

This statute authorizes the Secretary of Defense

> to carry out a program of planning for, and the development, maintenance and coordination of, wildlife, fish, and game conservation and rehabilitation in each military reservation in accordance with a cooperative plan mutually agreed upon by the Secretary of Defense, the Secretary of Interior, and the appropriate State agency designated by the State in which the reservation is located.

SOUTH PACIFIC TUNA ACT OF 1988, 16 U.S.C. §§ 973-973R

This statute implements the Treaty on Fisheries Between the Governments of Certain Pacific Island States and the Government of the United States, signed April 2, 1987.

TARIFF ACT OF 1930, 19 U.S.C. § 1527

This section of the Tariff Act of 1930 (also known as the "Hawley-Smoot Tariff Act" and the "Smoot-Hawley Act") prohibits the importation into the United States of any wild mammal or bird, alive or dead, or any part of product of any wild mammal or bird, if the laws or regulations of the country where the wild mammal or bird lives restrict its "taking, killing, possession, or exportation to the United States," unless the wild mammal or bird is accompanied by a certification of the U.S. consul that it "has not been acquired or exported in violation of the laws of regulations of such country. ..."

Any mammal or bird, alive or dead, or any part of product thereof, imported into the U.S. in violation of the above shall be subject to seizure and forfeiture under the customs laws. The Tariff Act of 1930 does not apply in the case of (1) articles the importation of which is prohibited by any other law, including 18 U.S.C. § 42(a) (the Lacey Act), (2) articles imported for scientific or educational purposes, or are migratory, or (3) certain migratory game birds.

TUNA CONVENTIONS ACT OF 1950, 16 U.S.C. §§ 951-962

This statute prohibits fishing in violation of any regulation adopted by the Secretary of Commerce pursuant to the Convention for the Establishment of an Inter-American Tropical Tuna Commission, and prohibits commerce in fish taken in violation of such regulations.

TWENTY-EIGHT HOUR LAW, 49 U.S.C. § 80502

Prior versions of this law were enacted in 1873 (Ch. 252, 42d Cong., 17 Stat. 584, R.S. §§ 4386- 4389) and 1906 (Ch. 3594, 59th Cong., 34 Stat. 607). The 1906 law was repealed and reenacted in amended form (but "without substantive change"[29]) in 1994 by P.L. 103-272. (It was previously codified at 45 U.S.C. §§ 71-74.) It is also known as the "Cruelty to Animals Act," the "Live Stock Transportation Act," and the "Food and Rest Law." As amended in 1994, it provides that "a rail carrier, express carrier, or common carrier (except by air or water), a receiver, trustee, or lessee of one of those carriers, or an owner or master of a vessel transporting animals" across state lines, "may not confine animals in a vehicle or vessel for more than 28 consecutive hours without unloading the animals for feeding, water, and rest."

It also provides that "[a]nimals being transported shall be unloaded in a humane way into pens equipped for feeding, water, and rest for at least 5 consecutive hours." The statute "does not apply when animals are transported in a vehicle or vessel in which the animals have food, water, space, and an opportunity for rest."

The 28-hour period is subject to the following exceptions:

> Sheep may be confined for an additional 8 consecutive hours without being unloaded when the 28-hour period of confinement ends at night. Animals may be confined for—(A) more than 28 hours when the animals cannot be unloaded because of accidental or unavoidable causes that could not have been anticipated or avoided when being careful; and (B) 36 consecutive hours when the owner or person having custody of animals being transported requests, in writing and separate from a bill of lading or other rail form, that the 28-hour period be extended to 36 hours.

The Twenty-Eight Hour Law is enforced by the Attorney General, who, "[o]n learning of a violation ... shall bring a civil action" to collect a penalty of at least $100 but not more than $500 for each violation. The statute does not provide for criminal penalties. The statute does not mention any federal agency or official besides the Attorney General, but its 1906 version provided, "It shall be the duty of all U.S. Attorneys to prosecute all violations of this Act reported by the Secretary of Agriculture," and, as noted above, the 1994 amendment was intended to be "without substantive change" to the 1906 version. In addition, in 1963, the USDA issued regulations under the act that remain in effect. 9 C.F.R. § § 89.1-89.5. Therefore, it appears that the USDA continues to play a role in enforcing the act.

In 2006, noting "that the plain meaning of the statutory term 'vehicle' in the Twenty-Eight Hour Law includes 'trucks' which operate as express carriers or common carriers," the USDA decided for the first time to interpret the act to include the transportation of animals by trucks.[30] In the same document in which it announced this decision, the USDA noted: "The Twenty-Eight Hour Law was never construed as being applicable to poultry, and ... USDA does not intend to change this longstanding interpretation of the statute."

UNITED STATES HOUSING ACT OF 1937 : SEE NATIONAL HOUSING ACT

UNITED STATES-RUSSIA POLAR BEAR CONSERVATION AND MANAGEMENT ACT OF 2006, 16 U.S.C. §§ 1423-1423H

This statute, which is part of the Marine Mammal Protection Act of 1972, makes it unlawful "to take any polar bear in violation of the Agreement [Between the Government of the United States of America and the Government of the Russian Federation on the Conservation and Management of the Alaska-Chukotka Polar Bear Population]." It also makes it unlawful "to import, export, possess, transport, sell, receive, acquire, or purchase, exchange, [or] barter ... any polar bear, or any part or product of a polar bear, that is taken in violation of" the agreement or other restriction that is adopted by the commission established under the agreement. The Secretary of the Interior is authorized to enforce the act.

WENDELL H. FORD AVIATION INVESTMENT AND REFORM ACT FOR THE 21ST CENTURY, 49 U.S.C. § 41721

This statute, enacted April 5, 2000, requires air carriers that provide scheduled passenger air transportation to submit monthly reports to the Secretary of Transportation on any incidents involving the loss, injury, or death of an animal. The statute requires the Secretary to publish this data in a manner comparable to other consumer complaint and incident data.

WESTERN AND CENTRAL PACIFIC FISHERIES CONVENTION IMPLEMENTATION ACT, 16 U.S.C. §§ 6901-6910

This statute provides for the representation of the United States on the Commission for the Conservation and Management of Highly Migratory Fish Stocks in the Western and Central Pacific Ocean.

WHALE CONSERVATION AND PROTECTION STUDY ACT, 16 U.S.C. §§ 917-917D

This statute directs the Secretary of Commerce to "undertake comprehensive studies of all whales found in waters subject to the jurisdiction of the United States."

WHALING CONVENTION ACT OF 1949, 16 U.S.C. §§ 916-916*L*

This statute prohibits whaling and commerce in whale products in violation of the International Whaling Convention for the Regulation of Whaling or in violation of any regulation of the International Whaling Commission or the Secretary of Commerce.

WILD BIRD CONSERVATION ACT OF 1992 , 16 U.S.C. §§ 4901-4916

The purpose of this act is to promote the conservation of exotic birds by assisting wild bird conservation and management programs in the countries of origin of wild birds, and limiting the importation of exotic birds.

WILD FREE-ROAMING HORSES AND BURROS ACT, 16 U.S.C. §§ 1331-1340

This statute makes it a crime, with respect to any wild free-roaming horse or burro, to (1) remove it from the public lands without authority from the Secretary of the Interior or Agriculture (depending on the public land), (2) convert it to private use, without authority from the Secretary, (3) maliciously cause its death or harassment, (4) process its remains into commercial products, or (5) sell it if it is maintained on private or leased land.

WILDLIFE AND SPORT FISH RESTORATION PROGRAMS IMPROVEMENT ACT OF 2000, 16 U.S.C. §§ 669-669K

This statute amends the Pittman-Robertson Wildlife Restoration Act to authorize firearm and bow hunter education and safety program grants, and to establish a multistate conservation grant program. Grants under the latter may not be used "for an activity, project, or program that promotes or encourages opposition to the regulated hunting or trapping of wildlife" (§ 113).

This statute also amends the Dingell-Johnson Sport Fish Restoration Act to establish a multistate conservation grant program, grants under which may not be used "for an activity, project, or program that promotes or encourages opposition to the regulated taking of fish" (§ 122).

YUKON RIVER SALMON ACT OF 1995, 16 U.S.C. §§ 5701-5709

This statute implements "the interim agreement for the conservation of salmon stocks originating from the Yukon River in Canada. ..."

End Notes

[1] A comparable provision, P.L. 110-329, § 528, 122 Stat. 3686 (2008), states, "None of the funds made available in this Act may be used to destroy or put out to pasture any horse or other equine belonging to the Federal Government that has become unfit for service, unless the trainer or handler is first given the option to take possession of the equine through an adoption program that has safeguards against slaughter and inhumane treatment."

[2] Regarding 7 U.S.C. 1901 note, see "Commercial Transportation of Equine for Slaughter," *infra*.

[3] For additional information, see CRS Report RS21842, *Horse Slaughter Prevention Bills and Issues*, by Geoffrey S. Becker. See also Libby Quaid, *Horse Slaughter to Continue Despite Action*, February 7, 2006, at http://www.boston.com/news/nation rss_id=Boston.com%2B/%2BNews.

[4] The Rehabilitation Act applies to federal executive branch agencies, federal contractors, and federal programs receiving federal financial assistance. The ADA applies to legislative branch agencies, the states, and the private sector.

[5] The transfer in 1985 did not explicitly appear in any federal statute; rather, P.L. 99-190, § 10 1(a), incorporated H.Rept. 99-439, and Amendment No. 31 to H.Rept. 99-439 incorporated a Senate amendment that appears at 131 *Cong. Rec.* 27449 (October 15, 1985). These provisions are set forth in "Federal Laws Enacted in 1985 Concerning Animals" (February 19, 1985), a CRS report by the present author. These provisions were declared "effective as if enacted into law" by P.L. 100-202, § 106, 101 Stat. 1329-433 (1987). The 1985 transfer to the Department of Agriculture was, according to the Washington Post (January 2, 1986), "to the delight of western cattlemen and sheep producers and the dismay of conservationists"; the issue is debated at 131 *Cong. Rec.* 27459 (October 15, 1985).

[6] The AWA defines "exhibitor" as "any person ... exhibiting any animals, which were purchased in commerce or ... will affect commerce, ... and such term includes carnivals, circuses, and zoos," but "excludes retail pet stores, ... State and county fairs, livestock shows, rodeos, purebred dog and cat shows, and any other fairs or exhibitions intended to advance agricultural arts and sciences." 7 U.S.C. § 2132(h). The Department of Agriculture added another exclusion: "horse and dog races." 9 C.F.R. § 1.1.

[7] Animal Legal Defense Fund v. Espy, 23 F.3d 496 (D.C. Cir. 1994).

[8] Animal Legal Defense Fund v. Glickman, 154 F.3d 426, 429 (D.C. Cir. 1998), *cert. denied*, 526 U.S. 1064 (1999).

[9] Alternatives Research & Development Foundation v. Glickman, 101 F. Supp. 2d 7 (D.D.C. 2000).

[10] A "dealer" is defined to include any person who buys an animal, and therefore could include a research facility. 7 U.S.C. § 2132(f).

[11] The regulations do not address this question. See 9 C.F.R. § 2.133(a).

[12] This section of P.L. 110-234, as well as the other sections of P.L. 110-234 cited in the text below, were also included, with the same section numbers, in P.L. 110-246.

[13] 7 U.S.C. § 2156(a), as amended by P.L. 107-171, § 10302 (2002); see also 39 U.S.C. § 3001(a). Prior to its 2002 amendment, 7 U.S.C. § 2 156(a) did not apply at all to fighting ventures involving live birds in states where such activity was legal.

[14] See also "Agriculture Appropriations Act, 2006, P.L. 109-97 (2005), and subsequent appropriations acts," *supra*.

[15] The bone trauma research involves the use of dogs; see H.Rept. 101-345, 101st Cong., 1st sess. 153 (1989).

[16] 18 U.S.C. § 1824a. This section was originally enacted as part of the Export Administration Amendments Act of 1985, P.L. 99-64, and was codified at 46 U.S.C. App. § 466. In addition, P.L. 107-171, § 10418(a)(2) (2002), repealed 42 U.S.C. §§ 3901-3902, which had authorized the Secretary of Agriculture to "prescribe regulationsgoverning accommodations on board vessels for cattle, horses, mules, asses, sheep, goats, and swine to be carried from the United States to a foreign country. The regulations shall prescribe standards for space, ventilation, fittings, food and water supply, and other requirements the Secretary of Agriculture considers necessary for the safe and proper transportation and humane treatment of those animals."

[17] Levine v. Conner, 540 F. Supp. 2d 1113 (N.D. Cal. 2008).

[18] The study has not been completed, but USDA has published estimates on the number of nonambulatory cattle, horses, sheep, and goats in the United States. Regulations on nonambulatory cattle are codified at 9 C.F.R. § 3 09.3(e). For additional information, see CRS Report RS22819, *Nonambulatory Livestock and the Humane Methods of Slaughter Act*, by Geoffrey S. Becker; see also Jennifer L. Mariucci, *The Humane Methods of Slaughter Act: Deficiencies and Proposed Amendments*, 4 Journal of Animal Law 149 (Apr. 2008), at http://www.animallaw.info/journals/jo_pdf/ jouranimallawvol4_p149.pdf.

[19] See, Kristin L. Stewart, *Dolphin-Safe Tuna: The Tide is Changing*, 4 Animal Law 111 (1998).

[20] 18 U.S.C. § 49 provides penalties for violations of the animal fighting prohibitions of the Animal Welfare Act, discussed above.

[21] P.L. 101-647, § 1206(a) (1990), repealed a section of the Lacey Act that protected carrier pigeons owned by the United States or bearing a band owned and issued by the United States. 18 U.S.C. § 45.

[22] S.Rept. 108-172, 108th Cong., 1st sess. 3 (2003).

[23] H.Rept. 100-970, 100th Cong., 2nd sess. 29 (1988); *reprinted in* 1988 U.S. Code Cong. & Ad. News 6170.

[24] This provision was opposed by animal rights advocates, who took the position that "NMFS has years of experience in monitoring this act, as well as other marine mammal issues. In contrast, the USDA has lacked both the commitment and ability to protect animals under the federal Animal Welfare Act." Animal Legal Defense Fund, *The Animals' Advocate* (spring 1994) at 2.

[25] This statute also required the Secretary to establish the Animal Health Science Research Advisory Board, which expired September 30, 1995. It was directed to advise the Secretary with respect to the implementation of animal health and disease research programs, and was required to have twelve members, one of whom had to be a "person representing an organization concerned with the general protection and well-being of animals." 7 U.S.C. § 3194.

[26] Regulations under this section are published at 24 C.F.R. §§ 5.300-5.380.

[27] Another section of the act, enacted in 1985 and repealed in 1988, authorized the Secretary to make grants to schools of veterinary medicine for "the development of curricula for training in the care of animals used in research, the treatment of animals while being used in research, and the development of alternatives to the use of animals in research. ..." P.L. 99-129, § 217(e) (1985), 42 U.S.C. § 295g-8(f); recodified by P.L. 99-660, § 601(a) (1986), as 42 U.S.C. § 295g-8(g); repealed by P.L. 100-607, § 613(a) (1988). Yet another section, enacted in 1986 and repealed in 1992, directed the Administrator of the Alcohol, Drug Abuse, and Mental Health Administration to establish guidelines for the following: "(1) The proper care of animals to be used in research conducted by and through agencies of the Administration, (2) The proper treatment of animals while being used in research ... (3) The organization and operation of animal care committee[s] [to assure compliance with the guidelines]." 42 U.S.C. § 290aa-10(a) (P.L. 99-570, § 420 (1986); repealed by P.L. 102-321, § 120(a) (1992)).

[28] H.Rept. 103-711, 103rd Cong., 2nd sess. (1994); reprinted in 1994 U.S. Code Cong. & Ad. News 1874.

[29] H.Rept. 103-180, 103rd Cong., 2nd sess. (1994) at 1; reprinted in 1994 U.S. Code Cong. & Ad. News 818.

[30] Letter from W. Ron DeHaven, Administrator, to Peter A. Brandt, Esq., The Humane Society of the United States (September 22, 2006).

INDEX

A

B

C

D

E

F

K

L

M

N

O

P

Q

R

S

T

U

V

W